ROY MAC

CLOUGH'S CHAMPION

ROY MAC

CLOUGH'S CHAMPION

Sport Media

Special thanks to my wife Lin and daughter Beth, who both encouraged me to tell my story. The boys, my two grandsons Heath, six, and Arthur, four: The major catalyst for this book is that in later years they will have a record of what their grandad did for a living. I have Mum and Dad to thank for all the support and help they gave me. Brian Clough and Peter Taylor: I count my blessings that I was with them every step of the way during their six years at Derby County. I owe a massive debt of gratitude to Dave Mackay – the best player I ever played with.

By Roy McFarland with Will Price

Published by Trinity Mirror Sport Media
Managing Director: Ken Rogers Publishing Director: Steve Hanrahan
Senior Editor: Paul Dove Executive Art Editor: Rick Cooke
Senior Sub Editor: Roy Gilfoyle Cover Design: Lee Ashun
Senior Marketing Executive: Claire Brown Sales and Marketing Manager: Elizabeth Morgan
Senior Book Sales Executive: Karen Cadman

First Edition
Published in Great Britain in 2014.
Published and produced by: Trinity Mirror Sport Media,
PO Box 48, Old Hall Street, Liverpool L69 3EB.

ISBN: 978-1-908695-78-9

Photographic acknowledgements:
Roy McFarland personal collection, Trinity Mirror, PA Photos.

Printed and bound by CPI Group (UK) Ltd, Croydon, CR0 4YY.

Contents

Acknowledgements

SPORTS journalist Will Price, of the Daily Mirror and Sunday People, who saw me make my debut at the Baseball Ground against Aston Villa in September 1967, has been a constant source of professionalism, diligence and good humour in helping me to complete this book.

My thanks also go to club historians Gilbert Upton, Steve Wilson and Peter Bishop, co-authors of Tranmere Rovers: The Complete Record, for jogging my memory about my earliest days in professional football. Lifelong Rovers fan Gilbert was particularly helpful in mining several golden nuggets regarding my fledging career at Prenton Park.

Everyone at Trinity Mirror Sport Media has been a delight to work with, particularly publishing director Steve Hanrahan, senior editor Paul Dove, senior sub editor Roy Gilfoyle and page designer Lee Ashun.

To all my many friends in football, and those I have gained through my passion for golf, I hope you enjoy reading my life story as much as I enjoyed my career.

Foreword

By Sir Geoff Hurst MBE

NO debate about who is England's greatest central defender will end in agreement, but all such arguments must start with Bobby Moore. As someone who grew up alongside Moore at West Ham, I think I know a thing or two about what makes a top quality centre-back.

For me, and perhaps I'm biased, Moore was the best of all-time and his 108 England appearances, 90 as captain, suggest that I have not been alone in that judgement.

But Roy McFarland is one of only two or three England defenders who approach Moore's stature as a centre-back of skill, intelligence and muscle. In fact, had it not been for the injuries he suffered, Roy may have challenged Bobby's longevity and illustrious position among world football's greatest defenders.

FOREWORD

It's an honour to be asked to contribute the foreword to this book; first because I played with and against Roy and, second, because, like Bobby Moore, Roy set standards on and off the pitch. At his peak he seemed to represent all that Derby County stood for, just as Bobby carried the banner for West Ham.

He was a formidable opponent in a team that was to become one of the great sides of the seventies. I first played against him in November 1969. Derby had run away with the old Second Division title a few months earlier and were still adjusting to life in the elite division. It didn't take them long.

Roy probably won't want to be reminded of this, but when we first faced each other West Ham beat Derby 3-0 at Upton Park. I remember because I scored twice. We travelled to the Baseball Ground later in the season by which time Brian Clough and his team had learned their lesson. They beat us 3-0.

I remember Roy marking me when West Ham lost 4-1 at the Baseball Ground in 1970-71 and a year later he marked me again in a real thriller at Upton Park. Derby were fourth in the First Division at the time. The match ended 3-3 and, memorably, they went on to be crowned champions after finishing their programme with a haul of points which neither Leeds United nor Liverpool could overhaul.

Roy's consistency, his confidence and his unobtrusive authority in the heart of the Derby defence had of course been noticed by England manager Alf Ramsey. A polished, classic centre-half with a crisp tackle, a sharp footballing brain and a good passing range, Roy was being talked about as the natural successor to Bobby Moore.

England's failure to defend the World Cup in Mexico in 1970 was forcing Alf to consider his options. Bobby was coming to the end of his long reign, and in February 1971, Alf dropped him from the team that was to play Malta in Valletta in the first qualifying match for the 1972 European Championship.

Alf left out several established players, myself included. He gave the captaincy to Tottenham's Alan Mullery and gave debuts to Martin Chivers, another Tottenham player, the Everton pair Colin Harvey and Joe Royle ... and Roy. It was a disappointing match but England won 1-0 and as far as Roy was concerned, he had staked his claim for a permanent place.

He played in the next three games – all wins with no goals conceded against Greece, Malta and Northern Ireland – and didn't experience defeat with England until his 17th cap, a 2-0 defeat in a World Cup qualifier in Poland in June 1973. It was the beginning of the end for both Bobby and Alf.

Roy looked increasingly confident at the heart of a new-look England defence, sometimes partnering Norman Hunter, other times his Derby County team-mate Colin Todd. They were in the team together, along with club mate David Nish, when England faced Northern Ireland at Wembley in May 1974.

Roy tore an Achilles tendon in that match, a serious injury in those days. He was just 26. It took a year out of his career. It was a great shame because at the time he was the best centre-half in the country with a great international career ahead of him. He returned to help Derby win the title again in 1975 and there were more good years to come, including four more England caps.

But he became increasingly prone to injury. Perhaps the best was over for him but, forty years on, Roy McFarland is still warmly remembered as a centre-half and captain of the highest quality.

Prologue

A WARM Friday night in the back streets of Liverpool at the end of the Summer of Love in 1967 and my teenage pals are out on the town, trying their luck in discos and parties, while I'm completely knackered after two games for Tranmere Rovers in 48 hours.

We've lost at home to Reading, I've sunk a couple of pints of bitter, and I'm relieved to be home in Edge Hill chatting about the match with Mum and Dad over a cup of tea before collapsing into bed, exhausted.

I'm not asleep for more than an hour when Mum comes into my bedroom and shakes me by the shoulder, whispering urgently: "There's two men downstairs to see you, Roy, and one of them is Brian Clough."

I recognise the name immediately. I know he scored a huge amount of goals for Middlesbrough and Sunderland and I saw him on television playing for England. What I missed over the summer was that he and his mate, Peter Taylor, had taken over the managerial reins at Derby County.

I can't be a pretty sight walking downstairs in my blue and white striped pyjamas, looking like a convict.

"Ah, here he is, the very man," says Clough, beaming from ear to ear.

Mum has miscalculated how many men have entered our house in Solon Street. I count four, including the Tranmere manager Dave Russell and a photographer.

Russell tries to say something first but gets a sharp look from Clough, who launches into a powerful, persuasive pitch, his sidekick Taylor reinforcing every point.

Clough points a finger at me, a raw 19-year-old Third Division centre-half, and says: "You, young man, are signing for Derby County and not only that, you will be playing for England within 12 months."

I'm wrong-footed, caught on the hop, trying to work out why Taylor keeps chipping away at me whenever Clough stops for a breather. I expect the manager to be in control of negotiations, but here's this other guy who is every bit as formidable and coherent.

Clough must think my attention is wavering because suddenly, in a tone half-friendly and half-challenging, he says: "You're not going to play for England if you stay at Tranmere now, are you, young man?"

On he storms: "But we three, you, me and Peter here, are going to win promotion to the First Division where we will be extremely successful and you will be playing Liverpool, Everton, Manchester United, Leeds United, Arsenal, Tottenham and Chelsea every week."

Alarm bells sound in my head. I am immediately uncomfortable. Liverpool? That's my team, my club. I never want to play against them.

I sit in a sort of stupor, I suppose. My grasp of geography

means I can locate Derby in the Midlands on a map but I know next to nothing about the club except that they aren't very well known, or successful, come to that.

I think: "Where are these guys coming from?" They are promising me the earth. I can't believe I will experience all this so soon. It is, frankly, incredible.

What I actually say is: "I'm not sure. I need time to think, Mr Clough."

"Sensible lad, you've got there, Les and Marjorie," says the charmer, whose charisma has already won over my parents. Despite the intensity of his argument, Clough suddenly relaxes and says: "Take all the time you need, Roy," before adding, "but we'll still be here in the morning and we're not shifting until you make a decision."

They want me signed on the spot. They don't want to waste time. They are in my house well over two hours convincing me Derby is the place to come to. They make it sound like Shangri-La.

When Russell manages to get a word in edgeways, it is to say: "The club have agreed a fair price for you, Roy, but it's entirely your decision now. If you decide you don't want to go to Derby, we will be delighted to see you on Monday for training."

At that, Clough and Taylor bristle visibly before banging on again about the riches football has to offer me if I come away with them. It's like someone opening the door to an Aladdin's cave of goodies and inviting you to step inside to have a look around and take whatever you want.

Their faith in me is total, their conviction that Derby will rise to power is absolute. They say they will turn Derby into one of the top clubs in the country.

The stalemate continues. Although I am impressed by their unshakeable confidence and how strong and forceful they are in predicting glory, glory days at the Baseball Ground, I am adamant that I want to sleep properly on the offer before reaching any decision and I go upstairs to change into a t-shirt and pair of slacks.

It's getting cold and I feel at a disadvantage negotiating in my pyjamas.

Dad is a heavy smoker and pleased to discover Taylor shares his vice. Tea and yet more tea is brewed. I just want them all to go and leave me in peace.

If I have my way, the decision will be a resounding "No" purely because I have set my heart on playing for Liverpool and would give anything to sign for them.

When I return, Clough is complimenting Mum on the quality of her tea-making, and she looks ready to blush at any moment, before Dad utters the immortal words: "If they want you that badly, son, I'd sign," and Clough says quickly: "You're dead right, Les Mac," as he sticks a pen in my hand before whipping out about eight forms, plonking them on the kitchen table for me to sign.

I've been on the back foot for almost two hours, defending for my life and playing for time, but now it's game over. My resistance is crushed.

I expect the Derby pair to say they are paying £10,000 for me. When I hear the fee is £24,000, I'm astonished. I think what a hell of a gamble they are taking in view of my limited experience, but they are all smiles and reassurances when I finally agree to join them.

Taylor does all the signing, guiding my hand to autograph the relevant forms before the photographer takes a picture of me shaking hands with Clough in front of our fireplace.

Moments later, Clough and Taylor have their coats on and sweep out into Solon Street like a mini tornado and away into the inky black night, thanking Mum and Dad profusely for their hospitality and promising to telephone over the weekend with instructions about precisely where and when we will meet again.

It will be in Derby on Monday. I'm told I'll be making my debut that evening for my new employers at Rotherham United.

Clough's parting shot to my parents is: "Mr and Mrs McFarland, your son has just made the best decision of his life."

My life? It's never the same again.

****

LATE September, 1978, and Football League champions Nottingham Forest are setting out in defence of their title under Clough and Taylor, when Pete phones to say simply: "Brian and me want you to come over here with us, Roy."

Derby County are in decline under Tommy Docherty. The turnover of players at the Baseball Ground is frightening.

I am a fool if I don't listen to the proposal – even if it is an illegal approach.

European Cup football is high on the agenda at the City Ground and Forest are already halfway towards eliminating Liverpool in the first round. Larry Lloyd and Kenny Burns are a formidable partnership in central defence, but Taylor insists: "We want you."

But not enough, it appears, to propose the sort of terms I feel

I am entitled to given my standing in the game, even though I have suffered more than my fair share of injuries.

I'm not insulted, but I'm not leaving Derby for a 50 per cent reduction in wages.

My old mentors promise that I won't be out of pocket and their incentive is a massive pay-as-you-play scheme plus assorted bonuses. That doesn't sit well with me. I'm dubious about the figures being mentioned.

Taylor calls a second time and presses me for an answer, asking: "Right, are we doing this or what, Roy?"

I tell him: "No, Pete. I'm not happy with the way it's going to be done. I'm staying here."

My answer might be different if Forest make an official approach, and if the board want to sell me to their fiercest rivals, which is not at all certain. But there are too many ifs and buts and maybes.

The bottom line is that despite all the considerable success I have enjoyed under Clough and Taylor, I don't see myself wearing red as a Nottingham Forest player.

Forest go on to win the European Cup eight months later, repeat the trick the following season and end up with four League Cups, yet I never regret my decision to turn them down.

Cups, trophies, silverware ... the big prizes are what you aim for when you go into the game.

It's clear those days are not returning to Derby any time soon.

But leaving would be an enormous wrench and a kick in the teeth for family, friends and our fans.

It's my club now and I feel as if I don't want to let them down.

I have seen too many good team-mates leave but I am comfortable about staying because this is where my loyalty lies.

1

Butcher's Boy

SOME local urchins were happy to investigate bomb sites but my playground was the tarmac and lamp posts of Edge Hill, in Liverpool, or the local park, two streets away.

I was no more than five when Mum untied her apron strings and allowed me to start kicking a tennis ball outside our front door at number 45. It was a safe environment because it was such a resolutely tight-knit, working-class community, strangers and cars stood out like sore thumbs. I knew of nobody in Solon Street who could afford to drive. I can't remember too many broken windows either. We must have been tidy players.

I knew early on that I had a certain talent for football. I found it easy and by the age of seven the bigger boys had taken me under their wing and were quick to choose me for their sides as

I was considered the pick of the young whipper-snappers.

The full-sized goal we chalked on the wall outside Clint Road Primary School meant you were on a hiding to nothing at four-foot nothing, as many of us were, and it was your turn to be 'in' for shooting practice.

It wasn't all football, not quite. For the fortnight of Wimbledon, our well-worn tennis balls were used for the purpose they were intended, if we could lay our hands on a racket or two. And if the only lad in the street with the appropriate gear was at home and available to play, we had a bash at cricket in the heat and the dust, attempting to bowl like Freddie Trueman and bat like Colin Cowdrey.

It was obvious where we had marked out our territory in the park, jumpers and coats for goalposts, naturally. Football all the year round had reduced the grass to a muddy patch – a bog in winter, a dust bowl in high summer.

We were a poor family, no escaping the fact, but never impoverished, and there was always enough food on the table. My dad Les worked as a butcher for the Co-op and my nan Ellen ran a grocery and vegetable shop. Despite Dad's job, I never saw any fillet steak, although meat and three vegetables was standard fare.

Mum Marjorie worked part-time in the Crawfords Biscuits factory, cycling to work for the afternoon shift. I never went short when it came to clothes either and I knew of several families in our street far worse off than us.

Our house was a very basic two-up, two-down with a small bricked yard and an outside toilet. My elder sisters Maureen and Pauline shared a double bed while I had a single in the same room before we grew older.

BUTCHER'S BOY

Dad's McFarland ancestry can be traced back to Scotland, although the family tree originated over the Irish Sea. Later in life, around 1960, he swapped the butcher's counter for a job working as a clerk in the office of Lucas Turbines, which was a turn up for the books because his generation tended to have a job or profession for life.

Dad was a decent footballer, a left-winger who once had a trial at Sunderland but he didn't fancy moving to Wearside. I suspect the wages on offer weren't much more than he was already earning for slicing bacon and jointing meat, and there was less security.

Money, or rather the lack of it, meant that treats were rare but Mum and Dad pushed the boat out to give me a very special early sixth birthday present. Hollywood legend Roy Rogers, the singing cowboy, was my hero principally because we shared a common Christian name and he was a cowboy, rather than my appreciation of his vocal talent.

And the three of us were in the audience at Liverpool's Empire Theatre in March 1954 when he appeared with his wife Dale, Trigger 'the smartest horse in the movies' and wonder dog Bullet. Trigger could count using his hooves but my abiding memory is Roy getting him to rear up high on his hind legs and stay in that position for ages. It was a magic day out – and I soon put Roy's Cowboy Annual on my Christmas list.

As I got older, I would join the local gang at the pictures for the Saturday midday matinee – and see Roy Rogers and Trigger in films such as Heart of the Rockies and, in glorious technicolour, Son of Paleface.

The first family holiday I recall involved a bus trip to a caravan park in North Wales, although Mum was brilliant the way she took us three kids for days out to New Brighton, Southport and other resorts along the coast from Liverpool. I didn't like Blackpool, though. I found it too big and noisy but perhaps my prejudice was coloured by the fact I got lost on my first visit to the Golden Mile, separated from Mum on that vast promenade. Several well-intentioned holidaymakers made a big fuss of trying to reunite us and eventually a policeman took charge of the situation. Obviously, he was only interested in a happy conclusion, but I was scared stiff because I thought, in all innocence, that I had done something very wrong and would be punished.

Solon Street isn't there any more, neither is Clint Road Primary School, both demolished during slum clearance in the 1970s, but the memories remain and spring vividly to mind whenever I return to my roots a mile to the east of Liverpool city centre.

2

Rebel Without A Cause

WOLVES invited me to Molineux for a trial and Tranmere Rovers were also keen. Far from feeling spoiled for choice, I tore up both cards and threw them in the bin. I showed such a marked reluctance to commit myself to the game as a youngster, it's a miracle I ever became a professional footballer.

Selected for my junior school team a year early, I didn't like it because I wasn't with my friends and didn't fit in with the clique of older boys. After a couple of matches, I told the teacher in charge that I didn't want to play for Clint Road any more. He evidently felt that I was among the better, more accomplished players, and didn't take the news very well. In fact, he immediately banned me from the annual school outing to the Isle of Man. I was distraught but Dad came to the rescue, marching up to see the headmaster on a morning he must have taken off work specifically for the purpose, and succeeding in getting me reinstated on the trip.

At Edge Hill Secondary Modern School for Boys, my pal John Wignall and I were picked to go training with Liverpool Schoolboys. Many lads our age would have jumped at the chance but I felt the slog to the north of the city was too much like hard work because it meant catching two buses. We didn't hurry and on the third occasion we arrived late. The manager Tom Saunders stopped the coaching session as he saw us dawdle up the path and shouted: "If you two can't make it on time, you might as well not bother coming again." So we didn't.

I was handed an opportunity to represent Liverpool Boys' Clubs after being spotted playing for Edge Hill Boys' Club on the left wing and left side of midfield. The trial matches lasted 30 minutes apiece and I knew I was not overly impressive when my turn came. Then the Norris Green centre-half couldn't be found for the next game and the organisers asked the two lads who had filled that position in my game if they fancied another stint. They didn't, so I volunteered and after half an hour I discovered my true vocation – although I didn't know it at the time.

I was thrilled to shake hands with my hero, former Liverpool forward Billy Liddell, at a mayoral reception at the Town Hall before a Liverpool Boys' Clubs tour to Germany. I captained the side and Billy presented me with the Liverpool city scroll I was to give to our hosts following a lengthy trek by bus and boat to rural Germany, where we played three games in five days.

As a Liverpool fan I already had Billy's autograph countless times but meeting him officially was very special and I was immensely proud when he offered me a few words of encouragement.

I just adored Billy for his goals, as any young kid would. We all love goalscorers, the golden boys of the game. From Liddell, a coal miner's son from a poor background in Dunfermline, through Roger Hunt, Ian St John, Kevin Keegan, Kenny Dalglish and John Barnes, and now Luis Suarez at Liverpool to Lionel Messi, at Barcelona, and Cristiano Ronaldo, at Real Madrid, they are the players who get the juices flowing in conversation down the pub.

I was fortunate to score a few coming up for corners and free-kicks, but I would love to have possessed the talent of an out-and-out goalscorer. They get paid the most, they get remembered the most, and that's perfectly in order. Putting the ball in the back of the net is the epitome of what football is about.

I watched Liddell and yearned to be him. He also happened to be a marvellous man, a lovely guy, who did a lot of charity work around the city after he retired. He didn't owe anyone anything but he put a lot back into the community which had supported him.

Following the tour of Germany, our last game together before we disbanded was against Tranmere Rovers' youth team at Prenton Park to prepare them for a Youth Cup tie. I played centre-half. Their centre-forward Kenny Beamish scored a hat-trick and we lost 5-0.

That result and Beamish's haul of goals would suggest I suffered a catastrophe, but Tranmere evidently saw something in me and a few days later I received a card from the club inviting me for a trial. Out of the blue, I suddenly received a similar invitation from Wolves – and snubbed them both.

For a 17-year-old who yearned to make his way in the game, it seems a ridiculous, immature thing to have done. Why I rejected those early chances is one of the hardest questions I've asked myself. Perhaps I had a perverse, rebellious streak. Perhaps I wasn't prepared to go the extra mile. In any event, I sometimes think I am the luckiest guy in the world to have become a professional footballer.

At the time, however, in mitigation, it must be said I was very happy and settled working as a trainee accountant for Ogden's Tobacco Company. Wolverhampton might have been a million miles away, rather than the Midlands, while I didn't want my comfortable life disrupted by going over the water to Birkenhead. I had left school after staying on an extra year to pass five O levels in Maths, Physics, Chemistry, Geography and History, and got a start at Ogden's.

It was ironic, because I have always been a dedicated member of the anti-smoking lobby but I loved the job, especially after six months when I was promoted from working on fledgling computers to the company's private accountants department. Instead of feeding cards into huge machines (the cutting-edge technology of the day), this branch of accountancy was much more old-fashioned, Dickensian even, writing by hand in ledgers and venturing from time to time to see the manager in his palatial, wood-panelled office with a deep-pile carpet. I loved it. My older colleagues were first-class people, extremely kind and helpful, and the pay was not to be sniffed at either.

I was happy when I was earning at last at Ogden's because my social activities had been a financial drain on Mum and

Dad during the year that my mates, fresh out of school at 15, had been enjoying their newly-acquired spending power. My parents were as generous as they could afford to be with a few shillings here and there, so I didn't feel uncomfortable going out with pals who were bringing in a regular wage as assorted apprentices, brickies and machinists.

At school, we'd been taken around factories to get an insight into what the world had in store for us in terms of manual labour and I was adamant that there was no chance I would ever work with heavy machinery or on a lathe.

A lifetime as an accountant for a company majoring in pipe tobacco might have been my destiny but for my good friend, Ronnie Todd.

I was happy turning out for a pub team in the rough and tumble of the Liverpool Sunday League. It was a school of hard knocks, where nothing could be taken for granted. The facilities were basic, hopefully some sort of shelter for stowing your clothes and a tap in a field for washing purposes, which was bracing, to say the least, in the middle of winter.

But Ronnie kept badgering me not to give up on Tranmere when I received a second chance, another card through the front door inviting me to attend trials one summer Sunday morning. "I'll go with you, Roy, I'll do it," he kept saying. He even paid his own fare over the water and I owe Ronnie a debt that can never be repaid.

I had my kit ready by Saturday tea-time, although my preparation for the big day was anything but sensible as my football boots came with me and Ronnie to an all-night party, a fairly frequent occurrence down our way thanks in no small part to one of our better-off friends, whose parents could afford weekend breaks. I spent the evening and most of the small hours drinking cans of beer, dancing badly to Beatles records and Tamla Motown music, chatting up the girls enthusiastically and generally having a lot of fun. Seven o'clock on Sunday found Ronnie and me in a daze, leaving the party and catching the bus into town for a ferry ride over the River Mersey. Then it was another bus to Prenton Park and a lift to the nearby training ground at Bebington, where several games were about to kick-off. The journey must have woken me up because I felt sharp and focused in front of the assembled Tranmere coaching staff during my 30-minute trial, after which I was told: "Roy, go and get showered, we'll speak to you when you're changed."

I had no idea what was about to happen and spent an anxious 10 minutes wondering what the immediate future held in store. The short wait ended and a mixture of sheer joy and immense relief swept over me as I learned Tranmere wanted to sign me there and then on amateur forms. The idea was that I would begin in the B team before hopefully progressing through the A team to the reserves. Beyond that, nobody was prepared to make any promises but I signed those amateur forms, which were duly registered the following Wednesday in August 1965.

After dillying and dallying, and messing people about who believed I might have a future in the game, everything seemed to happen so quickly. One moment I was perfectly content and feeling secure at Ogden's, wrapped up in the world of discovering how much money could be made in the manufacturing of St Bruno rough cut, Royal Navy medium Virginia flake and Aintree mixture, and the next I was being presented with what was, at 17, very probably my last chance if I wanted to become a professional footballer.

Soon I was knocking off at Ogden's to go training on a Tuesday and Thursday night at the back of Prenton Park. Myself and the other likely lads were not allowed on the hallowed turf itself but did a bit of work on the shale surrounding the pitch from time to time, and on the cold winter nights when the floodlights were switched on my imagination ran riot and I could anticipate the crowd coming in to watch me make my first-team debut.

I quickly made up for lost time. After a handful of appearances for the B team, I was promoted to the A team and within six months had made it into Tranmere's reserves.

My Saturdays were now spent pitting my wits and growing strength against fairly decent opposition in the Cheshire County League, which included Wigan Athletic, Altrincham, Bangor City, Macclesfield Town and the second-string sides at Stockport County and Wrexham.

I made my first appearance for the reserves against Stafford Rangers on March 12th, 1966 in a 2-2 draw, a debut looked upon kindly in the Birkenhead News by their reporter Bill Draper, who informed his readers: "The outstanding display for Rovers was, without doubt, by 17-year-old McFarland, a tall angular centre-half who must have a very promising future on this showing. He was the complete master in the air and rarely did he panic when under pressure."

I had the best 18th birthday present imaginable when I learned Tranmere were prepared to offer me a two-year contract and the club registered me as a professional with the Football League.

Signing that deal was made easier by the fact Ogden's provided a safety net, my boss promising: "Roy, if it doesn't work out, we'd love to have you back, but go out and give it your best shot."

It proved to be a hugely enjoyable summer, counting down the days until pre-season training commenced and watching England win the World Cup with a magnificent side. Little did I know that within five years I would be sharing the same stage at Wembley in a white England shirt with five of Alf Ramsey's heroes from the epic victory over West Germany – Gordon Banks, Bobby Moore, Martin Peters, Alan Ball and Geoff Hurst.

I went on to win 28 caps, mirroring my hero Billy Liddell's 28 for Scotland and, by coincidence, he too trained in accountancy.

3

Kop Idols

DAD gripped me by the shoulder and spun me round to see a man coming out of the Dublin Packet in Chester. "That's Dixie Dean, that is," he said in total awe.

A diehard Blue, Dad was forever telling me stories about the legendary Everton centre-forward – and here he was in the flesh, standing outside the pub he owned in the Market Square as we waited for the bus home after a family outing.

All I could see was a podgy bloke. He didn't look much like a footballer to me. But I didn't say anything to Dad. He was ecstatic. I could see tears in his eyes.

Watching football, Liverpool, in particular, became a passion from an early age, as did autograph-hunting.

Despite his strong Everton leanings, Dad took me to Anfield

for the first time in 1956 for an eighth birthday treat and Liverpool let me down, losing 2-1 to Doncaster Rovers, who had Charlie Williams playing centre-half.

Charlie prospered hugely as a comedian on TV in the 1970s after he hung up his boots and he had a great line in self-deprecation. Even though it wouldn't be acceptable to say it now, I still have the memory of him claiming the Barnsley manager once approached him to sign for the Tykes, and he responded: "Bugger off, it's bad enough being black."

I sat on Dad's shoulders at kick-off to enjoy a perfect view while he leaned against the back wall of the Kemlyn Road paddock. Although I was a scrawny lad, Dad kept putting me down to take a breather. I was frustrated at missing chunks of the action before two blokes in the seats above us came to the rescue, suggesting I was hoisted up to sit on the ledge in front of them, holding on to an iron pillar. I don't know who was happiest, me for being given one of the best seats in the ground or Dad, for having a weight removed from his shoulders. The friendliness of those two supporters helped convince me that I should follow Liverpool.

By the age of 10, I had graduated to standing in the boys' pen on the Kop, where our primary ambition was to escape the cage by sneaking past a steward to join the seething, swaying red and white mob behind the goal.

There was no escape, however, for the likes of the Tottenham Hotspur and Arsenal stars when they arrived by train to fall victim to my gang, the Lime Street 'graffers'. We were in the business of autographs. It was a closed shop and woe betide any little scally who tried to muscle in on our patch. All the teams who pulled in on a Friday afternoon in preparation for the following day at Anfield or Goodison Park were fair game, but Spurs and the Gunners carried a whiff of glamour about them, a touch of the exotic from north London. Tottenham signatures were highly prized among our gang, especially after they won the Double in 1960-61, and big names such as Danny Blanchflower, Dave Mackay and Jimmy Greaves were besieged with requests to "Sign please, mister" from the moment they set foot on the platform. They were escorted to the nearby Adelphi Hotel by the Lime Street 'graffers', pens in hand, and the whole scene would be re-enacted on Saturday morning when the likes of Arsenal's Joe Baker and George Eastham set out to stretch their legs after breakfast.

Our insatiable gang scurried back to Lime Street in search of more autographs after the match, even boarding returning trains before the guard blew his whistle. We knew it was time to jump off at the last possible moment when the trainers returned along the platform to join the players, having ensured the porters had stowed the kit hampers on board.

We were caught out on one occasion when I was convinced I would finish up in Crewe. One moment, I was happily chatting to Birmingham City's former England goalkeeper Gil Merrick, the next the train was pulling out ... first stop, Crewe! The trainers had sold us a dummy, walking back through the train rather than along the platform. Merrick and his team-mates sensed we were upset and started plying us with cheese and ham sandwiches and apples and bananas. Then just as we were settling into the party spirit and accepting our fate, the train pulled in at Edge Hill station and it NEVER did that. Someone must have tipped off the guard that the Lime Street 'graffers' were on board and had strayed offside.

If there were 15 boys in Solon Street around my age, 13 of them must have been Liverpool fans, even though Everton were considered the big club in the city at the time. With me, part of it was a simple colour preference for red over blue, but the most persuasive argument for supporting Liverpool was the fact the local senior boys I knocked around with were avid supporters at Anfield.

I sang my heart out on the Kop along with thousands of others as we belted out our versions of She Loves You by the Beatles, Cilla Black's Anyone Who Had A Heart and the song by Gerry and The Pacemakers synonymous with the club, You'll Never Walk Alone.

As a Liverpudlian, I'm ashamed to confess that music and Beatlemania never played more of a part in my teenage years. On the day I was born in 1948, Peggy Lee was top of the charts with Manana (Is Soon Enough For Me) and I couldn't get out of the famous Cavern Club soon enough on my only visit. I was too young to catch the Beatles before their last performance there in 1963, but felt I had to go with three friends after hearing about the buzz and live music scene. After leaving school one lunchtime and catching the bus, we walked down a flight of steps into the pitch black and could hear a group playing at the far end of what I took to be a brick tunnel. The place was heaving, people packed in like sardines, and the low ceiling added to the claustrophobic effect as we inched our way to the front of the stage. I was struck by a number of very attractive miniskirted shop girls and secretaries on their lunch breaks, while the sweat and heat generated was almost overpowering. Had there been a fire or another serious incident to induce panic, I dread to think of the consequences. If we stayed in the Cavern five minutes, it was four minutes too long, and I was mightily relieved when my friends decided it was time to fight our way back upstairs to gulp in some fresh air in Mathew Street and discuss the attributes of the prettiest girls we'd seen before catching the bus back to school.

The Fab Four left a lasting impression on me in terms of fashion, however, because I splashed out all my available cash on an expensive corduroy Beatles jacket, which I wore every time I went out for months. All my friends bought one too, and we thought we looked the business.

I didn't buy records, no 45s or albums, I just borrowed them from my sister Pauline's impressive collection. I quite liked stuff by Georgie Fame and, later, Frank Sinatra and Dean Martin.

The records I was interested in were those being set by Liverpool and there was a definite sense they were a happening club, especially after Bill Shankly signed centre-forward Ian St John, from Motherwell, and centre-half Ron Yeats, from Dundee United, in 1961. The following year promotion was achieved from the Second Division and the League championship followed in 1964.

As a professional with Tranmere, I received two free tickets to watch Liverpool and Everton on Saturdays, whoever was at home, if we'd had a Friday night match. It meant a 20-minute bus ride, followed by a five-minute walk to Anfield or a 10-minute stroll across Stanley Park to Goodison. If the weather was decent and I fancied stretching my legs, the hour-long walk to the rival grounds would be undertaken, joining the colourful crowds and growing sense of anticipation and soaking up the atmosphere. An afternoon at Anfield watching the team I loved, often with my cousin John Rowley, was a bonus. The tickets were always for the Paddock in front of the Main Stand, yet I'd try my best to get in the Kop. Stewards didn't usually object as we were transferring to the cheaper terraces but the Kop held a kind of fascination for me and I treasure my memories standing there.

I saw Ron Yeats, a colossus, dominate centre-forwards with his sheer physical presence and occasionally smash them over the touchline and into the crowd. Ron was such an imposing figure that when Bill Shankly first signed him, he invited journalists to come into the dressing room and "walk round him" as if the new No.5 was the statue of King Edward VII in front of the famous Royal Liver Building. In truth, Ron may not have been the most mobile of defenders but I rarely saw him embarrassed. Tricky inside forwards who fancied their chances had to answer to Ron's sidekick Tommy Smith, the Anfield Iron. When I first watched Tommy, he was a young man – three years older than me to the very day – who was relishing his introduction into a marvellous team. It was a privilege to get to know Tommy properly. We had some epic battles and although my emergence was probably responsible for him only winning a single England cap, he never held that against me.

The matches which really stand out are the big European nights, against clubs of the stature of Inter Milan and Ajax. It seemed as if half of Liverpool, the red half, converged on Anfield when Inter arrived for the European Cup semi-final in 1965, just days after goals from Roger Hunt and Ian St John in extra-time had seen off Leeds United to win the FA Cup. I never stood much chance of getting to the final at Wembley because I wasn't a season-ticket holder, but nothing was going to prevent me from standing on the Kop for the match against

Inter. It's a good thing that a pal warned me to get there early because I just managed to squeeze in before the gates closed two hours before kick-off. The effort and wait were well worthwhile because Liverpool triumphed 3-1 in a frenzied, emotional atmosphere, although Inter won the return match 3-0 amid dark rumblings that the Spanish referee had turned a blind eye to a couple of suspicious goals.

If Inter had been no match for Liverpool at Anfield, Ajax most certainly were when they landed on Merseyside in December 1966 on European Cup duty. Shankly was like an American circus showman after Amsterdam, where Liverpool were outclassed 5-1, urging people to roll up, roll up to witness the greatest show on earth and predicting we would win the return 7-0. And such was the hold Shanks had over fans, many believed him.

I thought the Dutch club wiped the floor with Liverpool, even if the result was a 2-2 draw. Thanks in no small measure to Johan Cruyff, who scored twice, Ajax played wonderful football. The real eye-opener was the manner in which Ajax came out on the pitch well before the kick-off for a thorough series of stretching exercises, sprints, shuttle runs, shooting practice and crossing. So energetic was their preparation, we convinced each other that Ajax were bound to be knackered before a ball had been kicked in anger. Traditionally, we never caught a glimpse of our heroes before they ran out five minutes before the start. Ajax were years ahead of their time, a point they proved emphatically with Cruyff, one of the all-time greats of world football, demonstrating his mastery before he had turned 20 years old.

I enjoyed watching Everton too, even if I wasn't concerned

whether they won or lost. I found them to be a very hospitable club, always ensuring I got a couple of good stand seats. Centre-forward Joe Royle was just emerging as a potent force in Harry Catterick's fine team and I was keen to see how he made life a misery for defenders deputed to mark him. Equally, I studied Brian Labone and John Hurst in the heart of the Toffees' backline and was struck by their movement, anticipation and positional sense. I thought I was a million miles away from them as they played in the First Division in front of a rocking full house at Goodison Park, while I performed in front of Tranmere's loyal faithful, numbering around 7,000.

4

Sudden Impact

NOBODY was going to take me for a mug. At least, not after my first costly experience of playing cards.

I had my L-plates on as a footballer and gambler when I succeeded in losing nearly all my wages playing three-card brag on the long train journey south to London for Tranmere's 1-1 draw at Brentford. It looked a simple enough game as I stood there in the gangway of the carriage, watching the old hands indulge in a spot of bluff and bravado. They suckered me in, wiped me out, and taught me that I wasn't as smart as I thought I was.

We were paid on a Friday, cash in a brown envelope, and fortunately I had remembered to give Mum a couple of quid for my bed and board. On the next away trip to Port Vale, the lads looked like innocence personified as they casually enquired if they could deal me in. "No thanks," I replied. I studied what was going on intently though, and in time I became adept enough to hold my own at cards – and even make a bob or two profit.

If things had worked out differently, I would have been standing on a packed Kop watching Liverpool beat Leicester 3-2 instead of making my first-team debut in a 0-0 draw at home to Chester in front of a crowd of 6,756 in August, 1966.

The occasion passed me by in a blur, although I do recall the build-up. Stan Storton pulled a thigh muscle in pre-season training and was clearly a non-starter. Our manager Dave Russell asked experienced left-back Barrie Martin to wear the No.5 shirt, only for Martin to openly defy him. He said: "No gaffer. Play Roy, he's our future." Russell wisely waited until the Thursday morning before telling me he was going to throw me in at the deep end. I was still as nervous as hell, but at least he spared me a week of sleepless nights.

My boss was a canny Scot who had coached Denmark to an Olympic bronze medal at the London games in 1948, and was consistently very honest and extremely helpful. He knew his football and surrounded himself with good coaching staff.

Goalkeeper Jim Cumbes also made his first appearance against Chester. Such an amusing man, he always had a broad grin on his face and was among the last of that rare breed of sportsmen who played both football and cricket professionally.

September brought a result which has provoked friendly rivalry for well over 40 years: Bradford Park Avenue 2, Tranmere 3. Kevin Hector has never let me forget that he scored twice on his farewell display for the Avenue before signing for Derby for £40,000. For my part, I have repeatedly pointed out the final score and the fact that it was our No.6 Alan King's job to take care of Kevin while I was busy coping with Bobby Ham.

Hector's blossoming reputation went before him, the paper talk was all about how good the young lad was who scored goals for fun in the Fourth Division and how so many clubs were casting envious glances in his direction. He was 21 and only Jimmy Greaves and Dad's hero, Dixie Dean, had scored 100 goals in the Football League at a younger age.

The start of my career proper was an ordeal because I quickly began to feel the pressure and how much results meant to Tranmere fans. After five matches, Storton recovered sufficiently to take his place in the side and I was glad of a little breather and the opportunity to take stock.

When Stan suffered a recurrence of his injury, the other senior players were extremely supportive and told the manager that I should be given another chance because they sensed my potential. Our left-winger Graham Williams, a Wales international, told me: "If I could buy shares in you, Roy, I would." That did wonders for my confidence.

Any trepidation I felt at becoming a fledgling first-teamer was dispelled. I think the players realised I could do a decent job in the Fourth Division and that it was in everybody's interest to work towards success.

One of Russell's strengths was that he listened to what the experienced members of the team said. All things considered, he didn't have much of an alternative to using me again. When I returned this time, in a 2-0 League Cup replay defeat at Carlisle, I wasn't to miss another match for six months and soon became fully accepted by my team-mates, my confidence growing all the time in training as I set about learning my trade.

I've seen dressing rooms full of cynical old pros who haven't got a good word to say for young players trying to make their way in the game. It's a combination of fear about losing their jobs and a warped sense of self-preservation. The old sweats think doing down the youngsters will somehow make their prophecies come true. It can be a bitter world.

The sense that I had fallen on my feet increased when, unbeknown to me, the club captain, Johnny King, went to see Russell in October and told him simply: "Boss, you need to increase the kid's wages."

Until then, I was still on reserve wages totalling £13 in total on a good week, comprising £7 basic, £5 in appearance money and a £1 win bonus while the top first-team players were on £18 basic. I accepted totally I wasn't worth that much yet, but there was a happy compromise. Now I found my basic was £12 a week and the fringe benefits went up accordingly.

King had seen at first hand how I quickly started to hold my own at centre-half and felt I was fully deserving of more money. I know the story is true because that is precisely how Russell relayed it to me when he called me in to sanction the rise.

November brought the first round of the FA Cup and two very difficult ties with Wigan. They were good value for a 1-1 draw at Prenton Park and two days later, for the replay, we found ourselves under floodlights which had recently been installed at Springfield Park. Heavy snow turned to a blizzard, making life distinctly uncomfortable for players and officials alike, although our fans in a bumper crowd of 14,306 weren't complaining when Williams scored. It reached the point where it was very difficult to see the white lines, and the drama continued until the final whistle which came just as a Wigan player was sticking the ball in our net. The home team's delight at apparently forcing extra-time turned to anger when they saw the referee with his arms crossed in front of his chest, signalling the 'goal' had come too late. King shepherded us off the pitch as quickly as possible while Wigan were incensed. They hadn't heard the whistle through the noise of the storm.

The following month brought a double-header over the Christmas period against Luton, who boasted England World Cup centre-forward Derek Kevan in their ranks alongside David Pleat and Bruce Rioch.

Some might argue it was a case of honours even as we beat Luton 1-0 at home on Boxing Day Monday before they gained their revenge 24 hours later, 2-0 at Kenilworth Road.

But my contribution to the victory was a sign I was maturing, the Birkenhead News match reporter Stuart Hooton noting: "Playing a centre-forward role in a No.8 shirt, Kevan was almost obliterated from the game. He would surely be the first to testify that McFarland's performance was one without blemish."

I felt I won a significant personal battle that day and had the satisfaction of knowing that, at 18, I had succeeded in snuffing out the threat of a former England World Cup goalscorer.

Kevan was a nemesis for Brian Clough in their heyday, keeping him out of the international picture on numerous occasions. There was never much finesse about the blond bomber whose nickname 'The Tank' was an apt commentary on his approach, but few could question his effectiveness. He had spent a decade at West Brom, scoring over 150 goals, and plundered 56 goals in 76 appearances for Manchester City, quite apart from hitting the target eight times in 14 games on England duty. He scored a couple of goals at the 1958 World Cup finals in Sweden – wearing the No.9 shirt Clough would have killed for – and was also a reserve for the 1962 World Cup finals in Chile.

Mum and Dad came with me to watch several Friday night matches and went home together while I stayed in the supporters' lounge for a beer and then returned to the city centre by train or ferry to catch last orders and a second pint. Mind you, I think I managed a third and maybe even a fourth beer after we bade farewell in style to 1966 with a 3-1 victory over Bradford City the night before New Year's Eve.

Tranmere wasn't much of a 'drinking' club, though. After training, we would invariably head to a local cafe for tea, coffee and sandwiches. Then the lads had to get home, several up the Fylde coast to the Blackpool area, others of us to Liverpool.

Although the opportunity for a money-spinning FA Cup run disappeared when we lost 2-1 at Barrow in the second round, fate looked kindly on me the following Friday in the shape of a visit from Hartlepools United (as they were then known), managed by the two men who were to walk into my life and turn it upside down, Brian Clough and Peter Taylor.

It's perhaps worth recalling the teams that evening:

Tranmere: Jim Cumbes, Stan Storton, Eddie Robertson, Johnny King, Roy McFarland, Barry Ashworth, Steve Hill, George Yardley, Alan King, Roy Sinclair, Graham Williams.

Hartlepools: Les Green, Tony Bircumshaw, Brian Drysdale, John Sheridan, Stan Aston, Tony Parry, John McGovern, Cliff Wright, Ernie Phythian, Jimmy Mulvaney, Mick Somers.

Les Green and John McGovern were destined to play a part with me in Derby's rise from Second Division mediocrity to become a First Division force, while two other Pools players also arrived at the Baseball Ground, Tony Parry, a tough midfield scrapper to feature in a handful of games, and John Sheridan as youth-team trainer.

Clearly, I wasn't the only one with a future in the game, as Derek Potter wrote in the Daily Express: "United's 17-year-old John McGovern drew a cluster of scouts including Wolves, who are closely watching his progress. McGovern made little impression on Tranmere's defence where centre-half Roy McFarland continued his season of progress."

However, it was a fifth Hartlepools player, Phythian, who was, unwittingly, to play a part in my destiny. Experienced centre-forwards such as Phythian could be distinctly awkward customers when the mood took them. To begin with, I thought I had to win every header, every tackle ... I didn't. And I quickly learned that when you weren't favourite to reach the ball first it was prudent to let your opponent gain possession before moving in to challenge.

We won 2-0, keeping a clean sheet, and that, for me, was always a priority. If nothing else, it meant I'd done part of my job correctly and the team had gained at least one point. I always maintained that a defender who wears No.5 on his back should defend. That's what he's paid for. Anything on top of that is a bonus. Keeping Phythian quiet was no mean feat. He finished the campaign as the division's leading marksman with 23 goals.

Taylor told me later it was my performance in preventing Phythian from making an impact that convinced him to write my name in his little black book of players to sign when he and Clough moved on to bigger and better things. I was hugely enthusiastic yet still very green, but Taylor picked up on my potential.

That Hartlepools team didn't possess a lot of craft or balance. Clough and Taylor had not had much to spend at Victoria Park and the side was little more than a loose collection of individuals, eager young thrusters such as McGovern and journeymen who had been around the block a few times and knew how to survive and earn a living.

I was fortunate to have caught Taylor's eye at that particular moment because the following month I suffered the injury which ended my season.

Before then, my learning curve continued when we travelled down to the South West to record a handsome 4-1 win at Exeter, who had Jim Ryan, a burly ex-Metropolitan policeman, out to make an impression on his home debut.

The Birkenhead News reported that Ryan "gave McFarland plenty of work, especially in the air. But he only got away once and, when he did, he scored. Even so, the youngster kept a tight rein on Exeter's new man." Three points to us then, and what I'd describe as a score draw in the personal stakes.

During a run of four successive 2-1 victories over Newport County, Wrexham, Port Vale and Crewe, I pulled my thigh muscle right at the top and the injury developed into a haematoma, or large blood clot, which grew to the size of a small boiled egg.

The lump was a worry but I was constantly reassured by our trainer and the doctor that it was a simple procedure to remove and that the club would never dream of jeopardising my career through negligence.

So I was happy to keep going for a few matches, but shortly after back-to-back home defeats by Barrow and Southend, it was clear to the management that I was struggling and that their policy of patching me up and pushing me out to play wasn't working. At least I had the satisfaction of helping us to a 2-1 victory at Rochdale before retiring hurt and missing the final 11 matches.

This time, Martin was happy to cover for me, and he made a decent fist of the job as I watched the home matches, nervously chewing my nails in the stands.

The tension eased when Stockport, the League leaders, came calling and were soundly beaten 3-0. A fortnight later, our biggest crowd of the season, 15,555, saw us go down 2-1 to promotion rivals Southport – but that was Tranmere's solitary defeat in the last eight matches. The finishing line was fast approaching now, we fought out a 0-0 stalemate at Notts County and then clinched promotion with a 3-1 win over Rochdale at Prenton Park. Champagne flowed in the dressing room and a night of celebration followed in a function room at the ground. It was a clean sweep for the North West, Tranmere going up alongside Fourth Division champions Stockport, Southport and Barrow.

As a team, we always felt that promotion was on because we were a decent side with a successful blend of youth and experience. I was fortunate to find such a good partner as Alan King. I was just a young wet-behind-the-ears lad, but he already had some worthwhile experience under his belt, despite only being in his early twenties. I learned a lot from King in terms of what to go for and when to back off an opponent and give myself some breathing space.

We received a promotion bonus in our wage packets, but that was immaterial compared to the fact I could point to my first honour on the board after just 33 League matches.

Within days of the final game, a 3-0 victory over Notts County, I found myself in a hospital on the Wirral undergoing surgery to remove the haematoma. I have a constant reminder of the operation in the shape of a scar.

I was buzzing after a week recuperating in hospital. There I was at 19, having helped my club win promotion in my first season and with a wad of bonus money burning a hole in my pocket. My mood soared on the journey down to Newquay in John Wignall's banger for our summer holiday and the chance to mingle on the beach and in the bars and nightclubs such as the Blue Lagoon and Coral A Go Go with a sprinkling of friends, Liverpool reserve lads such as Ian Ross and Doug Livermore, and their girlfriends. We stayed in a tidy little bed & breakfast place and all had a great time out dancing to Hi Ho Silver Lining by Jeff Beck at the start of the evening and Procul Harum's A Whiter Shade of Pale when the lights were dimmed.

5

Prison Pyjamas

PREMATURELY balding with muttonchop sideburns and a handlebar moustache, which gave him his nickname 'Pancho', Jim Fryatt was a casting director's dream for any Charles Dickens TV adaptation – and he guaranteed me hard times.

It seemed no sooner had I returned from Newquay and hurled myself into pre-season training, than it was time to head back to the South West.

And I was pensive on the trek to Torquay for the opening fixture of the 1967-68 Third Division season because I knew the man waiting for me there was capable of making my life a misery.

Fryatt was a tough old boot who should have been plying his trade at a higher level and I didn't discover for years what it was

I achieved against the stocky centre-forward which convinced Peter Taylor that I should become a Derby County player.

It was clearly by design rather than chance that Taylor took the opportunity to visit his brother Don in Plymouth that weekend, leaving Brian Clough on his own in Derby for a 3-2 win against Charlton.

My recollection is of Fryatt giving me a torrid time at Plainmoor, where we lost 1-0, yet Taylor reported back: "Yes, we're going to sign McFarland." I was surprised when he confided one day that my composure had impressed him. Taylor also said my cultured left foot and ruthlessness had caught the eye.

In years to come, Taylor regularly got me going in the dressing room before big matches by casually asking: "Is Jim Fryatt on the teamsheet today?" He knew Fryatt had got under my skin.

If we were adversaries in this day and age, I would be sent off eight times out of 10 games against him, and booked in the other two.

Fryatt always came with baggage marked 'danger' when he faced Tranmere, establishing a Football League record by scoring after four seconds against them for Bradford Park Avenue in 1964, and I knew I faced another nasty 90 minutes against him that hot afternoon in Torquay, having had a sample of what he could dish out when he was lining up for Southport.

I didn't consider myself to be a typical, big, strong lump of a centre-half, but I felt that at 5ft 11in I could compete with virtually any opponent in the air because I jumped well, getting powerful leverage from a decent spring. And I thought I could read the game fairly well, which helped in making interceptions, rather than being obliged to put in tackles all the time.

But Fryatt was also a formidable header of the ball and had

the knack of leaving me ragged, very frustrated and upset not only with myself but, for some reason, my team-mates. I would never give up, never, it wasn't in my nature, but the cunning Fryatt would constantly lean into me and knock me over. Ideally, I liked to see my opponent a yard or two directly in front of me, but he would manoeuvre himself into a position to the side, just out of my eyeline, before appearing at the last minute and smashing into me.

Fryatt gave me plenty to fret about on the journey home, but my mood improved four days later when we beat Wrexham 2-1 in the first round of the League Cup.

Forty-eight hours later we went into action against a visiting Reading side. They were a good unit who had gone close to promotion, so it was disappointing rather than any disgrace to lose 2-1 that Friday night.

My cousin John Rowley came back on the train to Liverpool after the match and we managed a last pint in a city centre pub before closing time, as was our custom, before catching the bus back to Edge Hill.

We said goodnight, went our separate ways – and in the morning I was a Derby player, and it felt worse than any hangover after being subjected to the whirlwind tactics of Clough and Taylor. My brain felt as if it had been put through Mum's mangle.

The first thing that sprung to mind was: "What the hell have I just done?" I was quiet at breakfast, very unsure of what the future held but unwilling to express my doubts and reservations as I didn't want to upset Mum and Dad. They were already fully paid-up members of the Brian Clough fan club. However, I was miserable, sitting at home wondering how I could get out of it.

At lunchtime, I set out to Anfield with John Rowley and we watched Liverpool destroy Newcastle United 6-0 in front of a crowd of 51,829 with a hat-trick from Tony Hateley, the new £100,000 signing from Chelsea, Roger Hunt's two goals and one courtesy of Emlyn Hughes. Normally, I would have been delighted but I don't think I ever felt more lonely standing on the Kop as I confided in my cousin: "John, I've made the biggest mistake of my life."

I couldn't have cared less when I heard Derby's result, a 1-0 defeat at Crystal Palace, on a fellow passenger's transistor radio going home on the bus. I couldn't believe I'd been so stupid. Derby County, who were they? I had just witnessed Liverpool, my Liverpool, the team I wanted to play for above anything else in the world, win 6-0, and it seemed to me that I had made a crazy decision to turn my back on them. The thought of never playing for Liverpool left me desolate.

I stayed in virtually all that weekend, which was unheard of. Usually, I would have been out on the town, partying and drinking on Saturday night then maybe playing golf or going to a bowling alley with the guys and their girlfriends on Sunday.

Still saddened by my decision to join Derby, I was very, very quiet, not myself at all, wracked with doubt and disappointment, as I tried not to upset Mum and Dad. They were both resolutely upbeat, however, and when I said I thought I'd made a huge error of judgement, they virtually spoke as one, telling me: "No, Roy, this is a great opportunity for you."

In fact, they were so positive about my future prospects that their attitude pulled me through my bout of depression. Their excitement was reassuring to see. My parents had been monumentally impressed by Clough and Taylor.

I spent Sunday trying to prepare mentally for Derby's next game against Rotherham, looking at worst-case scenarios and telling myself I needed to concentrate harder than I'd ever done before for 90 minutes and to make my passes simply and accurately to someone else in a white shirt, whoever that someone might be.

I slipped out for an hour in the afternoon to see a couple of pals and have a little chat with them, expressing my fears. One of the lads said: "Look, Roy, you've made a big decision and you've just got to get on with it. This doesn't mean you can't ever play for Liverpool some day." I knew he meant well and I felt better after that.

I have heard it claimed that Bill Shankly made a mistake and should have had me installed at Anfield before Derby came calling.

The theory goes that Shanks thought it was more beneficial to my development to be playing meaningful matches in the Football League, and performing regularly on Friday nights virtually on his doorstep for Tranmere where Liverpool could keep a close eye on me, rather than sign me to play in the reserves in the Central League, earmarked as the long-time successor to Ron Yeats. That simply isn't true. Like Clough and Taylor, Shanks was crucially aware of the competition to unearth nuggets in the lower divisions. That's why he wasted little time signing England stars Ray Clemence and Kevin Keegan from Scunthorpe United.

Shanks was never smug and had made a personal mission to see me in the second half of the previous season, besides Liverpool scouts monitoring my progress. That summer there was plenty of press speculation that I might be picked up by a First

Division club, and Liverpool were always mentioned as one of the interested parties.

Taylor had it right in my eyes when he said: "If we had waited until the morning, we would have lost the bargain of the century. When Bill Shankly heard next day that we had got Roy for £24,000 the things he called Tranmere manager Dave Russell were unprintable. If we had left it a few more hours, Bill would have found out and outbid us."

This was Clough's version of events, as he relayed them to a friend: "I got McFarland out of bed to sign for me. He was in bed when I got to the house. He came downstairs in his prison issue pyjamas with the blue stripes on. I said to him, 'Have you just come out of prison with those pyjamas?' Well, we'd been at it and at it and then his old man, who was a working man, took him in the back kitchen and Roy said, 'I want to talk to my dad'. And I heard his dad say, 'I'd sign for Brian'. He came in and signed. There and then. I said, 'We'll see you at the station Monday morning,' and he turned up with a suit on and said he nearly cried all the way coming to Derby. He said, 'I thought I'd made a mistake'. And I told him, 'Well, you didn't, mate'. Bill Shankly had his eyes on him all the time. Bill always used to ask, 'How is he doing, how is he doing?' I told him, 'He's progressing', I'd just give him that, but it was a very sore subject with Bill. And I think Harry Catterick wanted McFarland as well at Everton. They both wanted him."

I awoke about seven o'clock on Monday morning, thinking about the Rotherham game and donning my best suit over a shirt and tie. Mum, Dad and myself caught the train down from Lime Street to Derby, changing at Crewe. Having my parents with me eased the tension I inevitably felt.

We were met at Derby station by one of Taylor's scouts, who drove us to the Baseball Ground, where I was ushered onto the pitch to shake hands with the chairman Sam Longson and a couple of directors while Clough and Taylor looked on proudly. It would be a while before I tasted champagne in Clough's company. On this occasion, we toasted my arrival at the club with a pot of tea in his office.

I had played in front of a flowerbed behind one goal at Aldershot's Recreation Ground, and at The Shay, Halifax, where the pitch was surrounded by a speedway track, as well as Barrow's modest Holker Street, so Derby's home in Shaftesbury Crescent, although tight and compact, was not unimpressive because of a decent-sized main stand flanked by two huge stands which stood like sentinels at the Normanton and Osmaston ends. It wasn't Anfield or Goodison Park, but then I didn't expect it to be. I gazed out from the tunnel over to the Pop Side terrace's corrugated iron roof which bore the legend Offilers Ales on its roof and thought: "This will do for me".

Mum and Dad went to the York Hotel for lunch while I was introduced to the Derby team at the Clarendon Hotel, where I managed to swallow a mouthful or two of the pre-match meal before we boarded the bus bound for Millmoor. My new teammates were friendly. In fact, I was received very well, particularly by Bobby Saxton, who knew full well that I had been bought to replace him. The boss reckoned he had "shot it" and Bobby said to me quite casually: "You know who's leaving now, don't you?" I shook my head in silence as he replied: "Me" with a sorrowful smile. In fact, Saxton stayed until January because I was ineligible for the League Cup and Derby went on a lengthy run in the competition. But when his end came, it was brutal.

No.10 Kevin Hector I knew already in passing and the management were keen for me to get acquainted with another new boy, centre-forward John O'Hare who had just become their first Derby signing for £20,000 from Sunderland.

Hector, from the penalty spot, and O'Hare both scored at Rotherham in a 3-1 win along with a goal from Ian Buxton, one of several players that evening who must have sensed the wind of change about to sweep them out of the club.

While my old mate at Tranmere, Jim Cumbes, could happily combine two sports, the boss was never going to tolerate a forward who was unavailable for the crucial business of preseason training and divided his year between scoring goals for Derby County and making runs and taking wickets for Derbyshire. Buxton was gone a month later, sold to Luton Town for £11,000.

Millmoor held no great surprises, I'd played there before, but I did find it strange making my debut in a Second Division team without having enjoyed the benefit of a single training session. I didn't have a clue which players had a talent for tough tackling, for example, or which of them were especially skilful – although I had an inkling that it was a pretty sound idea to get the ball forward to Hector whenever possible. O'Hare looked as if he could become a focal point for attacks and bring others into play whenever the ball was pumped up to him. All things considered, I was happy with my contribution and I also got the thumbs up from the management, which was something of a relief.

I had settled quite well in a comfortable Derby win. Although it was a jump up in standard, I didn't notice a massive difference to Fourth Division football, but this was perhaps due to the fact Rotherham were quite poor. They didn't provide me with a stern test.

After the match, Mum and Dad were mightily impressed to be driven with me to Manchester by the chairman Sam Longson's son-in-law. Unfortunately, we arrived too late to catch our last train from Piccadilly station and my parents shelled out a small fortune for the 30-mile taxi ride down the East Lancs Road to Liverpool. It was money they could ill-afford and put something of a dampener on the occasion, but Clough was hugely sympathetic when he enquired if I had got home safely. I explained what had happened, and a cheque in the post to cover the cost of that taxi fare swiftly followed.

I honestly didn't have a clue how much I would be earning. Financial arrangements had never been discussed when I was hauled out of bed to sign. I had no idea of the contract details, I wasn't at all streetwise, but remember Taylor and Clough promising me: "We will look after you, Roy" and I trusted them implicitly. When my wages did come through, I found I was on £30-a-week basic – a considerable leap to what I'd been used to at Tranmere.

6

Crashing Through The Gears

MY height became an issue whenever I was beaten in the air for a goal at the start of my career, and the criticism frequently caused Brian Clough to lose his temper, sometimes using the most colourful language.

He explained: "I had an obsession with heading the ball. I was always under the impression that if you could head a ball it meant you could play because it meant you were brave for a start. McFarland was not very big, 5ft 11in, but he could get up like a gazelle. And one of the criticisms of McFarland was that he was too small to be a centre-half. What a load of bloody rubbish. I had a director at Derby County called Ken Turner, a suave, good-looking man who thought he was superior to everyone – even his colleagues on the board – never mind me. Their board meetings were a complete waste of time. I went to the first three or four and at one 'any other business' came up. 'Yes, I've got a suggestion to our manager,' said Turner. 'I suggest that Roy McFarland wears a lead belt round his waist during training five days a week, so when he takes it off on Saturday, with not having the excess weight round his waist, he will jump higher'. I just looked at him and he was head down with his notes. That was his contribution – I thought he was taking the piss. The chairman Sam Longson, who didn't like him at all because Turner was after his job, nudged me under the table with his knee and drew heavily on his cigar. So I just looked at Ken Turner and said: 'I've never heard so much crap in all my life. And he'll jump higher? If we nail you to that seat, you'll have trouble getting up and that's what we should do'. And I passed it off as a joke, but he didn't take it as a joke. That was the type of thing they came out with. Directors had not got the remotest idea. Sam Longson knew when the side won, like the other 20,000 knew, but he knew nothing about football. He couldn't tell a footballer from an armchair."

Woe betide anyone who didn't jump to attention when Clough or Peter Taylor made a point. There was a spark and fierce inner confidence in them that you couldn't fail to admire.

I liked them from week one and that never changed in all the years I worked for them. They reminded me of Morecambe and Wise, the way they sparked off each other all the time.

Clough and Taylor weren't a comedy act, but they could have topped the bill at the London Palladium with their razor-sharp wit and gift of timing. They were absolutely synchronised and complemented each other in terms of what they said about players. A lot of it was an act, said for effect, but a lot of it came perfectly naturally.

My first impression of Derby itself was something of a shock. Walking into town one lunchtime, a hooter made me jump as I passed a factory and I found myself engulfed by scores of men and lads covered in yellow or blue dye on their overalls and hats as they poured out on to the street in search of a pint and a pie.

It was surreal and I thought: "What the hell sort of a place is this?" As I recovered my composure, walking on to the town centre and the quaint old bits around Sadler Gate, the 17th century Bell Hotel and Irongate, it struck me how lucky I was to be a professional footballer and how many members of that odd yellow and blue band of brothers could be found inside the Baseball Ground on a Saturday afternoon. The people of Derby and Derbyshire took me to their hearts the moment I arrived and I think we've been good for each other.

Everything felt strange and new, and I was extremely privileged to be living in a hotel at the club's expense. I had been in the Clarendon a matter of days when I accepted John O'Hare's invitation to dine with him, his wife Val and their two small daughters at the York Hotel.

Despite only being a couple of years older than me, John was already a family man and certainly more experienced in the ways of the world.

The five of us sat down in the restaurant, menus were produced. I took a look and assessed the prices before informing the waiter that soup of the day and breast of chicken would do me nicely.

My mouth dropped as John ordered four prawn cocktails and

four fillet steaks. Prawn cocktail? I had never seen one before, but it sounded exotic. As I wondered about the cost, John read my mind and reassured me: "Don't worry, Roy, Derby County are paying for everything." I was back in the York the following evening with the O'Hare clan and this time the order was for five prawn cocktails and five fillet steaks.

John surprised me by relaxing with a cigarette after supper on one occasion, revealing: "I'm thinking of packing these things up." I said that was wise and he made me laugh, replying: "It's not my health I'm worried about, Roy, it's the cost. Peter Taylor's always in the dressing room nicking my fags when I'm playing."

The O'Hares and myself became regular dining partners for a few months before Clough decided that I needed a change of scenery because I was homesick.

Defender Ronnie Webster had recently married Doreen, whose mum and dad owned a farm in South Normanton, a mining village some 20 miles north of Derby. I would have considered it an imposition, quite frankly, but Clough thought nothing of asking Ronnie: "Would you take Roy in to make him feel more at home?"

The Websters were happy to oblige, so I moved into the spare room of their newly-built house in Red Lane, where the potholes in the unfinished road threatened untold damage to Ronnie's car.

We'd come back from training to find Doreen had prepared a lavish three-course lunch – topped off with a knickerbocker glory, Ronnie's favourite sweet. I'd been used to little more than grabbing a sandwich in the middle of the day and the excellent spreads were a challenge.

I would eat up, have a coffee and then Ronnie would try and persuade me to go to work with him in the fields for the afternoon, mending fences, baling hay and dealing with the cows. All I was fit for was sleeping like a baby on the settee.

Hours later, Ronnie would come in, bits of straw sticking out of his clothes before turning his hand to a spot of do-it-yourself, putting up curtain rails and other jobs which made me feel guilty as I couldn't change as much as a lightbulb.

I thought I was fit but Ronnie, our right-half soon to be right-back, was phenomenal and not only that, the outdoors life made him look distinctly Mediterranean such was his deep tan – a great advertisement for the north Derbyshire tourist board.

Ronnie stopped acting as my landlord and chauffeur after six months when I moved into digs. Eventually passing my driving test after about 40 lessons and at the third time of asking, I celebrated by buying myself a Ford Anglia.

Peter Daniel also did a bit of farming, while Brian Daykin used to buy eggs and sell them to us when Clough and Taylor first arrived at the club. Daykin's egg round on a Friday afternoon got shelved when the boss announced: "We're back in training this afternoon," but all the lads with outside interests were quickly reminded of the importance of focusing on football.

Derby were driven forward at breakneck speed with the odd nasty crash or two. Yet success was not going to be some idle boast, I could sense it from that very first night at Rotherham.

The promising start to the season continued with a string of League victories over Aston Villa, QPR, Plymouth and Cardiff, interrupted by a 3-2 defeat at Norwich. Our 5-1 win at Cardiff was memorable as it was my first encounter with John Toshack, who was destined for great things with Liverpool and Wales.

Four days later, Rotherham arrived for the return fixture, and interest in the town and county had soared to such an extent that 28,161 fans turned up to see us win 4-1.

The turnstile operators were caught on the hop with so many supporters arriving late, and quite a few missed the opening 15 minutes when we scored three goals. For everyone there, it was a first chance to see another new signing, winger Alan Hinton.

Nottingham Forest thought they got the better of the deal by selling Alan for £30,000 and that his best days were behind him, even though he was only 24.

Maybe the Forest committee men took that view because he'd won the last of his three England caps three years earlier. Maybe they simply didn't know a good footballer when they saw one.

I learned very quickly from the management that they signed players to do a specific job. They told me they would be entirely satisfied as long as I defended, headed the ball and kicked it clear.

Alan possessed a terrific shot with either foot but was identified specifically to deliver as many crosses as he could, which he did with unerring accuracy from free-kicks, corners or on the run, no mean feat given the notorious Baseball Ground pitch.

The Derby fans gave Alan a tough time to begin with. He stood out with his curly blond hair and a reticence to get stuck in but Clough educated the supporters and me, explaining just what it was that Alan brought to the team.

Taylor drooled over players such as Hinton. He defined players with real ability as those who did something constructive with the ball, and said to me with a grin and a friendly elbow:

"But don't you worry about that, Roy. Just keep winning your headers and tackles."

Alan Hinton possessed great moral courage, never hid and was always prepared to take responsibility. In awkward situations, certain players can make themselves anonymous – they can hide, but they can't run – yet Alan always made himself available, always tried to use the ball, manoeuvre it in a positive fashion or cut inside and take a shot himself.

Derby's development was like a whirlwind and at times it felt like you just had to cling on, things were happening at such a pace. I had shown enough already, though, to be considered useful to the cause and it seemed as if Clough and Taylor had grabbed me by the scruff of the neck and were carrying me with them. It was a wonderful feeling.

They made training on a nondescript patch of land at Sinfin Lane, Normanton, very simple – and it was a joy. Clough had different ideas about the best way to bond a team together and ensure we were in peak physical and mental condition for matchday.

Some clubs put a heavy emphasis on running, but with him it was all about what you could do with a football. He was big on splitting the squad into groups of two or three and challenging them to beat each other. It could be something as childish as passing a ball through each others' legs in a long chain then running to the front of the queue, or dribbling around cones, but he loved to foster a competitive spirit.

You always had to look sharp, and be on your toes. Lapse, miss the ball if your mind drifted off to what you were having for tea, and the punishment would be instant – five press-ups and a bollocking from the boss. He rarely missed a trick. His methods helped me enormously with my concentration.

We played matches in training, anything from seven-a-side to a full-scale 11 versus 11, but they always took place in a restricted area, nothing like a full-sized pitch. The emphasis was on passing the ball accurately and quickly, then deciding on your next move. Standing still wasn't an option.

Clough confided: "With me going into management so young I never sensed this age gap, you know. Dave Mackay used to kid his son on that he was definitely younger than me for a start, but he was about nine months older. But the players, even in their twenties, as McFarland was, for example, I was still in their bracket. I still played five-a-side with them. Never got a kick, but I played. I put a teamsheet up once for a testimonial at Peterborough and I put my own name on it. And clever bollocks Alan Durban turned up, saying 'Gaffer, you've dropped a clanger on the teamsheet'. He said 'What name's that at centre-forward?' I said 'It's my bloody name'. He said 'You can't play, gaffer'. I said 'Watch me'. The first one came over and I stuck it in. It bobbled in, like. I always remember Durban afterwards saying to me 'That's the type of goal you used to score, is it?'. And I said to him 'Does it matter how it goes in, as long as it bloody goes in?'. I could play 90 minutes in testimonials, so I got on with everybody in the sense that I was on their level."

Clough was a master at retaining information. He wouldn't let you off the hook for a misdemeanour and a severe dressing down often followed. I remember one early match when a cross came over and I ducked, letting it run out for a goal kick.

A fortnight later in training, there was a similar scenario, and I was pulled up sharply by the boss.

"Hey, Roy," he yelled. "You don't do that when you play for

me. It's lazy defending. You got away with it a few weeks ago. But you didn't see that forward who almost reached the ball then, did you? Almost cost us a goal. Good lad, play on."

Clough and Taylor reminded us every day how good we were going to be. I always valued Clough's opinion above anyone's in football. I respected him so much, despite his outspokenness – or perhaps because of it. He'd tell you bluntly what he thought of you, but he gained my confidence because of his honesty.

I had mixed emotions when the boss made me Derby's youngest captain at 19 for our match at Bolton at the end of October. Bobby Saxton was the skipper but on the Friday I was called into the manager's office and told: "I think the time has come for us to further your education, Roy. Let's see what you're made of – you can captain us tomorrow." Pride and fear washed over me in equal measures. While it was a huge vote of confidence, I honestly didn't want the job. After all, I was only a teenager, and the arrangement felt far from comfortable. Saxton had welcomed me into the club and played alongside me in the heart of the defence and although this decision wasn't my choice, it felt as if I was going behind Bobby's back.

But it was typical Clough, always one for testing people to see their reaction. Any pride I felt at running out at Burnden Park that afternoon didn't stay too long, and neither did the captaincy. Their centre-forward John Byrom scored twice as we lost 5-3 and Saxton soon regained his job.

Further disappointment came in December when I suffered a calamitous afternoon against Middlesbrough which did nothing to bolster my international ambitions.

My potential and that of the visiting No.9 John O'Rourke had come to the attention of Sir Alf Ramsey. I was distraught when told afterwards that the England manager had been in the directors' box at the Baseball Ground. I was so disappointed with my contribution and knew I should have performed to a much higher standard.

Our reserve goalkeeper Colin Boulton was making his first appearance of the season while Arthur Stewart, a £10,000 midfielder recruited from Glentoran, made his debut having travelled overnight from Belfast.

Others struggled, we were in poor form, struggling to buy a goal in successive defeats by Bristol City, Carlisle and Hull and we were not what I would call 'together' as a team.

Boro manager Stan Anderson, Brian Clough's captain in their playing days at Sunderland, must have relished the occasion as the Teessiders ran out convincing 4-2 winners. John Hickton, an out-and-out striker, wore No.2 on his back but bore a closer resemblance to Pele than any right-back I had ever seen. He rampaged down the wing in wave after wave of attack, terrorising our defence.

I was to blame for Boro's first early goal, failing to clear a shot from Hickton which fell invitingly into the path of O'Rourke, and midway through the second half I was struggling as Hickton took the ball past me and crossed to provide a second goal for O'Rourke, who went on to complete a hat-trick.

Hickton was a handful and formed a good combination with O'Rourke.

The talented pairing took full advantage of opponents who weren't at all with it. I found myself dragged around all over the place, trying to fill gaping holes. It was something like trying to fight five fires with a single hose, but the trauma taught me a valuable lesson: I had to learn to concentrate on my job. If I tried to do everyone else's I'd have a serious problem.

We knew we had a problem the moment we stepped into the dressing room and Clough, barely managing to keep a lid on the anger prompted by a thrashing from his hometown club, said: "You lot, I'll see you all back down here tomorrow. Ten o'clock sharp."

On Sunday morning at the appointed hour, he told us: "There's 11 of you and you were all crap yesterday, so you can do 11 laps round the pitch. Off you go – now." Clough stood there scowling next to our trainer Jack Burkitt between the dug-outs as we ran and jogged around the cinder track. We would reach a point furthest from him and ask each other: "Is he still there? Is he still watching us?" Nine laps down, two to go, one of the lads piped up: "He's not there, he's gone." All 11 laps were duly completed by all 11 of us, however, before Jack confirmed that Brian had, indeed, left after nine laps, telling him: "I've seen enough of that lot for one weekend."

Clough explained to me that he had decided to ruin everybody's Sunday because it was the only way he could deal with his frustration, how bitterly upset he was by the display against Middlesbrough and the result.

Stewart, a Roman Catholic, told us how he spent the rest of that day trying to find a Mass in Derby to attend, and there were a couple of others who would normally have gone to church.

Clough was still annoyed on Monday morning but after dismissing us as a "total and utter disgrace" he clapped his hands and said: "But, hey, it's a lovely day. Let's go to work." We knuckled down and the following two Saturdays brought us a 1-1 draw at Blackpool followed by a 2-1 win at Charlton.

Years later, Clough recalled: "I called them in on another

Sunday morning for a team talk and I said 'You bloody lot, I can't understand you. You can't stick a goal in the net'. We were missing plenty at that period of the season, something that comes to all teams. And I whipped round in my anger and said 'You call yourself players. I got 20 goals before Christmas one season." John O'Hare, who was the quietest of lads – he never opened his mouth from one week's end to another – he said 'It was 22, gaffer'. Just like that. Well, I laughed because John, of course, was at Sunderland when I was at my peak and he couldn't get in the side. He couldn't smell the side, never mind get in. But he counted all my goals, I know that, as a centre-forward does. And he said 'You got 22, gaffer' and then he never spoke again for another month."

I had a breather in the first half of the season. Playing for Tranmere against Wrexham in the League Cup meant I was ineligible for Derby's run in the competition which began with victory at Hartlepools, followed by success against Birmingham, Lincoln (after a replay) and Darlington – all fairly low-key stuff.

Before the club really knew it, we were in the semi-finals, and the ticket office was besieged by fans because Don Revie's Leeds were coming to town.

Fifteenth place in Division Two playing against one of the top sides in England, packed full of internationals with a World Cup winner in Jack Charlton at centre-half.

Suddenly, it looked as if we were going to be seeing quite a lot of each other as the draw for the third round of the FA Cup gave Derby a trip up the M1 to Yorkshire.

A crowd of almost 32,000 was shoehorned into the Baseball Ground for the League Cup first leg and saw Derby put in a magnificent shift. Leeds were certainly rattled and would have settled for a draw when the ground fell silent after an hour. It was one of those bizarre moments that leave fans asking each other: "Did I really see that?" as Jimmy Greenhoff sent a corner into our six-yard box and Bobby Saxton stuck his hand above his head to stop the ball.

It was as clear a penalty as you will ever see and Johnny Giles duly accepted the gift, tucking his spot-kick into the corner of the net.

Watching from the stands, I was as dumbfounded as anyone by Bobby's moment of madness. I felt for him afterwards as he apologised to the lads, constantly repeating that he didn't know why he had handled the ball and simply couldn't account for his actions.

I returned alongside Bobby 10 days later for the FA Cup tie, which Leeds won 2-0, but Clough could hardly wait to get shot of him and Saxton was immediately sold for £12,000 to Plymouth, who finished the season bottom of the Second Division.

For a fleeting moment, Kevin Hector's close-range header at Elland Road suggested the return leg in the League Cup might be a close-run affair but, valiantly as Derby performed, Leeds rattled in three goals before Stewart fired in a late consolation goal which caught Gary Sprake, not to mention the TV cameraman, by surprise.

So it was Leeds who prepared to march on Wembley, where they won the League Cup at the expense of Arsenal, while we took out our frustration on QPR and I had the immense satisfaction of scoring my first goal in professional football.

Boasting the talents of Rodney Marsh and the identical Morgan twins, Ian and Roger, QPR were a super side, on their way to a second successive promotion. But they held no mystique for us, having already beaten them 1-0 at Loftus Road during our purple patch at the start of the season.

Marsh tried his best but was eclipsed in the creative stakes by Alan Hinton, who scored one of our goals before beating his full-back David Clement and crossing for Kevin Hector to tee me up for an unmissable chance in the 82nd minute to seal a handsome 4-0 victory.

That was as good as it got in the second half of the season and we only managed two more wins, at home against Bolton and Bristol City, in our last 13 matches. We signed off with a 3-1 defeat by Blackpool at the Baseball Ground.

It might not have been obvious that day, but a crucial part of the Derby jigsaw slotted neatly into place in the shape of John Robson, a fearless 17-year-old left-back spotted by Taylor among the disused slagheaps of Northumberland when our assistant manager was on a mission to watch another potential recruit.

Robbo rattled in an early goal from 30 yards before catching the eye with some impressive work at the other end of the pitch to stamp his mark on the team.

The kid from Consett was a heady mixture of youth, unbridled enthusiasm and energy with a devil-may-care attitude. What you saw was what you got – he wasn't fazed by anything.

Webster's stout, solid defending at right-back and reluctance to commit himself to attack proved the perfect foil to rampaging Robbo.

This may sound as if I was suffering from delusions of grandeur, considering we finished the season way down in 18th place, four points clear of a relegation spot, but I was a bit surprised we didn't win promotion in 1968 – the progress and performances were so much better than the results.

We failed because we weren't good enough, of course, we lacked maturity, we might have scored a load of goals but conceded even more, and the main ingredients to transform us into a championship-winning side had yet to arrive.

Clough had taught me that you gain a foothold in a game with a strong work ethic, but that's not enough to win it. You require ability, talent and leadership – and that is precisely what he set out to find.

7

Mr Majestic

COLIN BOULTON was convinced his time had come when our veteran, chain-smoking goalkeeper Reg Matthews retired. A former police cadet, Colin had been at the club four years awaiting his breakthrough and then his hopes were dashed by the arrival of Les Green.

I sensed grievance gnawing away at Boulton – and when his temper snapped we all received a startling insight into the personality of Derby County's new star signing.

The apprentices had a habit of using our changing room as a short cut, which annoyed Colin, who sat nearest a door which kept banging open. His response was to try and clip the offenders with his hand to make them stop, but on this occasion Colin's frustration got the better of him and he lashed out, catching a youngster with some force round the ear. Tears welled up in the boy's eyes and nobody quite knew how to react in an embarrassed silence.

Dave Mackay had been idly chatting away on the other side of the room to Alan Hinton, but Boulton's behaviour had not escaped him. Nothing escaped him. Dave had seen enough, rose slowly to his feet and loomed over Colin, telling him: "If you ever do that again, you will have to answer to me."

Colin apologised profusely to the apprentice and also Dave, who held up a palm to signify the matter was closed before calmly carrying on his conversation while the rest of the team looked at each other in awe.

Mackay's message was clear: I don't like bullies and I'm not a man to be crossed.

I was back home in July with my parents in Liverpool, showing off my suntan from a fortnight in Ibiza, when news broke that Mackay had left Tottenham to join Derby for £5,000. I was astonished and thrilled.

Here was one of the legendary figures in football, a man who helped Spurs to the Football League and FA Cup Double in 1961, possessed a European Cup Winners' Cup medal and had represented Scotland with distinction.

Something else made him special – he had twice fought back after breaking his left leg in an era when that type of injury frequently meant career-ending catastrophe.

Not only was Dave fearless on and off the pitch, he was the most talented guy I ever played with.

The enduring image, and one he detested, is of him picking up Billy Bremner by the scruff of the neck at White Hart Lane after the Leeds player rashly decided to test how well his broken leg had healed, but I never saw him bully anyone into submission. Although Dave had a powerful physical presence which enabled him to snap into a tackle, and a cannonball shot, he had very nimble feet which cushioned a pass majestically and manoeuvred it to a team-mate with the minimum of fuss.

Those feet were also honed for marvellous tricks which captivated dressing rooms and hotel bars alike. Dave spun a half-crown in the air, trapped it on the toe of his shoe before flicking the coin into the top pocket of his jacket. He also demonstrated how to catch the piece on the back of his neck before it dropped into his pocket.

But most impressive of all, Dave caught the half-crown flat on his forehead and wiggled it over his right eye, then his left, before watching it slide safely into that pocket. We all practised like mad, discussing what make of shoe would give us an edge. I think there was a sudden run on suede Hush Puppies in Derby.

Brian Clough had not bought Mackay to perform party tricks, however. The manager persuaded him to forget about charging from box to box and, instead, settle down in the back four to sweep up next to me. Experience had taught him how to read the game and his positional sense meant he was rarely embarrassed.

Dave taught me so much, I received a fantastic education from him. He helped me enormously, mentally and professionally.

When he came into a group, he created atmosphere and held everyone's attention. He did a lot of our players good, especially the younger ones. He had style, tactical awareness – everything you look for in a footballer. There was no better tutor, in my opinion.

In short, Dave was a colossus at five foot, seven-and-half inches and I heard tales about how he and Jimmy Greaves used their height – or rather lack of it – to win bets when they were socialising in London.

Dave planted his impressive torso on a bar stool while slim Jim stood next to him, asking fellow drinkers to guess which one of them was tallest. Invariably, the answer was: "You are, of course, Dave," and it was wrong because Greavsie measured up at five foot, eight inches.

Dave might start an evening with a schooner of sherry before graduating to his trademark tipple in rounds – "a wee bottle of Mateus Rose". Sheer class, but then he did always stand out from the crowd.

At 33, he was a year older than Clough, who convinced him that playing alongside willing, young legs would prolong his career. Everything the Scot did seemed to be for a reason and had a valid point. His attitude to training was superb, he never shirked a thing. We ran 400-metre repeats and Clough said: "Dave, have a breather, sit this one out," only to be told: "No, boss. I want to do it." Long distance or the short stuff, he was an aggressive competitor – although he stood no chance of winning. The difference is that he still wanted to win and it was that do-or-die spirit that rubbed off on every player, from the experienced Alan Hinton to teenager John Robson. We all wanted to be like Dave Mackay.

Clough decided Dave should stay in the Midland Hotel when he was in Derby, and also that I would benefit from leaving digs to move in there too at a discounted rate for bed, breakfast and an evening meal.

The Midland was probably Derby's premier hotel. The club had started using it more and more, the food was top notch, and I was excited at the prospect of spending time with Dave.

Even the fact he had a plush double room overlooking the garden, while I was stuck away in poky, staff quarters with a view of a plain brick British Rail building, was of no consequence. Given what Dave had won in football compared to me, I thought the discrepancy was justified.

I was eager to learn from a master and he was generous with his time, although I exasperated him at dinner where I gave him a thorough grilling over every aspect of his career. I wanted to know all about his time at Tottenham, what it was like to play with Jimmy Greaves, Maurice Norman and Bobby Smith.

When I overdid it, Dave let me know in no uncertain terms, saying: "For crying out loud, Roy, shut up and finish your meal before it goes cold" and we'd concentrate in silence for a while on our steaks.

My abiding memory is how determined Dave was as a person, and his attitude to winning, which never left him. And he had an uncanny knack for winning – whether it was football, golf, cards, going to the dogs at Derby greyhound stadium, horse racing at Uttoxeter or tossing a coin nearest to the wall.

Never-say-die Mackay could be aggressive when he came second, and that aggression rubbed off on me. In many ways, he reminded me of golf legend Gary Player, who maintained: "The harder I practise, the luckier I get."

It was almost as if Dave possessed mental powers which could bend a result to his will. We watched the racing in the television lounge at the Midland when his horse was getting murdered, miles behind the field.

"Unlucky, Dave," I commiserated and he replied calmly: "Wait and see, be patient." I was staggered to watch as all three horses in front of his selection fell, two disputing the lead at the final fence, to give him a winner. He smiled knowingly as he informed me, very deliberately: "Never. In. Any. Doubt."

Dave commuted between his home in north London and Derby in a big American left-hand drive car at first and when we were going to Uttoxeter races once, he tossed me the keys and commanded: "You drive." I nervously protested that I'd never driven a car like his before. "You'll be alright," he insisted. And I was, feeling a great sense of achievement under my sweaty palms as I safely turned off the ignition and parked at the Staffordshire course.

Dave was a great one for building up your confidence like that. His motto for life and living life was: Get on and do it.

Dave swapped his American monster for a Mercedes, which drew envious glances from Jimmy Walker, who said: "I do like your car, Dave," to which he responded: "In that case, you'd better take it for a spin," and dropped the keys into Jimmy's lap.

The skipper barely needed his wheels during the week, so Jimmy took to swanning around Derby in that Mercedes, to such an extent he made us all laugh one morning when he came in to training and announced: "One of my mates wants to know what Dave Mackay was doing driving my Merc towards the motorway on Saturday night!"

Nobody doubted that Reg Matthews had been a great club servant and, equally, few doubted we needed a new goalkeeper, so Clough bought Les Green for £7,000 from Rochdale.

They had not always enjoyed a stable relationship together at Hartlepools, but Peter Taylor convinced the boss to concentrate on the level of performance he assured Brian that Les would guarantee.

Green became one of Derby's little big men. At five foot, eight inches, he was one of the shortest keepers in the Football League and, initially, over-ambitious.

Conscious of his height, Les persisted in leaving the safety of his six-yard area in search of high crosses to prove he was every bit as capable as six-foot stoppers in the business, and that size was no yardstick of ability.

After conceding a few unnecessary goals due to his bravado, Les eventually got the message: "Leave it, you stay on your line." He was a great organiser though, constantly bombarding us with information and shouting orders to his defenders.

Away from the pitch, Les increased the camaraderie in the team. Sometimes he wasn't what you wanted when the pressure was on, or if a player had an individual problem, but he kept a smile on our faces by and large.

A bundle of energy and fun, a larger-than-life character, Les was also incredibly strong and a great practical joker. On one alcohol-induced evening in Cala Millor, Majorca, he left our hotel room 10 floors up by way of a sliding door leading to the balcony.

After a few minutes, Jimmy Walker, John O'Hare and myself were gripped by a rising sense of panic. A light breeze was blowing the curtains into the room, but as we stared outside, blinking into the darkness, there was no sign of Les – until the three of us looked down and discovered him right underneath our feet, hanging on to the bottom of the balcony by his fingertips. It was a sobering moment, to put it mildly.

Our Second Division campaign started slowly in 1968, although I was on the scoresheet in the opening match with a header from a Hinton corner at Blackburn in a 1-1 draw. By far the most significant early result was a midweek defeat at Bramall Lane where we lost 2-0 to a Sheffield United side inspired by a spiky little Liverpudlian, Willie Carlin, who scored once and outwitted our midfield countless times.

He ran the show from start to finish, despite Robson trying to give him a good kicking.

Clough and Taylor knew all about Carlin, having tried and failed to sign him the previous summer from Carlisle. Those negotiations turned ugly when the Cumbrians' manager Tim Ward, who had been sacked by Derby, claimed Carlin had been illegally tapped up. Ward was happy to sell Carlin – just not to Derby – and the Blades had picked him up for £45,000.

If the management required further proof that Carlin was a "must" they received it under the floodlights in Sheffield and following another 2-0 defeat, at Huddersfield, they paid a club record fee of £63,000 to get their man.

Some of our fans questioned the wisdom of paying so much for a player who was nearly 28, standing just 5ft 4in with a fair few miles on the clock from plying his trade at Halifax and Carlisle, not to mention something of a reputation for getting into trouble with referees.

Willie immediately won over any doubters. If Dave Mackay was the general, then Willie was the catalyst which made everything tick, the signing that gelled us all together because he wouldn't take any crap from anybody, whether it was an opponent or, particularly, a team-mate.

Dave led by example, quite regally, he just strutted his stuff and was an inspiration that way, but Willie cracked the whip. Underperform, concede possession cheaply, miss a tackle, fail to mark your man and you were guaranteed an earful of Scouse spite. He read the game very astutely and dished out the bollockings rather than Dave. Their attitude was similar – both men had to win.

I was utterly convinced signing Mackay and Carlin was a double whammy for the rest of the Second Division and that we would be challenging near the top in next to no time, and I was right.

Everybody was in awe of Dave. He laid down the law, told us what had to happen and Willie was his enforcer. Carlin shook a fist, insisting: "If the skipper says that's it, then that's it. No arguments," and you would be a fool not to fall in line.

I won't pretend there weren't arguments, but when we came off the pitch there was a huge sense of togetherness.

Clough and Taylor were soon treating us to a unique side of their management – three-day mini-breaks in Majorca, Scarborough, Bisham Abbey and Blackpool. It was great for the bachelors at the club, but a strain on several of the married guys. However, we quickly became a remarkably tight unit, a team who would almost die for each other.

Another new face appeared when John McGovern landed from Hartlepools for £7,500. I had played against him for Tranmere, and recalled a slender, blond youth with an awkward, stooping running style which was eventually revealed to be the result of a missing muscle in his left shoulder.

In all honesty, he didn't look much like a footballer. Nobody knew whether John had come as an orthodox winger or to play in midfield. Equally, none of us doubted for a moment that he had been bought with a specific job in mind. His willingness to work hard was clear from day one.

With Mackay oozing confidence at the back, Carlin barking

orders in midfield and McGovern's presence on the sidelines increasing the competition for places, results improved dramatically and I scored my second goal of the season in a 2-0 win over a visiting Oxford side containing Ron Atkinson and his brother Graham.

The lads were congratulating me again when I was called up by Sir Alf Ramsey to make my debut for his England Under-23 side against Wales in Wrexham. He had been to Derby to watch me again in our first home game of the season, a 1-1 draw with Blackpool, and this time I had evidently done enough to make a positive impression.

Clough said nothing, though. He didn't need to, having seen the potential in me I never glimpsed myself and predicting that I would play for England within a year of joining Derby. He miscalculated by a matter of months.

There would have been no disgrace slipping quietly out of the League Cup in the third round when, following a couple of big wins over Chesterfield and Stockport, the draw pitted us against Dave Sexton's Chelsea.

When they weren't flaunting it in the clothes shops, clubs and discotheques of the fashionable King's Road, the flamboyant Chelsea boys were lording it over the First Division. Before our visit to Stamford Bridge, they had scored in every match – 26 goals in the League, Inter City Fairs Cup and League Cup – thanks to a potent attack featuring Peter Osgood, Bobby Tambling, Tommy Baldwin and Alan Birchenall. They travelled to both Manchester United and QPR to win 4-0.

The support act consisted of wingers Charlie Cooke and Peter Houseman, John Hollins and Derby-born forward Ian Hutchinson while in defence, Sexton could rely on an England goalkeeper in Peter Bonetti, the Scotland left-back Eddie McCreadie, Ron 'Chopper' Harris and another notable hard man in Dave Webb.

Yet while Chelsea were, in short, a very high-class act, Derby were absolutely fearless. We set out our stall to defend and frustrate them, succeeded and almost nicked a win. They didn't stretch us, which was a surprise given their reputation, and we made them look ordinary. With Carlin sitting in front of the back four, we were solid and difficult to break down, and we held Chelsea with the minimum of fuss.

My satisfaction at a job well done was tempered by the fact that the replay clashed with the England Under-23 game.

I knew where my priorities were and it took me about 10 seconds to decide the white shirt I'd be wearing the following week would be Derby's.

The club secretary sent the appropriate message to Lancaster Gate and Clough told me bluntly: "I'm so glad you made that decision, Roy. Otherwise I would have made it for you. If you'd made the wrong call, I'd have changed it."

The atmosphere inside the Baseball Ground for the replay was electric – and so was our performance.

Everything came together that October night as we battered Chelsea from pillar to post with a devastating exhibition of attacking play, even if it took us until 13 minutes from full-time to equalise Birchenall's goal midway through the first half. Then Dave Mackay drilled a dipping 30-yarder into the corner of Bonetti's goal and, with chants of "Der-by, Der-by" reverberating from all four sides of a stadium packed with 34,346 fans, Alan Durban headed us in front and Kevin Hector applied the coup de grace.

It was my first, thrilling realisation that when, rather than if, this Derby team was promoted, we had the potential not to merely survive in the First Division, but prosper. It opened my eyes to what we could achieve. This special, highly-charged night was possible only to appreciate if you were there, on the pitch, on the terraces or stamping your feet in the stands.

Chelsea had raised their standards from the stalemate at Stamford Bridge, they knew they had to, yet we played them off the park. It was a big game, in front of a big crowd against a big team and gave us the confidence to believe anything was possible.

Our fans had cup fever now and a fortnight later 10,000 supporters travelled up to Everton for our fourth-round tie by train, coach and car. Some fans, who could afford £5 10shillings for a return flight, went by plane from Castle Donington to Liverpool airport.

Harry Catterick's side was also filled with quality, boasting the 'Holy Trinity' of Alan Ball, Colin Harvey and Howard Kendall in midfield, England internationals in goal and at centre-half in Gordon West and Brian Labone respectively, and free-scoring Joe Royle up front with the dangerous Jimmy Husband.

I was relishing the prospect of going home and delighted to discover the club had booked us to stay the night before the match in the Adelphi Hotel.

As I registered my name in the guestbook, I was reminded of how far I had travelled in my career. It seemed like only a few years since I was one of the scallies hovering outside the Adelphi, autograph book in hand.

After dinner, Clough poked his head into the lounge where the players were relaxing, pointed to me and said: "Roy, would you mind stepping into the bar?" I wondered if I'd done anything wrong, or if he was poised to prime me for some tactical ploy against Royle and Husband, but any concerns disappeared as I spotted Mum and Dad, deep in conversation with Taylor – and Matt Monro.

Clough had phoned my parents and invited them to come down for a drink, and they looked as if they had won the pools. Mind you, I suspect Brian was equally impressed to see the great ballad singer.

He was a huge fan of Matt Monro's and always claimed The Man With The Golden Voice never got the acclaim he was due, despite recording the title tracks for successful films such as From Russia With Love and Born Free, not to mention his biggest hit, Portrait of My Love. I stayed in the bar for an hour, sipping a couple of soft drinks, before it was time for Mum and Dad to catch the bus home and me to go to bed.

A little over 12 months earlier, I had been in the crowd at Goodison Park watching Everton play a superior brand of football, but now Derby were a match for them and comfortably pulled off a 0-0 draw.

Unfortunately, the match is best remembered for a foul by Mackay on Husband, after which the striker was said to be never quite the same again.

Although I loved Dave as if he was my big brother, I was angry with him on this occasion. As Husband pushed the ball to his left, I sensed Dave wouldn't get there and moved to eliminate the danger, but Dave was fully committed to the tackle and caught him late. Husband went down, stayed down and everyone in the ground sensed it was a very serious injury. Dave made a genuine attempt to get the ball, Husband was too quick for him, but there is no way he would have passed me. The injury he sustained was due to the way he landed so awkwardly.

Fortunately, there were no recriminations in the replay. Hard as he undoubtedly was, I suspect Catterick's men knew Dave Mackay was not the sort of character to go around maiming opponents, especially having suffered the pain of two broken legs himself.

The atmosphere was crackling again but where Chelsea gave you a chance by playing an open style, Everton were more organised, regimented and compact. Kevin Hector made the vital breakthrough on the half-hour with the only goal of the game to book us a home tie against Swindon.

Mentally, I think a few of us were getting measured for our Wembley suits when Danny Williams brought his side up from Wiltshire, although this was only a quarter-final tie.

Having knocked out leading First Division sides in Chelsea and Everton, it seemed only natural to presume that Swindon, from the Third, would not prove too formidable a barrier.

Both games were a spectacular anti-climax as we were held 0-0 before losing 1-0 at the County Ground on November 5 when a freak deflected goal made a bonfire of our vanities.

They had Don Rogers, a genuine handful on the wing, and a Welsh international right-back in Rod Thomas, destined to become a highly valued team-mate at Derby, but as much as anything, we were guilty of underestimating shock troops who went on to win the League Cup at Arsenal's expense.

I couldn't afford to mope, however, as the following week found me preparing to make my belated debut for the England Under-23 side in a friendly against Holland at St Andrew's.

The emerging young Dutchmen were extremely accomplished

footballers, boasting Robbie Rensenbrink, a brilliant left-winger who was to feature in both the 1974 and 1978 World Cup final teams, and striker Ruud Geels, who also made Holland's 22-man squad in the tournament in West Germany.

Holland were good value for their 1-0 lead at half-time and we had it all on to fight back for a 2-2 draw with goals from Arsenal forward John Radford and our skipper, Everton's John Hurst.

It wasn't easy settling into a team drawn from 10 different clubs and difficult to assess how good my team-mates were, but I felt comfortable with my performance.

My abiding memory is the impact Peter Knowles made. The Wolves pin-up boy must have thought himself very rock 'n' roll, bowling into our city centre hotel in Birmingham the previous day with two young girls in mini skirts hanging onto his arms, dressed as if he was going to a nightclub.

As a footballer, Peter had no end of talent, but he was a very, very funny guy in a strange sense. It just didn't look or feel right at all to see him sitting there in the lounge, so flash with these girls, with all the other lads waiting to go into the restaurant.

If his intention was to impress us, he succeeded only in causing embarrassment. It was a huge relief when the time came to go and eat and, mercifully, he kissed the girls goodbye.

To be fair, Peter settled down after that and became one of the group, although he was the last player on earth I thought would hang up his boots and join the Jehovah's Witnesses.

My two days in Birmingham gave rise to another example of Dave Mackay's unstinting generosity. Three friends from Liverpool were in Derby briefly on a course at the Railway Carriage & Wagon Works.

When Dave discovered I would barely be around to entertain them, he volunteered his services.

My pals were huge football fans and enthusiastic drinkers, so they hit it off superbly with Dave, who met for aperitifs in the York Hotel, treated them to a steak at the Iron Gate Tavern, before moving on to the Embassy nightclub for more drinks and a little poker and roulette.

When I got back very late to the York after the match, I found two of my friends sitting on a sofa with their arms wrapped around Dave's shoulders. Five hours earlier, they had never met, now the young Liverpudlians were bosom buddies with Dave Mackay. It was typical of the effect the man had on people.

One unwelcome side-effect of gaining my first international honour was speculation that the Derby board might be tempted to cash in on their £24,000 investment and sell me for a handsome profit.

Agitating for a transfer was the last thing on my mind and I was relieved when Clough gave Sam Longson and his fellow directors this stark warning: "I've heard about clubs showing interest in McFarland. Even mention of a possible big bid. My answer is simple. If McFarland is transferred from Derby, I will be out of the door 10 seconds in front of him. I am building a side here. McFarland is an essential part of the general plan for progress. I bought him from Tranmere Rovers when everyone was still sizing him up. It's amazing. At least 14 clubs have since told me they were on the point of bidding when I moved in. It would be easy to sell Roy for a big fee, but where could I find a better prospect, no matter how much money I had, to replace him? It may be there are clubs prepared to spend six figures to get him. But I couldn't put a figure on his value to us and I don't intend to. If we sell McFarland all our talk about promotion ambitions will look ridiculous. This is one issue where there is no argument. If McFarland goes, I go."

I was perfectly happy where I was and had no intention of leaving. Promises made to me by Clough and Taylor the previous year at home in Edge Hill were starting to come true in front of my eyes.

The club had changed, the quality of new players arriving was improving us all the time and we were heading out of the Second Division. I had won my first England cap for the Under-23s and I was loving every minute of it.

There was talk of several clubs looking closely at me, but no one specific club. In any case, Brian had made it very obvious he wasn't open to entertaining offers, which was another boost to my confidence, and he was not duty-bound to inform me of any bids. So it was a shock when Clough met me in an otherwise deserted Baseball Ground corridor, fixed me with his eyes and said: "You know I rate you highly, Roy. But if I could ever buy a better centre-half, I would sell you tomorrow."

John McGovern got into the side in November and we soon began to appreciate his qualities, even if the critics and some fans asked: "What is it that McGovern actually does?"

Whenever our opponents' main creative force was obliterated and made to look anonymous, it was the result of John's diligence and hard work in front of the back four. He read the game brilliantly and broke up opposition attacks with his timing and anticipation before laying the ball off simply and accurately to another white shirt.

He wasn't big, he wasn't strong, he never had the pace to be a winger, he wasn't a great striker of the ball or a powerful header of it either, he was simply a genuine young lad who enjoyed playing football. John used everything he did possess to go on and achieve great things with us and also Forest, where he proudly lifted the European Cup in successive seasons.

Meanwhile, an away trip to tackle promotion rivals Crystal Palace was right up Mackay's street, especially when the management arranged for us to enjoy a three-night stay at Bisham Abbey before we headed for Selhurst Park, where I scored in a 2-1 win which took us top of the table by a point from Millwall and Palace.

This was Dave's first League match back in London since leaving Tottenham and he was serenaded from the terraces by a couple of dozen Spurs fans, who saw him turn on the pomp and majesty they were familiar with from his glory, glory days at White Hart Lane.

The management were in no mood to leave anything to chance now and they signed Frank Wignall from Wolves for £20,000 as cover should Kevin Hector or John O'Hare get injured. Wiggy was 29, an old-fashioned, bash-'em-up sort of centre-forward, with a couple of England caps under his belt. The fans loved him and chanted at the other team: "Six-foot two, eyes of blue, Frankie Wignall's after you."

Unrelentingly brutal, he was after me in training too and taught me more about the extreme physical nature of football. He deliberately roughed me up, tripping me, barging into me, seeking a reaction and doing his best to make me lose my rhythm and concentration.

"Hey, this is how tough it will be on Saturday," he insisted, well aware that I had a temper and whenever I responded angrily, he'd wag a finger at me and say: "Do that on Saturday when you get a bang and we're down to 10 men."

Wignall scored on his debut in a 4-2 home win over Blackburn when he came on as a substitute but then Palace deservedly beat us 1-0, after which Clough whisked the team away to Blackpool for three days before our match at Bloomfield Road with orders to "give the pinball machines some stick and forget all about football".

We squeezed out a fine 3-2 win beside the seaside, which I recall fondly as it featured a goal from the training ground.

Mackay signalled his intentions at a free-kick, gave me the nod and chipped the ball high over the Blackpool wall, enabling me to make a diagonal run, catch the ball on the volley inches off the turf and send my shot trickling inside the far post.

Growing in strength and stature, we won our last nine matches and proved ourselves the outstanding team in the Second Division as we ran away with the title.

The run included a satisfying 1-0 win at Aston Villa, where over 15,000 travelling Derby fans swelled the gate to 49,188. Tommy Docherty, the Villa manager, had raised the stakes in midweek, provocatively claiming: "All Derby are going to get is a cup of tea at half-time."

Typical Doc, he lived his career making wisecracks, but Clough was above all that and refused to rise to the bait.

When we went off, leading at the interval, Docherty was told in no uncertain terms by 15,000 mocking voices precisely where he could stick that cup of tea.

I was extremely pleased with my final tally of nine goals for the season, not a bad haul for a centre-half, and the last of them arrived, fittingly I thought, in a 5-1 home win to clinch promotion over Bolton on Easter Saturday, April 5, 1969 – my 21st birthday, which also guaranteed my party that evening in the York Hotel went with a swing.

Bristol City were beaten 5-0 in the final game of the season at the Baseball Ground, after which Dave Mackay was presented with the championship trophy. The skipper was soon celebrating another double, as he shared the Footballer of the Year award jointly with Manchester City's Tony Book.

There were celebration dinners and receptions, coach tours of the town and county, and a £30,000 promotion bonus to be divvied up among the team, but my work for the season wasn't quite done. Ron Suart claimed me for an England Under-23 tour in May and I went with the blessing of Clough and Taylor to further my international education. Results were mixed, a 2-1 defeat by Holland in Deventer, followed by a 1-0 win over a Belgium B side in Ostend, before we finished with a 1-1 draw against Portugal in Madeira.

The 1970 World Cup in Mexico was only a year away and I think all the players on that Under-23 tour believed they were in with a shout of catching Sir Alf Ramsey's eye – even if he had the bulk of the historic 1966 winners to call on. There were men such as Francis Lee and, significantly from my point of view, Norman Hunter and Brian Labone, in front of us in the pecking order.

We felt we had a chance of getting on that plane to South America. We were the young ones, the next generation and Suart was in charge of a talented squad. Emlyn Hughes and Peter Osgood both made it into Alf's 22 for Mexico, while Peter Shilton wasn't far away from full international recognition as well.

8

Terry's Turn To Make The Tea

WILLIE CARLIN feared he would be shot by a gun-toting Spanish policeman, while Jimmy Walker and Les Green nearly drowned on a boozy, two-week break in Majorca – our reward for winning the Second Division championship.

Brian Clough would not have been impressed but the boss wasn't around the night we spilled out of a Cala Millor hotel and went in search of another bar and discotheque.

A souped-up Mini car, driven by a young Spaniard, came hurtling down the narrow street towards us. Fortunately, he had the sense to slam on his brakes before mowing us down and was duly rewarded by Green bringing down one of his hammer-like fists on the roof, leaving a massive dent, as the rest of the lads scattered to safety.

The driver reported the incident immediately to the police, who duly turned up and arrested Carlin and John Robson, both of whom were totally innocent.

I crossed the street to remonstrate with the cops, only to stop in my tracks when Willie implored me not to make any sudden move. "Hold it there, Roy, don't come any closer," he shouted. "I've got a revolver sticking in my back and I don't want it going off!" My two team-mates were arrested and spent the night in jail.

As for the near-drowning incident, Walker was a non-swimmer and that became apparent when he wandered waist-high into the sea, only to fall victim to a steep shelf.

I was topping up my suntan on the beach when I was alerted to the sort of frantic thrashing more usually associated with a shark attack. Walker was panicking after going under and threatened to drag Green down with him when our goalkeeper went into lifesaver mode. To everyone's immense relief, he was powerful enough to fight off Walker and drag him into the shallows, from which both men emerged on their knees, exhausted.

We indulged ourselves totally over that fortnight with Peter Taylor loosely in charge. It was quite a shock to the system and we were shattered by the end due to a combination of lack of sleep and too much alcohol and sun. Club trips after that marathon bender were reduced to a maximum of a week.

When Clough did accompany us, he mixed business with pleasure as he revealed in this tale:

"I worked incentives and fines out sometimes at Cala Millor when we were away, all drinking San Miguel or whatever.

I'd explain, 'Right, we'll get the incentives sorted out now because I don't want it on my back when we get home'. Oh, everybody was in a good mood! I wasn't that bloody daft, like, you know. We'd sort it out and I implemented them when we got back. I'd ask them, 'Are you happy with it' and they'd say 'Yeah'. I insisted on them knowing how much I was going go fine them if they were late and I'd ask again, 'You're happy with what you're going to get fined if you're late' and they'd all say slowly together, 'Yes, gaffer, we're happy with that'. Everything agreed with, we'd all shake hands and have another beer.

"In those days money was so tight we talked in ten pounds. I argued with Willie Carlin at the Baseball Ground for three hours. That's the longest I've ever been in an office with a player. It used to be three minutes. And Willie was there and he sat it out and sat it out, and I argued with him over ten quid a week rise, and eventually I said 'Willie, I've had enough of you, get out'. 'Gaffer,' he said 'I wouldn't care if it was your money'. I said 'It is mine, I'm supposed to look after it and it is company money'. His head was down because I'd told him 'You're not getting it and that's it... and you can sit there all day. In fact, if you sit there much longer I'll fine you'. So anyway as he got up I said to him 'Go on, then, you've talked me into it'. And he whipped round thinking I'd given him a tenner. And I said 'I'll give you a fiver'."

Word of the incident with the Mini reached the Baseball Ground and the club compensated the driver. Although Peter pleaded the case for leniency, Clough was almost duty-bound to dish out a few club fines, but he didn't make a big issue of the trouble. He had more important things on his mind – a First Division campaign to prepare for.

Back home, an attractive blonde smiled across a crowded bar and I hoped it meant the end of a beginning which had seen more than its fair share of false starts. Many months earlier, you would have got extremely long odds on this equation working out: Idiot plus Blondie equals True Love.

Lin Webster didn't appreciate my clumsy attempt to break the ice the first time we met in the Khardomah coffee shop, around the corner from the Market Place. I was there with Dave Mackay, Jimmy Walker and Mick Jones when in walked a bunch of pretty girls who worked at Royal Crown Derby, less than a mile from the Baseball Ground.

After some banter, one of them, cheekier than the rest, said: "As we're virtually neighbours, why don't you come and join us at our table?" We didn't need any encouragement and it was then I focused on this gorgeous girl.

In the history of chat-up lines my opening gambit must be down there with the worst as I fished out a bag of toffees and asked Lin: "Do you want a sweet?" and just as she reached forward I added, "Fattie!" It was just a bit of harmless fun on my part but she was upset and very offended.

Lin had always sworn she would never get hitched to a footballer after all three of her elder sisters married local semi-professional players: Joyce wed Heanor's Jack Hallam, Jackie fell for John Page of Belper Town while Wendy went down the aisle to meet Alfreton's John Mycroft, who was on amateur forms with Nottingham Forest. Conversation in Lin's home tended to be pretty one-dimensional. Put bluntly, she was sick of the sound of football gossip among her sisters and assorted boyfriends, fiances and husbands.

If Lin had already been turned off by the game, my stab at

humour can only have reinforced her prejudice. She was mortified and hurried out of the cafe. There was an embarrassed silence until one of her friends informed me she would be in the Market Place, waiting for a bus home. I jumped up, went to get my Ford Anglia, found Lin and offered her a lift.

"You're an even bigger idiot than I took you for five minutes ago, if you think I'd ever get in a car with you," she said, which tells you how Lin got home that afternoon. A truce broke out when we saw each other in groups around town, but it seemed we would remain just good friends as either one or the other of us was always going out with someone else.

Clough was delighted when his young players settled into long-term relationships, preferably marriage, and he was happy for us to have a drink or two until midweek. If we had a match on Saturday, the cut-off point for drinking alcohol was Wednesday. Thursday nights we usually went to the cinema while Fridays generally found us all together in a hotel for away games and, increasingly, home matches.

The regime was relaxed that summer during pre-season training, which was thirsty work under our new first-team trainer Jimmy Gordon, and the evenings could invariably find the Derby County team holding court in the cellar bar of the Iron Gate Tavern.

It was there that Lin and I properly clicked. She was in the 'Gates' with her circle of friends, and we simply got chatting, hit it off and enjoyed our first proper date in a village pub, the Cross Keys at Turnditch.

We came from a similar background, but while I had been used to candyfloss-and-chips trips to the seaside at Blundellsands, New Brighton, Formby, Southport and Rhyl, Lin persuaded me to spend our Sundays visiting stately homes and on picnics in the Derbyshire countryside with her sisters in extended family groups.

Kedleston Hall was on our doorstep and we also got to know Chatsworth House and Hardwick Hall. We ventured into the Peak District to climb Thorpe Cloud at picturesque Dovedale, descending to eat our lunch al fresco by the stepping stones over the River Dove.

On another occasion we had coffee and sandwiches in the posh Peveril of the Peak, the hotel which hosted the West German national team for the 1966 World Cup.

Woollaton Park was explored in Nottingham and much further to the east lay Skegness, where the fish and chips were every bit as good as anything I had tasted on the Fylde Coast.

Someone else was only too happy to relieve me of the burden of driving and the Sunday experience was a constant eye-opener. It felt like a magical mystery tour to the kid from inner-city Liverpool.

Not so much fun was the heat and excessive coach travelling involved in a pre-season tour to Germany, where I felt discomfort in my groin during one of the friendlies and our results weren't too clever either.

Back at work, the moment of truth was fast approaching and the Baseball Ground looked a picture in the sunshine, having received a long overdue face-lift in the shape of the new £230,000 Ley Stand.

It was a steep, state-of-the-art structure, covering the full length of the Pop Side terracing below, and meant the obliteration of the famous Offilers Ales sign – but there was no room for nostalgia in Derby's brave new world.

Confidence was high among the bulk of the 29,451 crowd when we ran out to face Burnley at home in our opening game of the 1969-70 season, but I was never more nervous, even when I made my professional debut for Tranmere.

Burnley gave us a thorough working over, although the 0-0 scoreline might not suggest it. The difference in standard between the Second and First Division shocked me as Burnley dragged us all over the pitch with a performance of pace and power in the heat.

Harry Potts had brought his side to play football, rather than indulge in the sort of war games which had scarred our FA Cup tie at Turf Moor seven months previously.

Many of us were edgy and nervous with only Dave Mackay and Alan Hinton having previously sampled this level of football properly. It was quite an experience, and not a pleasant one. It might even have been personally disastrous when I handled a late shot from Brian O'Neil. Green had a knack of saving his team-mates, however, and spared me some stick by stopping Frank Casper's subsequent penalty. I was delighted and relieved to come off with a point.

While the management had total faith in our ability to hold our own, and I very rarely questioned anything Clough and Taylor said, I wondered how we would survive at this level when a middling sort of side could cause us such discomfort.

One reporter tried to ingratiate himself with Clough, saying: "It's a great vote of confidence in your players," only to be met with the put-down: "Rubbish. If I had someone better, he'd be straight in the team," and Taylor added; "We want a centre-half better than McFarland if we can find one."

My concerns disappeared when we settled down. For the second successive season, I scored Derby's first goal – a header from a Hinton corner – to give us victory at Ipswich in midweek. We were considerably more relaxed and ready to defend at Portman Road. The side as a whole was set up to defend away from home and the match was far less intense than the inquisition by Burnley.

I was on target again four days later in a 1-1 draw against Coventry, but it was a bittersweet afternoon at Highfield Road because I was badly at fault for their equaliser by centre-forward Neil Martin, who became one of my most awkward opponents.

Martin had a tremendous leap which made him very strong in the air, and you were in trouble unless you were prepared to time your own jump to challenge for the ball. On this occasion, I was slow off the mark, marooned at the back post, as the Scot got in front of me to connect with a free-kick. I held my hands up and confessed: "I was static. I should have run with him. It won't happen again."

In three matches, I had scored twice, conceded a penalty and made a schoolboy howler to concede a goal. It felt confusing but we kept learning, continued to improve and looked at the table in September to discover Derby top of the First Division after I headed the only goal at Newcastle. Mackay sent in a deep free-kick and the Magpies' striker, Wyn Davies, who was supposed to mark me, got his bearings all wrong and I connected with a firm header.

Bill Nicholson's Tottenham Hotspur all-stars were our visitors the following Saturday and all the talk centred around Mackay facing the club he had served with such distinction for a decade.

Sometimes he'd get on the coach for an away match, oozing confidence, and ask the lads: "Who are we playing today?" On this occasion he knew full well that Spurs were in town as did a crowd of 41,826, an interesting statistic in itself given that the Baseball Ground's official capacity was 40,500.

Professional from head to toe, Mackay had respect for Tottenham but he didn't betray the slightest trace of anxiety or nerves.

Match of the Day had screened our 2-1 win over Everton a fortnight earlier but this was our first genuine glamour game and the BBC cameras returned, no doubt anticipating another closely-fought match considering Spurs had won their previous four away games, and arrived on the back of a 3-2 victory at Arsenal.

Mackay was the model of serenity in the dressing room, radiating calm and authority, but I was pumped up because I knew Dave and I faced a formidable strike force in the shape of the famous Jimmy Greaves, who didn't need an introduction to anyone, and Alan Gilzean.

I rated Greavsie the best striker in the country, a forward with pace to burn who was denied the chance of a World Cup winners' medal because of injury. With the wily Gilzean alongside him, I felt I was going to be tested like never before.

It was the London club's misfortune to visit us at a moment when we felt settled, our football was flowing and they became the first of a succession of big-name clubs to be trounced at the Baseball Ground.

There were echoes of the League Cup triumph over Chelsea as Alan Durban scored twice and Bill Nick saw his players humiliated to the tune of 5-0, their biggest margin of defeat in the League since going down 7-2 at Burnley in 1964 when Mackay was on the receiving end. Tottenham could find no place to hide in their fetching change strip of yellow and white as they were cruelly taunted by our fans, who finished the afternoon chanting: "Derby five, Bananas nil."

Although we were rampant in attack, it was an incident at the other end that is still discussed by Derby players and supporters of a certain vintage. Trailing 2-0, Spurs had a chance to get back into it when Greaves went past me in the penalty area.

I stretched out a leg and clipped him slightly, but Greaves always preferred to put the ball in the net rather than accept a cheap penalty, and kept going before firing a shot.

Most goalkeepers would have settled for laying a glove on the ball, yet Green did better than that, arching backwards to catch it with both hands outstretched. Greaves couldn't believe it and neither could we. That save was as good as it gets.

In many respects, that was as good as it got for us, too. Durban went off injured and our lack of strength in depth began to catch up with us.

Because we needed to be at full strength each and every match with our best team on the park to compete, there was no time for players to take a fortnight or three weeks off to rest and recuperate.

Inevitably, something had to give and it was my groin when we were followed up to Hillsborough by around 20,000 Derby supporters in a crowd of 44,332.

Sheffield Wednesday were a poor side, bound for relegation, and we were dragged down to their level, the only goal going in off Alan Warboys' shins.

I was no help, though, struggling through 90 minutes with a nagging injury which restricted my mobility. The trouble I had suffered in Germany was back.

Manchester United were our next visitors, on a 10-match unbeaten run and boasting a front five of Willie Morgan, Brian Kidd, George Best, Bobby Charlton and John Aston.

Wilf McGuinness was the United manager and knew about my suspect groin because Bestie was picked to play centre-forward.

The plan was to get me twisting and swivelling sharply to aggravate my injury. When he wasn't doing that, George had the ability to drop off to collect the ball before turning and testing you for raw pace. Whatever United's tactics, the rest and treatment I'd had during the week was sufficient for me to cope with Bestie and we won 2-0.

I entered a strange routine whereby the entire week was designed around me getting through 90 minutes on a Saturday, and sometimes a midweek match too.

Rest was the major factor and when I didn't have my feet up, the physio was working on my injury. Clough and Taylor badgered me, saying: "We want you to play, we need you to play," and I just did it. I was so eager, so keen.

They kept reassuring me that I would not come to any lasting damage, and that a good summer's rest would cure everything. It was only autumn. June and July were a long way off, obviously, but I never doubted the management for a moment. I would do a spot of light training on Friday, play the following afternoon and be in a complete heap by the end of the match.

If the pitch was reasonably soft, it was not too bad, but eventually I had to miss a match against Manchester City at home, which we lost 1-0. Soon I was staying in bed on Sundays, but at least I got out there to play.

Knowledge of my condition cost me England Under-23 caps against Wales and Russia, and maybe even a summons into the full international squad and a chance to advance my claims to go to the World Cup in Mexico.

Liverpool, poised to embark on an incredible era of success, were outclassed 4-0 when Bill Shankly brought his side to Derby in November. It was the first time they had conceded four goals in a League match since 1965 at Chelsea and an odd feeling for me as the club I had supported as a boy was convincingly beaten. Kevin Hector and John O'Hare, who scored three between them, ran riot. There was no gloating from me, but I was very proud.

Another 4-0 scoreline arrived the following Saturday and this time we were on the wrong end of it. Up until our trip to Highbury, we had the meanest defence in the First Division, but everything that could go wrong did so against Arsenal.

I was doing next to no training and this caught me out as much as the injury. I was gingerly feeling my groin strain while Robson was pressed into service too soon after missing a few matches with a nasty ankle injury.

The Gunners' No.9 John Radford turned in a brilliant display at my expense in front of Sir Alf Ramsey. Normally, our back four of Webster, myself, Mackay and Robson, knew precisely how to operate as a unit, but we malfunctioned disastrously.

Ramsey and Clough never warmed to each other and when I did make the England squad, Sir Alf did not disguise the fact that he felt I had been poorly advised to continue playing. He told me: "When I saw you at Arsenal, I thought you had been silly playing with an injury. It could have finished your career."

By this time the trouble had spread to the other groin and I was swallowing painkillers and anti-inflammatory drugs galore, and undergoing x-rays. I felt like an old age pensioner.

TERRY'S TURN TO MAKE THE TEA

The London press wondered what all the Derby fuss was about when we returned to the capital for a 3-0 defeat at West Ham, but that disappointment was nothing compared to the angst to follow.

Our bitter rivals Nottingham Forest came calling and won 2-0 on an icy pitch. The match might easily have been postponed because keeping your balance was a lottery on the rock-hard, slippery surface – although I will concede that the Forest players adapted to the conditions much better than us, especially Ian Storey-Moore, who headed the first goal, and left Webster slithering on his backside on several occasions.

There was much discussion among the lads about what sort of footwear to use. Boots with a short stud or rubber-soled boots, training shoes even?

Forest had been struggling away from home but outplayed us, driven on by Terry Hennessey.

We came in on Monday and got it in the neck from both Cloughie and Taylor, which was a rarity.

They let us know in terms liberally laced with expletives that the standard of our play had been inexcusable and how poorly we had performed. Peter glowered as he said: "Don't any of you lot dare mention the pitch. Forest managed all right on it."

It was uncommon for both of them to have a rant simultaneously, and so soon after a defeat. Setbacks sometimes meant an order to get to the ground for eight o'clock on Monday morning for a three-day jolly and after the weekend we'd find Peter, certainly, had mellowed.

Alternatively, nothing might be said for several days, while we were kept stewing, before the negative result was forgotten in favour of praise for our overall achievements.

Then we might beat Liverpool 4-0 or get a great away win and Clough would charge in and accuse us of being "a bloody dozy lot" because he'd picked up on something relatively trivial that irritated him, and we'd look blankly and ask each other: "What the hell is that all about?"

We never knew precisely how the management would react. They employed reverse psychology all the time to keep us guessing. It had the effect of driving me on to improve, try to minimise my mistakes and prepare as thoroughly for games as injuries permitted.

Forest were mid-table at best despite possessing several extremely talented players – none more so than Hennessey, Storey-Moore and Henry Newton, and Clough tried to sign all three.

The trio were, in fact, introduced at the Baseball Ground as Derby players at various intervals but Clough jumped the gun with Storey-Moore. Crucially, that acrimonious deal was never signed off at Forest's end and the winger went to Manchester United instead.

The Saturday following Forest's win, Dave Mackay hurt me as we recovered to win 1-0 at Crystal Palace.

Dave and I had a fabulous relationship, I idolised the man even when he criticised me, notably when I once abused Hinton for shirking a tackle. He pulled me up sharply and said: "Just do your job, Roy. Leave Ally alone to put over the crosses for all your goals." But on this occasion I was really stung by a cruel jibe after collapsing in a heap from a tackle with about 15 minutes to go.

Normally I'd bounce straight up but I was in agony from my damaged groin. Jimmy Gordon ran on with the magic sponge to see how I was, and I said: "Tell the gaffer I'm struggling."

Mackay stood over me and said witheringly: "Get up, you coward."

That annoyed me intensely and struck home deeply because it was the first time he had ever turned on me like that. My pelvic problem had been going on for nine months and every movement I made was agony, as muscle and bone fragments had come away in my groin.

Through gritted teeth, I told Jimmy: "Leave it, tell the gaffer I'm okay." Dave had wounded me with the ultimate insult, using it to gee me up. The ultra professional, his attitude was to get on with it, get the game won, and he did spur me on even if I could only just about crawl off the field at the final whistle.

Hennessey looked an impossible signing in February 1970 but Clough and Taylor had the knack of making the impossible look commonplace when they were together in their prime, cementing their legendary status.

Signed for a club record £100,000, Hennessey would have been a big signing for any club in the country, let alone Derby. An established Welsh international, he was a high-profile name.

Some reputations, however, counted for nothing in Clough's eyes. To my knowledge, he never once pulled up Mackay, never rebuked the skipper, never confronted him over anything.

Yet Hennessey had only been at the club a matter of days when Clough chose to treat him like an apprentice in front of the team, telling him: "Get the lads a cup of tea, Terry."

There were several little incidents like that. It was Brian's way of cutting players down to size, letting Hennessey know that he was with new team-mates now and that he was to be part of it for the common good.

Clough didn't want egos and attitudes to develop in the dressing room.

I know Hennessey found the unorthodox style of management strange and difficult to handle, being reduced in the ranks one moment, then having an arm wrapped round his shoulders on Blackpool beach the next.

Although he was signed with the intention of becoming Mackay's long-term successor, Terry had a hard time because he rarely seemed to be 100 per cent fit and alternated between playing as midfield anchor in front of me and in central defence.

Derby never got full value from Terry because of an Achilles tendon injury and later trouble with his knees, which did not make him too popular with the management.

For £100,000, they wanted a player who was always fit and available for selection.

Make no mistake, he was a nice guy and very comfortable in possession. Terry's nickname 'The Glove' reflected his easy passing style and the fact everything fitted him immaculately – boots, shirts, suits. If he'd got any hair left, he could have been a film star. He wasn't the quickest but, much like England captain Bobby Moore, he sniffed out danger before it developed and proved to be a good tackler and an immense header of the ball.

To begin with, Hennessey replaced John McGovern in midfield and enjoyed perhaps his finest hour-and-a-half in a Derby shirt when we went up to Liverpool and he headed our first goal in a 2-0 victory which gave us the double over the Reds.

I vividly recall taking a breather in the second half and looking back at the Kop and wondering what I would be thinking watching my team losing 2-0 to Derby. It had always been my ambition to go back to Anfield and win, and if I had written the script myself it could not have worked out better.

I stayed with Mum and Dad for the weekend, and went out to the pub that night. Strangely, none of my Liverpool-supporting mates seemed to be around – although they had been falling over themselves to buy me a pint in September when we ended Everton's unbeaten start.

The following month saw me make my fifth and final appearance for England Under-23s against Scotland at snowbound Sunderland, where no fewer than five current or future Derby players were on view.

I faced John O'Hare in an England line-up which included local hero Colin Todd and Leicester's David Nish, while Preston's Archie Gemmill was scurrying around in midfield for the Scots.

Clough and Taylor gave the other Derby lads the 'option' of travelling up with them on the team bus to watch John and myself do battle. Nearly all of them took the hint that it would be prudent to make the journey, despite the horrendous weather forecast.

I gained useful experience alongside Toddy, we complemented each other confidently, but it wasn't a genuine test because the conditions became atrocious to the extent the referee had little option but to abandon proceedings due to the thick snow after 62 minutes with England leading 3-1. Soon afterwards, Clough and Taylor had the engine of the bus running outside Roker Park so I could jump on for the long return journey.

Ten days later in Nottingham, with Hennessey wearing a white No.4 shirt, we kicked off at the City Ground with vengeance in mind and the Forest centre-half Sammy Chapman suffered.

Forest feared what Kevin Hector might do to them and there was a big buzz leading up to the match that he was going to get a kicking. Kevin played in 51 of Derby's 52 games all told in the First Division, FA Cup and League Cup that season.

He was, however, conspicuous by his absence at Forest, where Clough summoned up the heavy brigade aka Frank Wignall.

We were on the up and there was a lot of talk about Forest disrupting us although, to be fair, they were not a notoriously physical team. The ball was cleared on the halfway line and Frank sorted Sammy out in no uncertain terms.

We turned round to see Sammy lying flat on the floor and Frank standing about 10 yards away, as cool as you like. Battering ram Frank had waited for his opportunity and, when it came, he did Sammy in cold blood.

The shell-shocked Forest defender had to be helped off the pitch and out of the contest. As a statement of intent that Derby were not prepared to be bullied into submission, it was brutally effective and we went on to win comfortably 3-1.

Clough was all in favour of the beautiful game yet pragmatic when the situation demanded it.

He told a friend: "I actually bought Frank Wignall as the most expensive insurance document in the country at that time. I paid twenty thousand quid for him and had no intentions of playing him. And he said to me, 'Where am I going to play, when am I going to get in?' and I said, 'You're not. I've got 15 players and you're just coming in if any of the strikers get injured' and that's exactly what he did. He sat weeks and weeks out the side, never cribbed. I told him at the start, 'You don't have to sign' but Frank was then nearly 30, experienced and that's all I needed. I needed a cover. He played a few times, didn't he? He was a bloody vicious centre-forward as well. I know I played Frank once just because first of all he was ex-Nottingham, wasn't he? And if there was any sign or link that they were going to try and rough us up, Frank was the ideal man. Nobody was going to go near him. And his reputation before I even picked him in the side got to them and they thought, 'Oh, bloody Wignall's playing...' because they'd worked with him, they knew what he was like. So nobody was going to mess with him – so we were halfway there. Sammy Chapman? He'd have snapped Sammy Chapman in two. So that was the thinking behind that."

I was understandably proud to be named in Sir Alf Ramsey's World Cup 40 for Mexico. There were 28 likely contenders to be trimmed to a final 22-man squad a week before the tournament kicked off, plus 12 reserves – of which I was one.

The dozen on standby were inoculated and received medical certificates because there was a chance any one of us could be called up in an emergency.

I was fervently hoping to go to Mexico, despite being uncapped. After all, I argued to myself, Martin Peters didn't make his England debut until May 1966 and still managed to force his way into that World Cup team and score in the final triumph over the Germans.

There was always that story to keep me going but, deep down, I knew the groin injuries had taken too heavy a toll on my body and that it wasn't really going to happen.

The value of Hennessey's versatility became apparent when injuries forced out first Mackay, then myself, and 'The Glove' fitted seamlessly into the back four for the last handful of matches. In a brilliant climax to the season, we ran through

February, March and April unbeaten in the First Division, winning eight of our final dozen games to finish fourth – behind runaway champions Everton, Leeds and Chelsea – and qualify for the Inter Cities Fairs Cup.

No sooner were we looking forward to parading our skills on the continent, than we were hanging our heads in despair.

A joint Football Association and Football League commission investigated the books and discovered gross negligence in administration of the club.

Derby were fined £10,000 for financial malpractice but, far worse, banned from Europe for a year.

It was a vicious punishment for the players, and I felt it keenly after the way I had played so many matches in pain. We were bitterly disappointed having qualified for Europe on the pitch, only to have the prize snatched away from under our noses because of what had happened due to substandard accounting.

Clough, being Clough, gave the FA a mouthful, then he and Taylor told us: "It's gone, forget it. We're professionals, we move on. Enjoy your holidays."

There was a brief discussion about whether I should undergo surgery to fuse the groin ligaments to the bone, but I wasn't at all happy with the idea and it was agreed that a summer of careful rest might be a better bet.

I suppose there were times when I should not have played. But Clough and Taylor always left it to me. Half-a-dozen times I went to the ground knowing that I was not fit to play. I would set off to walk along the corridor to the manager's office to tell him and then turn back and get stripped. I always wanted to play for the club. I never wanted to let anyone down.

9

Jumping To Alf's Tune

WHEN the working men and women of crisis-ridden Derby cried out for a messiah in the winter of 1971, Brian Clough duly obliged and bought me the best present money could buy – Colin Todd.

I was almost embarrassed to celebrate my first England cap against Malta, my excitement contrasting with the fear and despondency which descended on the town.

Rolls-Royce had gone bust and the official receivers were to be called in. It was devastating news.

It's no exaggeration to say that everyone in the town knew someone, directly or indirectly, connected with the business of manufacturing aero engines at Rolls-Royce.

All three of my future brothers-in-law had jobs surrounding the company, as did legions of our fans. The news that thousands of jobs were in danger of disappearing hit Derby hard.

Clough was always very politically minded, marching with miners and supporting local Labour candidates on the campaign trail.

Now he sat us down and gave it to us straight: "The workers of Derby have just had a right kicking, so it's your job to go out there and put a bloody great smile on people's faces. They support us through thick and thin and we must support them through entertaining football and winning football matches."

We felt that connection, the gaffer's words struck a chord and we reeled off four straight wins against West Ham, Crystal Palace, Blackpool and Arsenal that February.

The 2-0 home success over Bertie Mee's Gunners, who were destined to complete the Double in May, was a highly satisfactory afternoon's work as I scored, took my revenge on John Radford and our supporters were treated to their first sight of Todd in a Derby shirt.

I'll let an England team-mate, Arsenal's Peter Storey, give his version of events: "It was a typically awkward uneven Baseball Ground surface, but you'd never have guessed it from the performance of Roy McFarland. Derby's England centre-half had been taken to the cleaners once or twice before by Raddy, but not this time. He not only found time to score the opening goal but totally dominated too for good measure."

Clough called the Sunderland manager Alan Brown's bluff in a classic bit of brinkmanship to pay a British record fee of £175,000 to take Todd from Roker Park.

He told a friend: "I bought Colin Todd and Derby were bust at the time, the club and the city. Rolls-Royce had got padlocks on the gates and British Rail were on their knees. I know Rolls-Royce was going into liquidation, I do know that. And I went up to Alan Brown and I said, 'Colin Todd?'. 'Yeah,' he said, 'he's not for sale'. I said, 'Well, would you consider £100,000? I started off at £100,000. I went up and I went up and the conversation went on for ages because he was a good talker, Alan Brown, but about himself. So there we were talking, talking and he used words like 'you've got a lot to learn in management if you stay in it' and it was true. I did have a lot to learn. I was a novice. And I said, 'I'm having trouble at Derby' giving him the sob story. And he fell for it lock, stock and barrel. 'Anyway,' he said, 'you couldn't get him for all the money in the world'. I said, 'Mr Brown, you can buy everybody'. I got to £150,000 and then he said, 'Well!' and clapped his hands – I thought, 'I've cracked it' – 'well, I'm sorry if you think I've wasted your time but it's been lovely to talk to you again, as manager to manager and I've got a busy schedule'. I've been there two hours and he's got a busy schedule? I went on the floor and I said, 'I'll still have to say that every man has got his price'. He said, 'It would take £175,000 to get him'. I said, 'Done' and he was so conceited he couldn't back down. He wasn't big enough to back down and say, 'I was only kidding'. He said, 'You'd pay £175,000 for Colin Todd, a 22-year-old?'. Brownie had forgotten I'd looked after Toddy from 15. Long before Brownie became manager of Sunderland I was working with Colin Todd. Because when I was injured, George Hardwick told me, 'Don't mess about on a Saturday. We don't want to see you in crutches and plasters and you injured with your face on the floor'. He said, 'Go with the youth side'. Bill Scott was 69 years old, in charge of the youth side. George said, 'He's about shot it, you get with them, so I had Toddy from 15'. So then Brownie is fraternising and taking the mickey and said, 'Go on then. Done. £175,000'. And I just saw him for all his strength of character, he just couldn't stop a smile – thinking he'd done me."

Sam Longson, our chairman, was on holiday in the Caribbean and almost choked on his cigar when he learned of the cash involved, but I wasn't surprised.

It had reached the stage where if there was a vacancy, you expected Clough and Taylor to get the top bloke in.

In terms of signing players, they were prepared to break the bank and target whoever they fancied.

I knew Todd was a high-class operator from the England Under-23s, but I didn't know just how good he was until we formed a natural partnership.

Dave Mackay was the best I ever played with but Todd was the perfect successor. He actually let forwards run past him because he knew he'd catch them. That sounds crazy, but his pace and power made it easy. He'd slide in, hook his foot round the ball as the forward fell over, then stand up and pass. All in one move. Toddy was quick, strong, better in the air than some thought and a great passer. We just gelled. Whatever I missed, he tidied up and vice versa.

Malcolm Macdonald, a prolific goalscorer for Newcastle and Arsenal, acknowledged that we became a pretty useful pairing.

Supermac said: "There were many great defenders – and a few scary ones too – that I faced in my decade at the top. But, for me, without question, the most difficult to play against was the combination of Colin Todd and Roy McFarland. Roy was hard as nails, mobile and unstoppable in the air while Toddy just sat off a little, clearing everything that Roy missed and prepared to outpace anyone who had the temerity to think they could run through the Derby back line."

The World Cup in Mexico had come too soon for me in the summer of 1970 when I took every opportunity to rest and return to full fitness. Now the Watney Cup, a new pre-season competition, was my immediate goal.

Manchester United's presence guaranteed prestige for the sponsors and we reached the final against a team including Bobby Charlton, George Best and Denis Law, plus Alex Stepney, Tony Dunne, David Sadler, Pat Crerard and Brian Kidd from Sit Matt Busby's line-up which had won the European Cup in 1968. Nobby Stiles was there too, coming on at the Baseball Ground as a substitute.

United were still, clearly, a huge scalp and on a scorching day we beat them every bit as convincingly as the 4-1 scoreline suggests, a huge confidence-booster. I delighted in scoring the first goal, blasting a shot beneath the angle of bar and post when I reacted quickest to Mackay's 25-yard free-kick which rebounded off the other upright.

Dave had this habit of rubbing his left boot on the back of his right leg, to let the opposing wall know he was poised to let fly with one of his specials. He shot so powerfully that I always tried to be alert to the possibility of a rebound from the woodwork or a parry by the goalkeeper.

Critics derided the Watney Cup as tin-pot stuff but we treated the contest as if it was the European Cup final and I saw no reason why we couldn't emulate the previous season's fourth-place finish. Derby County were in it to win it.

Decades later, Sir Alex Ferguson compared United to a moving bus, making the point that you had to be up to speed or you would be dropped off and a replacement taken on board. It was just like that with us.

My great friend and fellow Scouser, Willie Carlin, felt like he had been run over by a bus when Clough camped out overnight in Preston and signed Archie Gemmill for £66,000.

The intention was clear – Carlin out, Gemmill in – and I was as shocked as Willie because he was unquestionably our best player in the first few months of the season.

Even when we were losing, he was outstanding, with a regular position in midfield. It wasn't as if he was some kind of in-and-out fringe member of the squad. He was tremendously popular in the dressing room and also with the Derby fans.

Willie was bitter. The last thing he wanted was to leave the club, and it was the last thing we thought likely to happen at the time. I felt desperately sorry for him but football can be a cruel business.

Clough and Taylor decided Willie had done his job, there was no room for sentiment, and his departure was part of the general scheme of things at Derby: recruit, absorb, mould and eventually replace.

Taylor picked the optimum moment to decide Willie needed to go. Just 30, he was still doing the business in the First Division, and good enough to persuade Leicester to pay £40,000 for his services.

At least he had the satisfaction of helping the Foxes gain promotion from the Second Division. The management were conscious of the need to balance the books and Willie's sale, in effect, meant they had paid only £26,000 for Gemmill.

Archie was aggressive and confident from the word go, but didn't find it easy to settle in Derby.

His wife Betty was heavily pregnant with their son, Scot, and stayed in Lancashire while he moved into the Midland Hotel with me for several months.

I was conscious of the fact John O'Hare and Ronnie Webster had gone out of their way to help me adjust when I came down from Liverpool, so I tried to do the same for Archie, inviting him out to Sunday lunch with me at Lin's house.

Archie struggled to adjust to the tempo we played at, but it wasn't long before he was displaying the gifts which made him a human dynamo in midfield – enthusiasm, pace and energy.

Just like Carlin before him, Gemmill was a born winner, and a blessing for our defenders because when he picked the ball up and ran 70 yards towards the opposition's area or the corner flag, it eased the pressure and gave us time to get organised.

Archie matured into a very creative, excellent player. One of the most influential midfield players in Britain.

Clough was delighted to find Gemmill and Alan Durban complemented each other, because they were almost total opposites and he gave this insight into the Welshman: "Alan Durban didn't have anything Archie had. He used no pace, he'd got a bit of ball control, experienced, very experienced. An international, tons of caps, but what he had was the ability to get a goal believe it or believe it not. He would sneak in and tap the ball in the net there and then before you knew he was coming. Yeah, he weighed in with double figures, Alan Durban did. A good-looking lad, suave, he was a right busy bugger on the pitch. I used to give him stick all the time. I used to make Durban's life a misery. But he had endurance as well. He'd keep going and going and going. And he wasn't the favourite at Derby County by any stretch of the imagination. When I went there he wasn't the favourite. Mind you, they didn't have a favourite, but he was the type of player that attracted criticism because he looked as if he wasn't really trying. People say: 'You're not trying' ... all this bullshit. He's trying his balls off. But he didn't give that impression. But as soon as he got in a good side, as soon as he got surrounded by players, then he looked a bloody player then. And once again, right-hand player, left-hand player – he was the perfect fit with Archie."

A torn hamstring caused me to miss a clutch of matches before returning for successive 2-0 defeats by Leeds and Arsenal which left us in 20th place at the end of October.

The management's response was for Taylor to whisk us away from Luton Airport to Majorca on a four-day sunshine break.

These mid-season trips when a nip in the air at home was starting to develop were highly beneficial to recharge our batteries. The opportunity to get some sun on our backs, relax, swim, play a little tennis and train in a less-pressured environment gelled the team together even tighter.

Boxing Day brought another visit from Manchester United, a dramatic 4-4 draw – and two brutal sackings.

Les Green was ruthlessly axed after suffering something close to a complete systems shutdown. The end was as swift as it was surprising because entering the Christmas period, supporters would have been hard-pushed to detect any signs of deterioration in his displays.

But behind the scenes our goalkeeper was beset by serious problems of a financial and personal nature and, in retrospect, they were bound to surface at some stage.

All was well from Derby's point of view in the first half on the snowy, icy pitch as we took a 2-0 lead thanks to goals from Mackay and Frank Wignall.

Then from Ebenezer Scrooge at his most tight-fisted we turned into Lady Bountiful, gifting United three goals in four minutes through Denis Law (2) and George Best. Stung into retaliation, we edged 4-3 ahead with goals from Kevin Hector and Gemmill but were caught out badly again when Brian Kidd equalised.

A draw against United was never to be sniffed at in my view, but the fact we had emerged from an eight-goal thriller with just one point after leading twice was bitterly disappointing.

Green was distraught, a picture of misery in the dressing room, apologising as he said: "I let you down, lads. That was a really poor performance." He owed us nothing, having been fantastic for Derby from the first day he arrived and, of course, we had done a substandard job of protecting him against United, especially from corners.

The back four were responsible for dealing with crosses. We always tried to support each other, and I told Les I should have done better myself in those situations.

Clough and Taylor were not inclined to mess about, and Green never played League football again.

Colin Boulton's big chance had arrived at last and the club was in reliable hands between the sticks.

That Boxing Day also ended in a broken heart for United boss Wilf McGuinness, who was busted down the ranks to his previous role as reserve-team trainer, enabling Busby to return as manager.

My star was in the ascendancy, however, and I made my

full international debut as England launched their European Championship qualifying campaign with a 1-0 win over Malta in a less than daunting group which also featured Switzerland and Greece.

I was relaxing in the Midland Hotel on a Sunday when a phone call came through from Jeff Farmer, the Daily Mail's Midlands football writer, who told me he had a nice surprise and that I had been called up by Sir Alf Ramsey because Everton's Brian Labone had torn his Achilles tendon playing at Tottenham.

I didn't believe Jeff at first, but he assured me that the Football Association had issued an official statement.

I drove down to the England headquarters at Hendon Hall and any trepidation I felt at mixing with the 'big boys' evaporated when I was welcomed into the fold by a clutch of familiar faces, such as the boisterous Emlyn Hughes, Peter Shilton, Alan Ball, Colin Harvey and Joe Royle. There were guys like me, graduating from the Under-23s, and I immediately felt at home.

The composition of the England team was changing slowly, yet we were still indebted to a couple of the 1966 World Cup heroes for a narrow 1-0 win in Valletta where the 'field' did not boast a single blade of grass.

The sandy pitch was as hard as iron after being squashed flat by a steamroller before water was sprayed on to eliminate the dust and turn the surface dark red.

Martin Peters scored the only goal while Gordon Banks came to my rescue when the veteran Maltese centre-forward Joe Cini slipped past me to smash a shot which was destined for the top corner of the net before Banksie took off and pushed the ball behind for a corner, ripping his shorts and grazing his thigh when he landed on the horrible, gritty surface.

I felt that losing Cini was the only mistake I made all match, but it was one mistake too many – and the incident taught me how vital it was to be vigilant at all times at this level and never to underestimate a fellow international.

Six weeks after Malta, I represented the Football League against the Scottish League in Glasgow, where we won 1-0 with a goal from Ralph Coates.

It was not a match which set local fans alight as a crowd of only 17,657 congregated at Hampden Park, but it did give me my first opportunity to play alongside Bobby Moore in this line-up: John Jackson (Crystal Palace), Paul Reaney (Leeds), Derek Parkin (Wolves), John Hollins (Chelsea), McFarland (Derby), Moore (West Ham), Ralph Coates (Burnley), Tony Brown (West Brom), Geoff Hurst (West Ham), Brian O'Neil (Southampton), Ian Storey-Moore (Nottingham Forest).

Bobby had been temporarily in disgrace the previous month, dropped by England after West Ham suspended him following a late-night drinking escape in the boxer Brian London's night-club in Blackpool with Jimmy Greaves, Brian Dear and Clyde Best before an FA Cup tie they were convinced, wrongly as it happened, would be postponed because of a frozen pitch.

A 4-0 hammering by the Seasiders did not endear the quartet to manager Ron Greenwood when word reached him they had been spotted out on the town.

The representative fixture in Scotland was a brief in-and-out job and it wasn't until a few months later that I started to learn more about Moore.

I returned to Derby and was celebrating a 'win double' later that week when the House of Commons announced the acquisition of Rolls-Royce from the receivers. Ted Heath's Conservative government had saved the business from going under completely by nationalising the company, and the threat of mass redundancies receded.

I was beginning to gain a reputation and, without sounding too big-headed, I knew my time had come.

Jack Charlton's England career had finished at the World Cup the previous year, his successor Labone was really struggling with his Achilles injury and I thought I was a little bit ahead of Sadler and Liverpool's Larry Lloyd, certainly in Sir Alf's eyes.

Banks bailed me out in Malta and put in another sterling shift on my behalf in his weekly newspaper column, when he informed readers: "Roy McFarland looks to be making the England centre-half position his own. Sir Alf Ramsey praised him highly after his appearance in the Football League side against the Scottish League recently, and Roy will probably be England's centre-half in the next full international against Greece in the Nations Cup at Wembley on April 21. Roy is a really skilful centre-half, not just a stopper. We haven't had a centre-half of this type for some years. He likes playing the ball around. Joe Shaw, of Sheffield United, was similar in style. Is it an advantage to be skilful at centre-half? I reckon so, but you have to be careful with the skill bit. It's all very well beating an opponent inside your own box, but if you then lose the ball, then you're in trouble. When Roy McFarland first came into the First Division, I think he tended to overdo it. There has been a noticeable change in his play. He still uses the ball well, but he's not quite so adventurous. Perhaps Brian Clough or Dave Mackay at Derby has had a quiet word with him."

Banks' suspicions were on the mark because the gaffer had told me: "Roy, you can't pull the ball down in the 18-yard box every time. Occasionally you've got to whack it into the stand. Only thing is, I can't tell you when to do it. You've got to make that decision."

In other words, I had to think more, assess situations swiftly and take responsibility for my actions. That advice was imprinted on my brain from the moment it was uttered by Clough.

I kept my place for the match against the Greeks which we won 3-0, with Moore restored, in my first appearance at Wembley.

It was a nice, comfortable England team to slip into alongside five World Cup winners plus Alan Mullery and Francis Lee, who was another bubbly character like Alan Ball. They were an immense group of players who had all been tested and stretched to the limits in Mexico. I felt some sympathy for them because I was convinced England were almost there as the best team in the world and not far off meeting Brazil in the final.

I found my England No.5 shirt hanging next to Moore's iconic six in the dressing room, and that happy state of affairs continued for the best part of three years.

Bobby possessed charisma, a blond god with a suntan from somewhere even in April.

He never said much, he wasn't a great talker and I never saw him give anyone any advice, but everyone respected him and we were a perfect match, comfortable together from the start.

Although naturally left-footed, I was used to playing on the right at Derby and I discovered that Bobby, despite being predominantly right-footed preferred to operate on the left, so there was never a conflict of interests over our positions.

There was a misconception that Bobby was weak in the air.

He wasn't but he was a great reader of the game, as good as anyone I ever saw.

He broke down attacks simply and effectively by reading passes and stepping up to cut them out, taking possession and moving the ball on accurately.

Very rarely did you witness him give it away cheaply. Bobby was a tremendous, disciplined defender with great positional sense.

He never felt the need to go meandering off, unlike me on occasions when I sensed an opportunity to supplement the attack.

Most players have their quirks, superstitions and little routines they go through and I quickly picked up on the way in which Bobby treasured the tools of his trade.

He was a craftsman and just as a master builder might clean his favourite trowel and apply a light coat of oil to avoid rusting, Bobby would take off a sock after a match and use it to carefully clean any mud off his boots and then rub them dry if it had been raining or there had been a lot of moisture on the pitch.

I copied this practice and took it back with me to Derby. Anything that was good enough for Bobby Moore was certainly good enough for me.

At heart, Moore was a normal, regular bloke. He just had this aura surrounding him. It was nothing to do with anything he said. He was never a great communicator, yet he was in control of everything he did.

Socially, Bobby mixed easily with the guys. There were no cliques but it was only natural, and accepted by all, that he might drift towards a corner of the bar to chat with Geoff Hurst and Martin Peters, while nobody was more popular with both the Famous Five and the new kids on the block than Ball, who loved being with the younger set.

Back in the quest for points at Derby, with Gemmill developing more of a rapport with Alan Hinton down the left wing and Todd coping with anything that came his way, we ended the 1970/71 season strongly with five wins and two draws in our last eight games to finish in ninth place in our second term in the First Division.

Frankly, that was a disappointment given the impact we had made 12 months earlier and we only had ourselves to blame this time for failing to qualify for Europe.

Derby's good fortune in the transfer market continued when the management turned a £25,000 profit on Mackay.

The man who had left Tottenham three years earlier for £5,000 was sold for £30,000 to Swindon, who wanted him as their player-manager.

There was nothing mournful or poignant about Dave's departure for Wiltshire and the Second Division. He had helped us enormously, done his job and it was time to move on.

It didn't feel sad and he realised it was time to go. It was the natural order of things – when your time was up, you left, no matter who you were.

With Todd and Hennessey on the books, nobody was surprised Dave went, even if he had been good enough to play all 42 League matches.

My season had another fortnight to run on England duty – and it was during this time that I learned a valuable lesson from Sir Alf.

As we trained, Ramsey walked round, observing carefully and having a private word as and when he felt necessary.

I was surprised one morning when he detected a flaw in my game and pulled me to one side.

He noticed that from a standing jump, I didn't get the same spring as I did from a running jump and he advised me to practise leaping from a standing start carrying a couple of handbell weights.

I did as he suggested regularly a dozen times on my own after training sessions and it certainly did improve me.

Sir Alf's training routine itself was similar to what I was used to at Derby – sharp stuff, warm-up sprints and five-a-sides, six versus six and eight against eight.

And just like at Derby, the England manager was very keen to involve the entire squad in any enterprise. Whether it was going for a walk, to the cinema or out to a show, we all went together, everybody was required to attend.

May saw Malta duly brushed aside 5-0 at Wembley in the return European Championship qualifier. Once Martin Chivers opened the scoring after half an hour, the outcome was never in doubt and the only issue at stake was how many more goals we would score. It turned out to be four, thanks to another from Chivers, Lee, Allan Clarke with a penalty, and right-back Chris Lawler.

My winning start for England became five out of five in the Home International Championship with victories over Northern Ireland in Belfast and Scotland at Wembley.

Best was up to his tricks at Windsor Park, impudently whisking the ball off Banks' toes, as the goalkeeper threw it up to clear downfield, before lobbing the ball over Gordon and winning their race to head home. The effort was disallowed for ungentlemanly conduct, which this most certainly was.

Had Banks rolled the ball out on the ground, he could have had no complaints at being mugged by Bestie, but the Ulsterman had taken things a step too far, although he was within his rights to complain that the ball was not actually in Banks' possession when he robbed him.

Football was changing in terms of the protection afforded to goalkeepers, certainly in Europe, and what happened abroad seeped into British football.

Best was my toughest opponent. He was a great player with tremendous skill and great balance. George could head it, score from all angles and tackle like Mackay. He was the fifth Beatle, the media chased him and it didn't end happily. George indulged himself off the pitch but as a footballer he was the best I faced by a mile.

The following Saturday, I sampled a Wembley full house for the first time with 91,469 fans packed inside to see England see off the Scots 3-1.

My abiding memory is not the match itself but Ball's rapport with a battalion of the Tartan Army as we travelled to and from the famous old stadium.

You could sense the atmosphere building outside our team coach when we were about a mile away from Wembley, especially when we navigated a roundabout covered in Scottish supporters singing and chanting.

The racket reached fever pitch when they spotted us and Bally loved it. He was in his element goading them from the safety of his seat behind a reinforced glass window, gesticulating what he thought the result would be.

A few hours later, victory secured, we returned the same way to Hendon Hall, passing the roundabout which was now strewn with Scottish bodies, most of them absolutely plastered.

Bally was up to his tricks again, gesturing to them and emphasising the score with his fingers – banter rather than anything malicious.

It was quite hilarious because those fans who did react, did so with humour and the acceptance that their heroes had been beaten by a better side. All credit to them.

10

First And Best

DAMNED if you do, damned if you don't . . . the saying played repetitively on my mind as I studied two immense fixtures in three days and wished I could make one of them simply drop off the calendar.

Derby County's push for the club's first Football League championship in 1972 threw up the ultimate club versus country dilemma as England were poised to take on West Germany for a place in the European Championship semi-finals.

Sir Alf Ramsey wanted me to play at Wembley on Saturday, April 29, and Brian Clough was claiming me to line up for him in our final match of the season, against Liverpool, two days later on Monday, May 1.

Ramsey must have choked on his cornflakes at the start of

international week when a storm broke over my head, the Daily Mirror back page trumpeting the banner headline: INJURY BLOWS FOR ENGLAND – Clemence out, McFarland and Todd battle to face the Germans.

Harry Miller wrote: "The pressures of the frantic chase for the First Division championship are biting deep into England's bid to beat Germany in the European Nations Cup. Yesterday, title contenders Liverpool and Derby were involved in situations that affect England. Liverpool goalkeeper Ray Clemence, who hurt an ankle against Ipswich on Saturday, is definitely out of the squad for the quarter-final against the Germans at Wembley next Saturday. And last night there were serious doubts about Derby defenders Roy McFarland and Colin Todd, both injured against Manchester City. McFarland, England's first choice centre-half, has a groin strain, Todd an ankle injury. Both had treatment yesterday."

I was perfectly fit and so was Toddy, but the following day Clough ordered a phone call to be made to the Football Association to the effect that both of us had been declared unfit to report for international duty.

I would have started against Gerd Muller, while the best Colin could have hoped for realistically was a place on the substitutes' bench.

Clough released both Archie Gemmill and John O'Hare to represent Tommy Docherty's Scotland in a midweek friendly against Peru at Hampden Park.

He was taking no chances in defence, however, where we were resigned to coping without right-back Ronnie Webster, who took a bang on the knee in a potentially disastrous defeat at Manchester City.

I felt uncomfortable letting down Sir Alf, but Clough made the decision very clear on the way back from Maine Road, telling me sharply: "England. You're not going."

If I had played for England and picked up a knock which prevented me from facing Liverpool, and Derby hadn't won, I would never have forgiven myself, never heard the end of it and my relationship with the gaffer, Peter Taylor and our supporters would have been badly damaged, perhaps beyond repair.

Of course I wanted to play for England and help the nation gain a measure of revenge for that World Cup defeat in Leon two years earlier.

But I would have sold my soul for a championship winners' medal, and who could tell if I would ever be in that position again?

Winning the title was a long shot, as demonstrated by the bookies' odds, but the management were never men given to conceding an inch and insisted they wanted Toddy and myself fresh, fit and strong for the final push.

While Ramsey was inwardly raging at Clough and disagreed vehemently with him, he would have understood the logic and motives. Of course, he would.

Sir Alf was hugely patriotic but had the situation been similar when he was manager of Ipswich, I suspect he would have pulled exactly the same stunt.

Saturday came and I was in the doghouse with England fans, who saw Bobby Moore badly exposed at centre-half against Muller, who scored the Germans' last goal in an emphatic 3-1 win. Someone said to me charitably that given Muller's form and the eye-catching passing of Gunther Netzer, it was probably a good game to miss.

No it wasn't. It was a horrible game to miss and I was gutted not to be there at Bobby's side.

I also knew I wasn't going to look very clever if we flopped against Liverpool.

Getting changed at the Baseball Ground on Monday, I considered the enormity of the next 90 minutes and the progress the club and myself had made since the 1971-72 season kicked off without me... as I spent three weeks recovering from a savage bout of pneumonia at St Mary's Nursing Home, near Ashbourne.

I must have become run down and vulnerable to infection on holiday in Ibiza, and on my return to the Midland Hotel I woke up one night sweating like a pig in a sauna.

Three times I got up to towel myself dry and change the bed linen, and first thing in the morning I made an appointment to see the club doctor, David Eisenberg.

I was sure I was suffering from a heavy dose of flu, but he checked my lungs with a stethoscope before promptly diagnosing something much more sinister.

The appropriate phone calls were made to place me under the tender care of the Catholic sisters of the Institute of Our Lady of Mercy.

I was really quite poorly for five days while huge doses of penicillin were pumped in and worked their magic. I perked up when Lin and several team-mates came to visit and, eventually, I was allowed out of bed in dressing gown and slippers to visit the television room, where I watched the afternoon racing and rang the lads to place my bets to kill the boredom.

It was a tedious time and a struggle to keep my mind active, but I was warned that rest was of paramount importance.

No sooner was I up and about than the club paid for Lin and myself to spend a long weekend at a hotel in Skegness, with two provisos – absolutely no running or drinking.

Whether the team were on the front at Scarborough, Blackpool or Cala Millor, Taylor preached the stimulating benefits of sea air. Long walks along the promenade at Skeggy and endless cups of tea proved to be the ideal tonic before I was eased gently back into training.

Only opponents could have benefited from learning the truth about my pneumonia, so a smokescreen went up to explain my absence from the opening three games of the season – a 2-2 home draw with Manchester United, followed by successive 2-0 victories over West Ham and Leicester.

The official word was that I had been laid low with flu, then picked up a little niggle in pre-season training.

I had my own itinerary to follow under trainer Jimmy Gordon and our physio, Gordon Guthrie, to get me up to speed.

With Dave Mackay at Swindon, it was time for me to step up and captain the side. I was an England international now, which gave me status and presence in the dressing room.

I thought my opinions should carry some weight and that it was right and proper that I made myself heard.

There were no speeches or anything like that when I inherited the mantle.

Although Colin Boulton, Alan Durban and Kevin Hector were the senior professionals, and Durbs had an opinion about everything under the sun, I think everyone in the club naturally assumed the job was mine and there was no dissent.

We welcomed a new face, someone few, if any, of the lads had seen before, when Taylor's antenna twitched in the direction of

Southern League Worcester City, who accepted £14,000 for their 6ft 3in centre-forward Roger Davies.

He was a big, raw-boned boy and was evidently bought with an eye to the future – but his arrival soon heralded a surprise departure.

Davies made an immediate impact and he spent the next two years regretting the day he banged into me in his first five-a-side and sent me crashing to the floor.

I was none too pleased at being assaulted by this gangling, 20-year-old rookie, but at least Davies, mortified by his clumsy foul, had the good grace to pick me up and say: "I'm so sorry. I didn't mean to do that."

Big mistake. Clough and Taylor were great wind-up merchants and would have us doubled up in laughter with some of their banter. Taylor never missed a trick and sometimes he could inject that little bit of needle, like he did by constantly referring to the hard time Jim Fryatt caused me. That was designed to concentrate the mind, and it worked.

So it was with Davies. The words: "I'm so sorry, I didn't mean to do that," were seized upon by Taylor, the apology used as a weapon to galvanise the striker.

Taylor mocked him unmercifully and said: "I'm so sorry, Roger, but we don't want a big, soft fairy out there. We need a big, nasty 'effing villain."

A tip from Frank Wignall paid off at Chelsea, where I equalised in a 1-1 draw in September. Big Frank had noticed that when a chance fell to me, I invariably took a touch to compose myself before shooting with my natural left foot. "You haven't got time to fanny about like that, Roy," he barked. "Just strike it first time."

So when Alan Hinton's low corner from the right squirted away in my direction 15 yards out, I took Wignall's advice and simply spun round to connect with a screamer into the top left-hand corner of Peter Bonetti's net. All this with my right foot. It was one of the best goals I ever scored.

Having underlined my fitness, Ramsey awarded me my sixth international cap against Switzerland as England resumed the straightforward business of qualifying for the European Championship quarter-finals.

I was always going to play in Basle, primarily because Sir Alf named me as the only recognised centre-half in the squad.

Although Larry Lloyd and David Sadler weren't forgotten, it did look as if I had beaten off my rivals, but I flinched a little when Clough said: "McFarland is so far in front of his competitors, that if it were a boxing match it would be declared a no-contest."

For all Clough's immense self-confidence and the brusque manner in which he asserted himself, he did let slip occasionally that there were moments when he wasn't Mr Know It All – and that he owed a debt to his biggest foe in football.

The boss revealed to a friend: "Don Revie paid me a compliment once, which I couldn't understand at the time. I was working with him in television, and he said, 'I want a quiet word with you, Brian'. I said, 'Right, what is it?' He said, 'How good's your centre-half?' I looked at him, I thought he was taking the piss out of me. I said, 'What do you mean, Mr Revie?' ... because I used to call him Mr Revie. He said, 'How good's McFarland?' 'Well,' I said, 'if you don't know, who does know in the game?' He said, 'You. If you don't know how good your players are, nobody knows'. He taught me that. And of course he was dead right. If I didn't know who could play at the club, spending seven days a week, 52 weeks out the year with them, who the hell did know?"

Speculation that superstar treatment might come my way reared its head when a publicity agent connected to the England team reckoned that I would make a fortune from commercial activities involving modelling suede wear, books, annuals, pop posters and endorsing football boots and tracksuits.

I was sceptical, but when I talked to the lads at Liverpool, Everton, Arsenal and Leeds, it was evident that a few lucrative off-field avenues were opening up for them.

I had a deal through athletics legend Derek Ibbotson, the man who set a world record for the mile in 1957, to wear Puma boots but other proposals petered out.

In reality, the only serious money to be made off the pitch would come through the England team being more successful and reaching tournaments.

Posters of me adorned His 'n' Hers, the most fashionable clothes store in Derby, and another upmarket menswear shop in Ashbourne, but the modelling work never reached any dizzy heights.

We all admired George Best. He was the fifth Beatle, the epitome of style on and off the pitch. Clough loved what he could do with a football at his feet but he would have hammered any of us if we had attempted to copy other aspects of Bestie's lifestyle. While Brian was quite happy to sell himself to the BBC and ITV, he frowned on activities which might have impacted on a player's core business on the pitch.

Switzerland's pitch in Basle seemed huge, surrounded by a running track, but there was no hiding place for Gordon Banks.

Our goalkeeper dropped a couple of clangers to present the Swiss with sloppy equalisers after goals from Martin Chivers and Geoff Hurst, and we were ultimately grateful for an own goal to give us a 3-2 win.

My mind drifts back to Basle whenever I look at the magnificent engraved watch the players were given to commemorate the match.

Time was about to run out on the last remaining unbeaten record in the First Division after a dozen games. Derby's encouraging start ended following five wins, seven draws and seven clean sheets.

Never discount the value of shutting out the opposition, it's a cast-iron guarantee of at least one point. Clough constantly preached the need to keep a clean sheet and it also became a mantra with Taylor, a goalkeeper in his playing days at Coventry and Middlesbrough.

Manchester United were going frighteningly well, despite playing two home games at Liverpool and Stoke City, because Old Trafford was closed following crowd violence.

They topped the League with eight wins from 12 games and Best was in electric form when we arrived in October. He improved his tally of goals to 10 in as many matches to send us packing.

We weren't very good that day and I anticipated a hostile reaction from Clough, but he came into the dressing room only to say: "We haven't performed, the bus is outside. Let's go."

Arsenal, Nottingham Forest and Crystal Palace were beaten in successive matches as the attack began to function again with Wignall on the mark against Palace to become our joint top scorer with five goals.

Days later he was shipped out to Mansfield for £8,000. Wignall fell from a lofty perch near the summit of the First Division into a Third Division relegation dogfight overnight.

It was similar to Willie Carlin's fate 12 months earlier and you couldn't help but feel sympathy towards another valued teammate. The management looked at it this way – Frank was 32 years old, there was a bit of cash on the table for him, young Davies was in the bag and it was time to move on.

Losing at Old Trafford was understandable, but the boss was not so forgiving after successive 2-1 away defeats at Wolves and Huddersfield.

Our inability to perform competently on the road was driving the management up the wall. We were locked in a spell of four successive away defeats, yet smashing everyone in sight at the Baseball Ground, where the run of straight home League victories was to eventually reach the dozen mark.

Leeds Road was as bad as it got. Normally, when we lost, you could trace defeat down to a silly individual mistake but Huddersfield was different because nobody emerged with one iota of credit.

It was our worst display of the season, by some distance, and I feared the worst when I glanced up to see Taylor fidgeting, almost hopping up and down as if he needed a pee.

He was desperate to let rip, but knew his place and that he had to wait until Clough had run out of steam and expletives.

Our heads were down, staring into our mugs of tea and Jimmy Gordon was attempting to raise our spirits, when the gaffer launched into a bitter tirade.

First we got it in the neck as a team, then he went around the bench picking us off one by one with verbal blows. Clough always preached the team ethic but he was never afraid to single out individuals, and if our coach driver had been inside that dressing room he would undoubtedly have been torn off a strip for good measure.

The essence of Clough's complaint was that he didn't think we were up to the job of matching our opponents physically.

Poor Taylor was itching to get in his two penn'orth when the boss told him: "Leave them, Pete. They're not worth talking to, save it," but our assistant manager had the last word.

"You lot are a disgrace. Play like that again and you'll never play for this club again," he said before the pair turned on their heels and left us to stew.

I escaped to Greece with England for a 2-0 win which sent the team through in the Euros to meet West Germany.

Injury ruled me out of a disappointing 1-1 draw with Switzerland at Wembley the previous month when Lloyd took my place, but there was no pressure on us in Athens because only a defeat by four or more goals could prevent England from qualifying.

Colin Bell, Alan Ball and Martin Peters dominated the Greeks in the middle of the park, and Hurst and Chivers supplied the goals. It was the sort of occasion when Bobby Moore and myself might have had a cigar and Gordon Banks could have planted a sun lounger in his goalmouth.

Within a fortnight, I found myself back in Greece, this time for a harrowing experience.

The background was a classic home display to beat Manchester City 3-1, a match memorable for Webster's only goal of the season.

We had to look twice to confirm the identity of our scorer

when this bronzed figure came tearing into the area to head home a centre from Hinton. We couldn't believe it, Ronnie never got that far forward.

That victory was followed by O'Hare's two goals at Liverpool being trumped by a hat-trick from their reserve centre-forward Jack Whitham in a 3-2 defeat.

In Robson's absence, Todd was playing full-back at Anfield and went off in the second half with a broken nose when he took an elbow to the face in a challenge with Kevin Keegan, but Toddy's discomfort was nothing compared to the torture a desperate Terry Hennessey went through that afternoon a fortnight before Christmas. None of the defence emerged with any credit, but the Liverpool goals destroyed 'The Glove'.

We flew out to Greece for rest and recuperation on a four-day break, during which Olympiakos beat us 3-1 in what was billed as a 'token friendly'. In fact, it was a tough, tough game, one of the hardest of my career. Given Derby's pre-season experience in Europe, there was a feeling in the camp that we would brush them away but what a talented team we discovered in Piraeus.

Olympiakos kept the ball superbly, had us chasing shadows and constantly dragged us out of position. As a confidence-building exercise designed to get the Liverpool defeat out of our system, I'm not sure it was a success.

We returned to beat Everton 2-0 only to go down 3-0 at Elland Road to a Leeds side which had turfed us out of the League Cup in September.

There was never any love lost between Clough and Revie, and the fact Leeds regularly got the better of us haunted the gaffer, who complained: "We're not big enough or strong enough to dish it out when it needs to be dished out."

The new year started in encouraging fashion and we went through January unbeaten, courtesy of home wins over Chelsea and, at last, Coventry while demonstrating the resilience to come from behind at The Dell, never a happy hunting ground, to beat Southampton 2-1 with a late goal from Durban.

Now the FA Cup occupied our minds and, after beating Shrewsbury 2-0, we welcomed back Willie Carlin, now plying his trade in the Third Division at Notts County.

Jimmy Sirrel's teams never laid down for anyone but we produced some very high quality football to beat them 6-0 with Durban slipping in from all angles to claim a hat-trick.

Willie had a rueful smile in the players' bar afterwards, as if he had just been wrestled into submission by his big brother. In a way, he was still among us because he lived in Allestree, a Derby suburb popular with the players and home to Clough and myself. I had moved from the Midland Hotel to a swish apartment in a block of flats at Park Farm centre and regularly saw Willie there, helping his wife Marie with the family shopping.

Willie accepted defeat like the man he was, although he was still hurting and smarting from the manner of his dismissal from the club. That feeling stayed with him for quite a time.

The miners' strike plunged Britain into darkness, with a three-day working week in places, but the sparks flew in three epic FA Cup fifth-round ties against Arsenal.

Boots were flying all over the place at the Baseball Ground, where Charlie George incited our fans by racing over to them on the Pop Side terraces, flicking V-signs with both hands after scoring both the Gunners' goals in a 2-2 draw.

That was typical of Charlie, a streetwise kid with a volatile personality from a tough Islington upbringing. He was replying the only way he knew how after the Derby supporters had spent the match goading him.

I thought we were a shade fortunate to still be in the competition thanks to a Hinton penalty with two minutes to go because Arsenal played well, although we had them on the back foot three days later when a huge crowd of 63,077 crammed into Highbury for the novelty of a Tuesday afternoon kick-off.

We had to start early to avoid the need for floodlights because of power cuts in the capital, and with so many Londoners on a restricted working week, the replay between two of the best teams in the country was an obvious attraction. We started and finished strongly, repaying Arsenal for the onslaught they had subjected us to at Derby but neither side could manage a goal, despite extra-time.

The second replay took place at Leicester and was a personal disaster for John McGovern, whose underhit backpass was seized on by Ray Kennedy, who scored the only goal of the game. John was distraught and quite rightly so. We all were. We felt we played well enough to win that evening at Filbert Street.

Although we were contenders for the League title, the FA Cup looked as if it might be our best bet for a trophy.

Durban made a rallying call as we sat around moping, cursing our misfortune.

Even Clough was subdued and didn't appear to know what to say but Durban, for some reason, seemed almost euphoric as he told us: "Don't worry, boys. Maybe this is a sign that we'll go on and win the League."

He meant that, it was a statement of intent, almost a prophecy, even though it didn't ring true with me. Durban had surely lost the plot and I thought: "What the hell is he going on about?"

Between the replays, the boss made an audacious bid to snatch Ian Storey-Moore from Nottingham Forest for £200,000, trying to push the transfer through by the force of his personality.

Forest were in a sorry state, sinking fast in the quicksands of relegation, and we had recently beaten them 4-0 with Storey-Moore still managing to look a class act on the left wing.

We were in the Midland Hotel for an overnight stay on Friday, preparing to watch It's A Knockout on television before dinner, playing cards and generally having a laugh, with Wolves due the following afternoon, when Ian turned up.

I was under the impression the deal was done and dusted because he told us he had signed transfer forms. My reaction was: "Here we go again – another quality player".

Storey-Moore was paraded in front of the fans before we beat Wolves 2-1 as "our new signing" but, crucially, the deal was not signed off by Forest, who must have feared, and rightly so, total outrage from their supporters who had seen another of their favourites, Hennessey, come to Derby.

Hinton's career was totally revitalised with us after leaving the City Ground and Clough still had designs on former Forest midfielder Henry Newton, now settled at Everton. Seeing Storey-Moore strut his stuff on behalf of their bitter rivals would have been the last straw for the Forest faithful.

So it was that he went to join Frank O'Farrell at Manchester United, but I am convinced Ian would have loved it with us. We were really going places. He had glimpsed that and wanted to be part of it. Storey-Moore's greatest asset was his versatility, he could play anywhere along the front line – right-wing, centre-forward, left-wing – and it would have been intriguing to see where he would have slotted in.

To the public, Hinton might have appeared under the greatest threat but I was rooming with Ally and he did not betray the slightest signs of concern. He was a confident guy, knew his value to the team and there were those who thought he was even good enough to play again for England.

Out of the FA Cup and with Storey-Moore slipping through the net, we put on blinkers for the last two months of a title race which always threatened to go down to the wire.

It was a four-horse race between ourselves, Leeds, Liverpool and Manchester City. March proved highly profitable: six matches, five wins and a draw.

Easter Saturday, All Fool's Day, arrived and brought a visit from Leeds along with an immense performance which defined John O'Hare's career.

Nobody in that Derby team put his body on the line for the cause more often than John, who took such a kicking from defenders that when he peeled his socks off in the dressing room we could see his calves and ankles had turned black and blue.

John's lips must have been bruised as well, from the times he had to bite them in refusing to rise to the bait and retaliate to the provocation.

While Archie Gemmill had the ability to run the ball out of trouble and right up the other end of the pitch, John was the man we always looked to as the focal point to launch attacks.

We knew we could chip the ball up to him and it would stick, nine times out of 10.

His innate positional sense took him into little pockets of space where he could control the ball on his huge chest or trap it on a thigh.

Then he would look to lay it off, or maybe catch a run by

Hector out of the corner of his eye, or wait to be clattered from behind to win free-kicks which Hinton would seek to exploit.

O'Hare's bravery and tactical nous more than compensated for a lack of pace. He may not have been eye candy for the supporters, but he was the consummate professional.

Leeds arrived, favourites for the title, going for the League and FA Cup Double, a multi-skilled side which always loved to battle and came with the guarantee of giving all their opponents a hard time.

This was a must-win match. We rarely found it easy to beat them, but on this occasion we summoned up an outstanding team display.

Making Jack Charlton look every one of his 36 years, O'Hare headed the opening goal and later saw his shot rebound off Gary Sprake and Norman Hunter into the net to clinch the sweetest of 2-0 wins. We came off the pitch to find we were top of the table for the first time.

After the Lord Mayor's show came a monumental let-down on Easter Monday when we resembled a bunch of dustbins, swept away 1-0 at home by Newcastle. They had a few good individuals, including Malcolm Macdonald and John Tudor in attack, but we let ourselves down badly.

We failed to maintain concentration levels pumped to the maximum for the visit of Leeds and paid a high price. I needed stitches in a head wound from a clash with Tommy Gibb and came back out swathed in a large white bandage.

As inquests go, it was a decidedly long one and I was glad to miss some of it, getting my head repaired.

Clough and Taylor had to air their frustration somehow and did so by giving the team a full two hours in detention, emphasising again and again how disappointing it was to recklessly throw away the precious advantage we had all worked so hard to achieve against Leeds.

Their mood was not helped by learning Liverpool had won 3-0 at Manchester United and within a couple of days Manchester City beat Arsenal 2-0 while Leeds were too good for Huddersfield.

After Newcastle, we asked ourselves: "Have we blown it now?" Certainly, there was no margin for error.

Each and every one of the final five matches was critical and the general acceptance was that we could not afford to lose one of them.

The sequence began with a goalless draw at West Brom before a 4-0 romp at Sheffield United followed by a 3-0 home win over Huddersfield.

Rodney Marsh was never far from controversy and when he went from QPR to Manchester City for £200,000, at the time we were trying to sign Storey-Moore, many thought he was the final piece in Malcolm Allison's jigsaw which would bring the championship to Maine Road.

But Marsh wasn't fit enough by Big Mal's standards and his arrival coincided with City losing form. Allison did, however, promise to bring him back for the last few games and it was our misfortune to run into a Marsh determined to prove a point to his critics when we went there.

Marsh, who had shed 10lb in weight since joining City, scored one very fine solo goal and found himself unceremoniously wiped out in the penalty area by Hennessey to win a penalty, converted by Francis Lee, as City ran out 2-0 winners in their final game of the season to go top.

City's sense of satisfaction was diluted by the fact their goal average meant they could not stay there while, privately, even Clough and Taylor felt the title was too tough an ask for us now and that we wouldn't recover.

Publicly, the boss was as bullish as ever, saying: "After we've beaten Liverpool, we'll have to sweat it out until the middle of May. It's going to be agony."

City had 57 points from 42 matches, Liverpool 56 from 40, Derby 56 from 41 and Leeds 55 from 40. Bookmakers generally made Revie's men 10-11 favourites, Bill Shankly's team an 11-8 shot and ourselves the 11-2 outsiders.

I expected Peter Daniel to wear the No.2 shirt against Liverpool but Clough instead threw Steve Powell in at the deep end.

Our 16-year-old apprentice had a fine pedigree, being the son of Derby legend Tommy Powell, and had only been in the game 10 minutes. But the maturity he showed in dealing with the threat of Steve Heighway made him look as if he had been playing First Division football for 10 years.

The management always felt if you were good enough, you were old enough, and they had the courage and confidence to put Powell in. He was fearless, not the tallest but he had a great spring and was prepared to put his head and foot in where it hurt. He would put his body on the line to defend.

Shankly paraded a super side at the Baseball Ground that sunlit evening: Clemence, Lawler, Lindsay, Smith, Lloyd, Hughes, Keegan, Hall, Heighway, Toshack, Callaghan.

Unbeaten since a little slip at Leicester in January, they had since reeled off 13 wins and two draws in what looked like a juggernaut's charge to the title.

We matched Liverpool every step of the way until the 63rd

minute when we got our noses in front. And fittingly, John McGovern scored the goal, the self-same player who redeemed himself more than we could ever imagine for our FA Cup exit. He looked awkward, almost clumsy, the way he hit the ball – but his aim was true and that's all that mattered.

More than the goal, I remember how close Liverpool came to equalising. With time running out, Chris Lawler found himself clear on the edge of our penalty area after selling a couple of dummies.

Lawler had a clear sight of goal and smashed a shot which beat us all. It looked a goal all the way from where I was, watching in desperation, but somehow the effort curved wide of the far post.

That's when I knew, instinctively, that we had won 1-0. Sometimes, a side will just have one chance to score a vital goal – this was Liverpool's opportunity and they missed it.

It was a magical feeling when Clive Thomas blew the final whistle to appreciate we were back on top of the League and had a chance of staying there.

There was elation among the majority of the lads, but we knew both our rivals still had an opportunity to leapfrog us to the prize we all craved.

You didn't need to have an IQ for Mensa, or be a fan of the Reds like me, to suspect Liverpool were on the verge of greatness, while Leeds had been either champions or runners-up for the previous three seasons.

Meanwhile, the club versus country issue was bound to add another level of frost to the icy relationship between the boss and Sir Alf, who couldn't even bring himself to utter Clough's name when he said: "The Derby manager sent a message that it was impossible for Roy McFarland and Colin Todd to play on the Saturday night against Germany; they had both failed try-outs. Yet on Monday they both played against Liverpool and, I was told, without either showing sign or semblance of injury."

All we could do was wait on the outcome of two matches the following Monday – "sweating it out in agony," as the boss predicted.

While we were beating Liverpool, Leeds overcame Chelsea 2-0, so only required a draw at Wolves to move above us while the Reds needed victory at Arsenal to knock us off top spot.

Job done, Clough decamped for Tresco's Island Hotel in the Scilly Isles with his family while Taylor took the players on holiday to Cala Millor, our customary retreat in Majorca, where it was a case of sombreros, swimming, suntan oil and bottles of San Miguel round the pool of the Castell de Mar Hotel.

However, Todd and myself had to go easy on the lager because of imminent international duty – the return leg against the Germans in Berlin.

We flew back together to East Midlands airport at the weekend and on Monday evening Lin and I drove over to Toddy's house in Littleover.

We sat in his car with Colin and his wife Jenny with our ears glued to the radio commentary from Highbury and Molineux, where Leeds had pitched up confident of completing the Double having beaten Arsenal in the FA Cup two days previously.

The tension was unbearable, especially when Billy Bremner scored to cut Wolves' lead to 2-1.

Colin and I exchanged glances as if to say: "They'll go on and equalise now," and we all got out of the car to stretch our legs and try to compose ourselves.

Liverpool kept pressing hard to gain the vital breakthrough against Arsenal and there was a heart-stopping moment at the end when Toshack had the ball in the net, only to be ruled marginally offside.

Deep into injury-time, the final whistle sounded at Highbury on a 0-0 draw, then it was all over at Molineux too. Leeds had failed to score again and it dawned on us that Derby County had done it, we were Football League champions for the first time in the club's history.

The four of us leaped out of Colin's car and started hugging and kissing in an otherwise deserted road. There wasn't another soul in the street, many of the other residents indoors listening to the radio or waiting for the results to appear on television.

It was weird travelling sedately down the M1 to meet up with the rest of the England squad at Hendon Hall two hours later, knowing all the other Derby lads were going out of their minds in Majorca.

Colin and I would have given anything to pull off the motorway into the countryside to find a pub and crack open a bottle of champagne to toast our success.

We were dubious about the reaction we could expect from Sir Alf on our return to the England fold, but we need not have worried.

He congratulated us warmly on our title success and the matter of our withdrawal for the West Germany game at Wembley was never mentioned.

A few of the squad started to arrive from Highbury. Emlyn Hughes was gutted but still managed a generous smile as he shook my hand and whispered: "Lucky so-and-so, McFarland" while Arsenal hard man Peter Storey came in with a little grin as if to say: "We played our part," and Alan Ball, now with the Gunners after a £220,000 transfer from Everton, was simply delighted to have prevented Liverpool from winning the championship.

It was a while before the Leeds contingent, including Norman Hunter and Paul Madeley, turned up and they were deathly quiet and downcast.

That was perfectly understandable, because in some ways it had been Leeds' title to lose.

Resentment was there, a little shred of bitterness, some of it directed at the Football League, which had made them play so soon again after the Cup final.

Colin and I went to our room and celebrated in style – with a pot of tea and biscuits.

Shankly was characteristically magnanimous as he said Derby had been the best team Liverpool had encountered all season, yet there was plenty of sniping from other quarters, allegations we had somehow become champions by default while sitting on the beach.

No one wins a championship by luck, so we did not get involved in all that nonsense and it was hardly our fault the way the fixtures fell when it came to the crunch. We won it because we had more points than anyone else.

As Clough said, it's about how many points you have after 42 matches – and we had the most.

I remember him telling us: "You are the champions of England, not Leeds, not Liverpool – Derby County."

Points were not the issue on the international scene, it was goals everyone was talking about on the plane to West Berlin. England needed to beat the Germans by a two-goal margin to force a play-off for a place in the semi-finals of the European Championships.

Unfortunately, it ended in a sterile 0-0 draw and Sir Alf suffered fearful criticism for setting up the team very defensively, drafting in Storey at the expense of Lee and preferring Hunter to Peters.

The England manager thought our best, in fact only, chance was to soak up as much pressure as we could withstand in a backs-to-the-wall operation and hit the Germans on the break.

The conditions were appalling, heavy rain throughout the match saturating the pitch, and that made it all the harder to implement our counter-attacking strategy because the soggy ball got stuck and refused to run.

The German coach Helmut Schoen said afterwards that he wanted England to be adventurous because then he would have fancied his side to score six. Much as it pains me to admit it, Schoen was right.

If Sir Alf had sent us out all guns blazing with a gung-ho mentality, they could have picked us off and won 6-0.

England were not equipped to compete with that West German team, which was the best in the world, with so much natural technique.

They were so very effective, organised and fluid with full-backs Horst-Dieter Hottges and Paul Breitner flying on past their wingers Heinz Flohe and Siggi Held, the capability of Gunther Netzer to murder you with passes in tight situations, the authority and arrogance of Franz Beckenbauer, striding around as if he owned the place, and a demon striker in Muller.

The one thing Sir Alf wasn't, was anyone's fool. He had seen more than enough of the Germans' potential realised a fortnight earlier to know that if England came out to play, the result could be catastrophic.

It might have been a different story had I scored from the sort of chance I stuck away maybe seven times out of 10.

The ball reached me from a set-piece and I headed it back over the keeper, Sepp Maier, but also too powerfully and the bar got in the way.

My main job was at the other end marking Muller, when I could see him! The guy was never in my eyeline, constantly positioning himself to the side and poised to sneak in behind me.

It needed a supreme mental effort to keep tabs on Muller and I had Storey to thank on one occasion when the Bayern Munich star gave me the slip and was poised to shoot.

Sitting just in front of myself and Moore, Storey was never more effective in an England shirt, and on this occasion he surpassed himself with a monumental physical challenge which blocked Muller's route to a certain goal.

There had to be a bit of ball in the tackle, or it would have been a penalty, but it could only have been a very little bit. Schoen criticised our "brutal methods" while captain Beckenbauer snorted dismissively that we had confused the laws of the jungle with those of the football pitch.

It was inevitable, West Germany would go on and be crowned champions of Europe, which they duly did, eclipsing Russia 3-0 in the final.

I felt tired and weary on the flight back to Heathrow, despite the warm glow of satisfaction from Derby's triumph, but my season still had matches to run in the Home International series.

Wales didn't possess the quality to harm us in Cardiff, where

England won 3-0, before Ramsey rang the changes for the visit of Northern Ireland – which I watched – and he must have wondered why he'd bothered as that genial Ulsterman Terry Neill scored the only goal of the game.

Moore, Paul Madeley and myself were swiftly recalled for the trip to Scotland and an encounter with the famous Hampden Roar from a massive crowd of over 119,000.

The Scottish supporters created a fierce and ferocious atmosphere which was reflected on the pitch as the two sides went to war and we were grateful for a goal by Ball for a narrow victory.

Back home in Derby, and now I sensed it would be 'home' for a long time, there was a magical feeling and it was a fabulous time with a real buzz and sense of excitement about the town.

It wasn't just winning the title, but the realisation that we would be representing England in the European Cup – with the chance of meeting Real Madrid, Juventus, Benfica, Ajax, Celtic and Bayern Munich.

They love their football in Derby and the surrounding county, and the community took great pride in us winning the championship.

Success put us on the map nationally, and Clough and Taylor relished that.

They enjoyed looking at the big-city clubs of Liverpool, Manchester and London, and saying: "Look what we've achieved."

The title was always the big thing with Clough. He talked about Liverpool incessantly and, of course, there was the rivalry with Leeds and Revie.

There was an acceptance that if you finished above Leeds, Liverpool and Arsenal, you always had a great chance of becoming champions.

I had done enough in the minds of leading football writers to merit inclusion in this Rothmans Golden Boots XI for 1971-72: Gordon Banks (Stoke and England); Paul Madeley (Leeds and England), Roy McFarland (Derby and England), Bobby Moore (West Ham and England); Billy Bremner (Leeds and Scotland), Johnny Giles (Leeds and Republic of Ireland); Jimmy Johnstone (Celtic and Scotland), Martin Chivers (Tottenham and England), Francis Lee (Manchester City and England), Eddie Gray (Leeds and Scotland).

My citation read: "Roy McFarland becomes the first Englishman to wear the Golden Boots No.5 shirt. This is fitting reward for a player who had, by the end of the season, gone a long way towards solving a problem position for England since the decline of Jack Charlton and Brian Labone. As well as establishing himself as an international, McFarland played a memorable role in Derby County's League Championship success. A bargain signing from Tranmere Rovers, only seduced to the Baseball Ground by some nocturnal persuasiveness from Brian Clough, McFarland, with Colin Todd, cemented one of the tightest defences in the country. His international development has been hindered by injury, often a nagging groin complaint, and he missed the crucial first leg of the European Championship quarter-final. Essentially a footballing centre-half, particularly strong on his left side, McFarland has the dual ability to destroy and construct."

11

Mugged By The Old Lady

THE power and plotting of Juventus stood between Derby County and the European Cup final in 1973. As omens go, there was no encouragement to be had the night I first realised there was a dark side to Brian Clough's relationship with Peter Taylor. It wasn't all sweetness and light.

A couple of card schools were in play after dinner in the lounge of our lovely hotel in the picturesque mountains outside Turin.

Relaxed and sitting in his shorts, Clough was absorbed in a hand of bridge with Alan Durban, Ronnie Webster and another player while a further six of us were having a laugh and frantically trying to outdo each other at shoot pontoon.

The only trouble was that the manager and his assistant should soon have been somewhere else.

They were due at a pre-match reception down in the city but, in this mood, the gaffer was going to take an awful lot of shifting.

Three times Taylor, visibly upset, came down from his room to remind Clough of his responsibilities, tapping his watch, becoming more annoyed, aggrieved and aggressive on each occasion.

Finally, Clough turned his head to his partner and said casually: "You go for me, Peter, if you want to go so much. You represent Derby County for a change."

That was it. Taylor snapped, starting with a few 'bloody hells' before calling Clough 'a disgrace' and turning the air blue with a tirade of abuse.

Taylor would have detested going to that reception as the club's figurehead, and Clough knew it.

The boss could be awkward and contrary like that and I felt for Taylor. He didn't deserve such treatment. I had been with them for six years and had never witnessed a previous public disagreement.

Eyebrows were raised as the players looked at each other because the management had always displayed an overpowering sense of togetherness.

For all Clough's attempts to portray a man at ease, there was tension surrounding one of the biggest matches in Derby's history.

Another scene suggested the pair had fallen out when, to our huge surprise, Tony Parry was selected in midfield. Clough had done Hartlepool (as they were now known) a favour by giving them £3,000 for Tony, when they were more skint than usual, but he had only started two previous League games.

I thought it very odd that he was going to be thrust into a European Cup semi-final.

Something was definitely going on, however, because the following day Parry was out and Durban was in.

We found ourselves in exalted company alongside Juventus, Ajax Amsterdam and Real Madrid when the draw for the last four was made and pitted us against Italy's famous 'Old Lady'.

The mood on the flight to Turin was very positive, despite a warning given by Clough's good friend and fellow ITV panellist Malcolm Allison, the new Crystal Palace manager.

Big Mal nearly became Juventus coach in 1969 before loyalty to Manchester City swayed him to reject their offer.

He said: "No one goes to Italy and wins. Most teams get cheated because there is skulduggery and the referees are put under so much pressure. Corruption, it's endemic."

Clough brushed away the doubts. He thought Allison was imagining ghosts.

On our first night in Italy, the quiet, low-key build-up arranged by the management was disturbed by a procession of cars and motor scooters which arrived at midnight, horns blaring and huge black and white Juventus flags waving.

You could put the 'welcome' down to typical Italian exuberance or a scheme dedicated to disturbing our sleep.

Maybe it was a bit of both.

Clough was a great student of the history of football and almost painfully aware of his place in the great scheme of things.

He was besotted with statistics, his own – those 251 League goals in 274 games for Sunderland and Middlesbrough, and the grinding disappointment that his phenomenal scoring record had earned him only two England caps.

He had his heroes too, though, and extended an invitation to Juventus legend John Charles to join our trip and train with us. John was kicking around as player-manager of Merthyr Tydfil but was revered in Turin, a fact I discovered the day before the match when I went shopping with him and saw the Gentle Giant worshipped and fawned over by a succession of middle-aged men and women. He had all the time in the world for them. There was nothing brash about John and his nickname suited him perfectly because of his gentle demeanour.

The old cleaner in our dressing room dropped to his knees and began weeping when John walked in. The Welshman was plainly embarrassed as he picked him up, hugged him, and said: "You don't have to do that, it's only me," but the old boy was inconsolable.

The Stadio Comunale was packed with 72,000 fans, but there was no sense of intimidation or an oppressive atmosphere because the crowd were quite some way from the pitch, separated by a running track.

As we kicked off, I thought in my naivety that it would be a level playing field, a decent contest against a technically excellent team with a chap called Fabio Capello playing in midfield.

Juventus went ahead when Pietro Anastasi lobbed a pass between me and David Nish, and the cagey old Brazilian striker Jose Altafini timed his run to perfection to drill a left-foot shot past Colin Boulton.

The Italians were soon in for a nasty surprise, however, when John O'Hare found Kevin Hector, who beat keeper Dino Zoff to equalise and carve out a niche in history as the first British player to score a European Cup goal on Italian soil.

So much for the football in the first half, there was dirty work afoot as Archie Gemmill and myself were booked by the German referee Gerhard Schulenburg – unbelievably harsh, unjust cautions which were to have serious ramifications.

My offence was so innocuous that I have never been able to recall it, although Gemmill says I jumped for a high ball and simply clashed heads, while he made a sliding tackle to keep the ball in play and clearly reached it before his opponent.

Those yellow cards were a set-up because the two of us had been booked earlier in the competition and they meant we would miss the return leg.

I didn't give that any thought at the time. The implications didn't sink in until afterwards.

I went into our dressing room at half-time far from depressed because we had upset Juventus with the quality of our counter-attacking and scored a precious away goal.

Just as Clough was about to speak, the door burst open and in rushed Taylor – heading straight for the bathroom, followed by three or four security guards and policemen, and there was a big commotion, a lot of agitation with people shouting, bodies being pushed and fingers jabbed.

Clough went ballistic at the Italian mob, yelling: "Get out, get out. Who the hell do you think you are? This place is off limits to you bastards" and he effectively kicked them out.

Later, it transpired that Taylor had spotted the Juventus substitute Helmut Haller chatting to his fellow countryman Schulenburg and walking with him towards the referee's room at the interval.

Taylor, who knew precisely what Schulenburg's use of the

TOP OF THE CLASS: Clint Road Primary School football team (seated, second from right)

NEW BOY: First day at the Baseball Ground in August 1967 with (from left) Brian Clough, Ken Turner, Sam Longson, Peter Taylor, Fred Walters and Sydney Bradley

ROY OF THE ROVERS: In Tranmere kit in July 1966

FIT TO DROP: Worn out after pre-season training at Colwick Woods, Nottingham in 1968

DEN AND DUSTED: Walking off with Dave Mackay and John Robson at the Den in April 1969 as Second Division champions in borrowed Millwall away shirts – after we forgot to pack our change strip

HAPPY GANG: Time for a laugh... (back row, from left) Peter Daniel, Kevin Hector, Alan Hinton, Colin Boulton, Tony Rhodes. (Middle) me in a stranglehold from Willie Carlin, a muffled Alan Durban, skipper Dave Mackay, Barry Butlin, John Robson

ON A TIGHT REIN: Marking future team-mate Franny Lee closely in September 1970

SIMPLY THE BEST: Up against George Best in 1971

MASTER BLASTER: Firing a shot just inside the near post as Derby beat Manchester United 4-1 in the Watney Cup in August 1970

WORDS OF WISDOM: Sir Alf Ramsey imparts his knowledge to Allan Clarke, myself, Ralph Coates Peter Shilton, and Francis Lee during an England training session at Roehampton in 1971. In the same year Sir Alf has us all jumping to it during another international gathering (below)

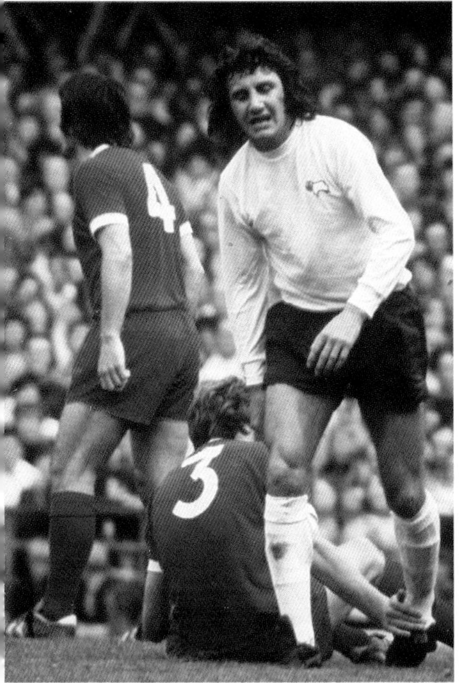

BOYHOOD HEROES: In action against Liverpool in 1971 at the start of our championship-winning season

HOLDING TIGHT: With Kevin Hector and the championship trophy in 1972

CLOSING IN: An aerial battle at Highbury as Frank McLintock rises highest with Derby closing in on the 1971-72 title

WE ARE THE CHAMPIONS: The Football League trophy is proudly on display with the squad as we prepared to defend our title at the start of the 1972-73 season

WALKING WITH A GIANT: Juventus legend John Charles (left) accompanied Derby to Turin in April, 1973, and the Gentle Giant passed on advice during training before our European Cup semi-final

STAR IN STRIPES: A tense moment up against Jose Altafini, who scored twice for Juventus in our European Cup semi-final in April, 1973

WHAT A TEAM!: Lin and I share our big day in July, 1973, with the lads (standing from left) Kevin Hector, Alan Hinton, Jimmy Gordon, best man John Wignall, Alan Durban, Dave Mackay, Colin Todd, John O'Hare, Steve Powell, Colin Boulton. (Front) Ronnie Webster, John McGovern

GLOWING RECEPTION: Brian Clough was fully in favour of my marriage to Lin in July, 1973

POLE-AXED: The dejection is written on our faces as Peter Shilton and I trudge off the pitch after we failed to beat Poland in 1973, and therefore missed out on going to the 1974 World Cup

SUMMERTIME BLUES: Resting after surgery to repair my torn Achilles tendon in 1974

GETTING ACQUAINTED: Up against Charlie George in an Arsenal shirt. The skilful forward would later be my Derby team-mate

TEA AND SYMPATHY: Lin tries to cheer me up with a cuppa after Achilles surgery in 1974

yellow card meant, thought he and Haller were colluding and called the official a cheat.

Juventus scored again through Franco Causio, while we missed the quality an injured Hinton would have provided, especially from the corners and free-kicks we won.

Those set-pieces saw me venture upfield to be assaulted by the opposing centre-half Francesco Morini.

When he wasn't punching me in the back and on my arms, he was grabbing my shirt and spitting at me.

Schulenburg was blind to it all and, following one particular piece of dirty work right in front of the referee's eyes, Malcolm Allison's warning came back to me: "You go to Italy and you don't get anything. Corruption, it's endemic."

Morini can count himself doubly fortunate. His attempts at intimidation should have brought us a penalty and had it dawned on me that I wouldn't be facing him again in a fortnight, I would almost certainly have retaliated and decked him with a punch.

Altafini scored a third Juventus goal seven minutes from the end to seal our 3-1 defeat, which hurt me deeply.

From their point of view, it might have been a wonderful piece of skill by the South American, who picked up a pass, motored past two of our players and sidestepped me before shooting into the roof of the net.

From our point of view, it was a lousy, wretched, stupid goal to concede. We were all at fault. The defence certainly should have been tighter as a unit, we were too spread out and I should have made the last tackle.

It was just all so unnecessary and rankled deeply with me on the journey home, more than the knowledge I would be watching the second leg. I fervently hoped Altafini's second goal would not prove terminally damaging, while Clough and Taylor were insistent we could still retrieve a two-goal deficit.

After all, they argued, we had needed two goals against Spartak Trnava earlier in the tournament and got them.

A repeat performance was surely not beyond us.

The more the management assessed the situation and clarified our position, the greater our conviction grew that we could beat Juventus 2-0 and reach the final on away goals.

Sitting alongside Gemmill in the directors' box at the Baseball Ground, it was apparent that the Italians felt their two-goal cushion would be enough and they hardly bothered to venture over the halfway line.

Archie and I were on our feet in the 56th minute when Hector was tripped by Luciano Spinosi and the Portuguese referee Francisco Lobo had no hesitation in awarding a penalty.

Lobo probably enjoyed pointing to the spot because it later emerged he turned his back on a set of car keys and £5,000 in cash from the notorious fixer Dezso Solti before the game to favour Juventus.

Even as the ultra-reliable Hinton stepped up to take the kick, some of our fans were checking their watches and telling themselves: "Half an hour, we've got half an hour now to get one more goal and we're in the European Cup final."

If there was one immutable law, it was this: You could stick your life savings on Ally scoring a penalty.

The guy was phenomenal from 12 yards, his record virtually immaculate, he must have had ice running through his veins to have retained his composure so often. All through his career at Derby I had never recalled him missing.

It was, to put things mildly, a very intense situation for an individual returning from two months sidelined through injury.

The pressure, the tension must have been unbearable but not a single Derby fan in the crowd of 38,350 would have wanted anyone but Hinton, even if he was a little rusty, to be taking the penalty – and a split-second after he sent it wide I swear you could have heard a pin drop.

The ground went deathly quiet, nobody could quite believe what they had witnessed because the rule was: Hinton doesn't miss penalties.

I knew then that we were fated to go out and my mind raced back to the third Juventus goal at their place.

The Italians celebrated Hinton's error and were slapping each other on the back again five minutes later when Roger Davies's patience snapped.

For an hour, the despicable Morini gave him precisely the same dirty, sly treatment he'd meted out to me – and Davies retaliated by felling Morini with a headbutt to leave us with 10 men.

The result was a foregone conclusion and 0-0 it duly finished.

Clough and Taylor were far from impressed with Davies but, in time, Clough inevitably mellowed and I heard him relate this anecdote, which shows that he wasn't the only member of our management duo with a harsh tongue: "I fell out with Roger Davies once when he got sent off against Juventus – and it was one of the funniest laughs, but only afterwards. He went into the dressing room, got changed and came out. I used to sit in the dugout with whoever was with me, and Taylor used to sit on a chair out of the dugout with another couple of players, coaches, whatever. Roger walked along, strolling along, and we're in the bloody thick of it in the match and I heard him say, 'Where can I sit?' and Taylor, quick as a bloody flash, says, 'Well, you can fuck off, 'cos if you get near the gaffer he'll kill you. You're no fucking good out here, fuck off!' Well, Roger went from about six-foot three, which was his true height, to about four foot ... and I just heard it all. He scarpered, couldn't get away quick enough obviously. But afterwards, it was funny."

So Juventus went through to the 1973 European Cup final to meet Ajax in Belgrade, where again they were in negative mode, rarely venturing into the Dutch side's half and deservedly losing 1-0.

Johan Cruyff's Ajax were a fabulous side, clinching their third successive European Cup.

We might not have beaten them but I am convinced we would have given them a much better match than Juventus and genuinely tried to win.

A week before the 1972-73 season, Derby should have been at Wembley for the first time since the 1946 FA Cup final to contest the Charity Shield against Leeds.

Instead, we found ourselves at home losing 2-1 to FC Den Haag while Leeds were away in Greece, drawing 2-2 with Olympiakos.

In place of the traditional curtain-raiser between the League champions and FA Cup winners, the Shield saw Manchester City beat the Third Division champions Aston Villa 1-0 at Villa Park.

I felt sorry for our supporters, who had been denied a glamorous trip to Wembley, but few of them were inclined to criticise the manager.

Clough was already in the process of totting up a crime sheet at the Football Association and the Football League, but he didn't give two hoots for upsetting the men in suits.

Given the antipathy between Derby and Leeds, he didn't have much appetite for what was in essence a high-profile friendly. It might have ended in tears and, quite possibly, injuries. Bearing in mind what happened two years later when Leeds and Liverpool players turned their Charity Shield encounter into a battlefield, he probably made a wise call to Don Revie to get the whole thing cancelled.

As champions, we were up there to be shot at, the team all the others wanted to beat and having come so far, so quickly, it was inevitable that we lacked the experience to deal with certain situations.

Clough and Taylor soon decided it was time for another infusion of new blood.

They popped down the road to Leicester waving a British record cheque for £225,000 to sign left-back David Nish.

I knew David from the England Under-23s, where he had been a regular for several seasons, so I was ready to greet a very skilful player with a lovely touch, who could see and play a pass as well as anyone and rarely gave the ball away. Technically, he was excellent, a clean striker of the ball with great balance.

David was a right-footed left-back with a gift of dropping his shoulder, selling opponents a dummy and coming inside to beat them, rather like Stanley Matthews.

He was as far removed as possible from your archetypal rough left-back, with two broken noses, who would tackle everything.

The management knew they had acquired another treasured item, but they weren't quite sure where to put him on show, and it took time for David to settle into his natural position in the

No.3 shirt. Certainly, an early run on the right of midfield did him no favours.

One particular match there for him didn't work at all – and neither did Clough's abrasive style.

David's problem was that he was a little bit sensitive. Not in a wimpish way, but the pressure got to him when Clough said: "I hope I haven't wasted my money on the most expensive player in Britain."

Nish found that difficult to deal with. He couldn't relax and it affected his performances.

Derby fans never saw the best of him until Clough and Taylor had gone.

The glamour of the European Cup was not immediately apparent when the first-round draw brought us a visit from the Yugoslav side, Zeljeznicar, and I managed a little footnote in Derby's history by scoring the club's first goal in European competition.

Archie Gemmill added another and we kept it tight and compact to ensure we had a satisfactory 2-0 advantage for the return leg in Sarajevo, where my knowledge of history reminded me the First World War began with the assassination of Archduke Franz Ferdinand.

We prepared by taking a trip into the hills to see where the Yugoslav patriots fought against Hitler's troops in the Second World War, but there was little drama on the pitch – just a watchful, professional show to complete a 4-1 aggregate win. I still raise a toast to that success in one of four surviving brandy glasses, from a set of six, which I bought in a glass factory in Sarajevo.

If Derby supporters asked: "Zeljeznicar who?" they needed

no introduction to our next opponents Benfica, or their star player, the legendary Eusebio.

The Portuguese champions were right up there with the most successful clubs in the world to my mind – Real Madrid, the Milan sides and Ajax.

Benfica were the first club to win the European Cup after five years of domination by Real and between 1961 and 1968, the Eagles of Lisbon contested no fewer than five finals.

They were, by any yardstick, genuine blue chip opponents, while Eusebio would rank among the world's best players in any era.

Peter Taylor went to spy on Benfica before we met them in October and was far from impressed.

More than that, he returned to tell us: "You have nothing to fear, they are beatable," which was very reassuring.

Taylor going to watch opponents was most unusual in itself, as he and Clough always preached the game was all about us.

It was an indication that the management were in no mood to be embarrassed by the Portuguese, who arrived in England unbeaten in seven domestic matches in which they had plundered over 30 goals, Eusebio claiming 16 of them.

There was embarrassment, however, and it all belonged to Benfica as we produced a very special performance to win 3-0.

Clough got plenty of water onto the pitch to ensure the ball zipped about.

I opened the scoring with a trademark header at the far post from Hinton's cross from a short-corner routine and we increased our lead when Hector scored a truly magnificent goal.

This time, Hinton's corner was slightly too strong for me, the ball brushing the top of my head, only for Hector to watch it like a hawk, rocking back to connect with a dipping left-foot volley inside the far angle of bar and post. John McGovern pounced for our third goal inside 40 minutes.

Benfica looked to Eusebio in vain for a spark of inspiration. The Black Panther was 30 and had lost half a yard of the pace which had made him such a formidable competitor.

I thought he looked a fading force, and Todd and I spent most of the second half defending on the halfway line as Benfica were penned back and restricted to nothing more threatening than a couple of half-chances.

Clough and Taylor were at their inspirational best in the return leg, where we were tucked away in the Hotel Miramonte in Pinhal Colares, 20 miles outside Lisbon, and the relaxed pre-match routine included paddling in the Atlantic, a couple of glasses of beer and a plate of shrimps.

The local police told us we had to get to the ground early and we were in the dressing room over two hours before kick-off, not ideal before such a big game.

All of a sudden, Clough and Taylor started with their stories and jokes and the place was full of laughter.

Before we knew it, there was only half an hour to go and we ended up rushing to get ready to play.

Benfica had their tails up from the first whistle, forcing a string of corners and winning free-kicks in dangerous areas in the first 30 minutes but they foundered on the rock of Terry Hennessey, who produced an heroic performance just in front of Todd and myself.

It was Hennessey's best display in a Derby shirt and just a shame finances dictated that not more of our supporters could afford to be there to witness it in a crowd of 75,000 fans.

Benfica came at us from the off. They seemed to have 15 players on the pitch and Hennessey marked five of them!

With 15 minutes to go, a series of bonfires were lit on the vast banks of terracing in the Stadium of Light as the Portuguese started to walk out of the ground, accepting a 0-0 draw.

The fires symbolised Benfica's hopes going up in smoke, we learned, although it was a little distracting at the time.

The stalemate also meant Benfica had failed to score in a European tie for the first time in a decade.

On the flight back to Castle Donington, Taylor told me he had been less than frank with his scouting report on Benfica and let slip: "Roy, they might have been unbeaten but they were dreadful when I saw them, so poor I couldn't tell you. If I'd been honest, the lads might have become over-confident and vulnerable. Or they would have thought I'd been drinking and lost the plot."

Europe was a blessing to us. With things not going right in the First Division, we went out in all our first four European legs completely relaxed and with the pressure off.

Playing relaxed football, we reached our peak in those games.

The European Cup went into hibernation for the winter and we needed to attend to a poor away record which ran to seven straight League defeats.

I wasn't responding well to losing matches, I never did, and I was suddenly pulled up short after six bookings cost me a two-match ban by the Football Association, promptly followed by a £100 fine – a week's wages – from Cloughie.

To say I felt disappointed and let down by the manager would be an understatement.

I was relaxing at home one afternoon when one of the lads

rang, asking: "Have you see the Evening Telegraph, Roy?" before going on to spill the beans.

Plastered all over the back page was a verbal assault on me by Clough. He pilloried me for those six cautions, insisting he would not tolerate that sort of behaviour, especially from the club captain. He said that the team could not afford to be without me, my ill-discipline would cost me £100 and that he hoped it would prove to be a valuable lesson.

I was very upset to have to read all this without Clough first pulling me to one side and explaining his actions.

Despite feeling foolish and belittled, I kept my cool when I went into work the following morning, saw the gaffer and asked him: "Can I see you after training, boss?"

The moment arrived when I went into his office to have it out with him. I had rehearsed what I was going to say, how demeaning it was to see him slagging me off in print without a warning. I wasn't going to argue the toss over the £100 fine, but couldn't he see how I had amassed all those bookings, doing everything I could to prevent us leaking so many goals when we were considerably less than watertight at the back?

I was going to plead my innocence and tell him I was being punished financially for trying to do my best for the football club – his club, my club, our club. I couldn't believe he hadn't spoken to me first, but simply hung me out to dry.

As I entered his room, the gaffer smiled and held up his hand, waving two airline tickets at me.

"Before you start with all the moaning and whining," he said. "You're off to Spain on holiday at Derby County's expense with that charming young lady of yours – just try not to kick her. And please don't give me anything about that hundred quid fine, because this little break is costing considerably more than that. Behave in future. Now get out of my bloody sight."

I found myself outside his office, clutching tickets providing Lin and myself with a passport to four days' five-star accommodation at the luxurious La Manga sports resort.

Clough knew that I would return refreshed and revitalised from getting some Spanish sunshine on my back.

He knew that would benefit the team.

Equally, he knew that he could not reward, or be seen to reward, what he considered to be inappropriate behaviour.

That was typical Clough, a slap with one hand, a present in the other.

I led a tight-knit bunch, but some of the lads believed I enjoyed a special relationship with him.

Gemmill stated: "I thought Roy got preferential treatment. Maybe he'd get an extra day off here and there, and the gaffer tended to back him in an argument or dispute. At the time, I resented that," while Colin Todd said: "Brian Clough used to pick on me something terrible, but he wouldn't say anything to Roy."

What Archie and Colin had to remember was that I joined the club several years before them, and had already had my fair share of run-ins and verbal batterings long before they set foot in the Baseball Ground.

I took on board Brian's advice, learned from his informative bollockings, and he had moulded me into what he thought a club captain and England centre-half should be.

In the manner of many Yorkshiremen, he sometimes explained things strongly, which could be interpreted in a different manner – as outright criticism – but much of what he said was inspirational when you fully digested it and put it into practice.

If Gemmill and Todd thought I was always the blue-eyed boy, they should have been with me on one early occasion when I was called to the manager's office and went to sit down.

"Who said you could sit down?" he snapped. I quickly stood up. "Sit down," he said. "Just what do you think you're up to?" I was completely taken aback and replied: "I don't know what you mean, gaffer." He shot back: "Yes, you do. The way you're living your life. You're in the Midland Hotel drinking every night with Dave Mackay, then out clubbing it. I know everything that goes on in this town." I was mortified, hung my head and could only apologise. "Don't say you're sorry," he continued. "Just mend your ways or your career will be over before Dave's. Sort yourself out, stop the boozing and stop going out every night. Now get out of my sight." I was left, my mouth gaping like a goldfish, with no chance of defending myself.

Gemmill ended up as an extremely loyal friend to Clough, although the gaffer labelled him "a miserable little so-and-so at times, and cantankerous, as awkward off the field as he was on it," and in their initial dealings, our dour Scot was the butt of some fearful teasing.

Clough would come into the dressing room, turn to me and say: "Morning, skipper. How is he today?" before enquiring: "Has he said hello, skipper?" and I'd respond: "No, gaffer," and so we would proceed, "Has he spoken to anyone, skipper?" "No gaffer." "Has he smiled, skipper?" "No gaffer."

Archie must have been inwardly seething to be spoken about this way, but he took all the mickey-taking and responded by putting in some monumental shifts in the only place it mattered – on the pitch.

Gemmill was probably right on occasions about my days off.

There were times when Clough would tell me after training early in the week: "See you on Friday morning," and tell some of the others, "I'll see you lot tomorrow."

You did what you were told or bollockings and fines were dished out. If the boss calculated a light week would benefit me on Saturday, then my workload would be reduced accordingly – especially when my groin was playing up.

The Baseball Ground remained a stronghold and, before I started my ban, we demonstrated our class in late November by pulverising Arsenal 5-0 – a scoreline sealed in the 47th minute when Davies scored his first League goal.

The Gunners were reduced to rubble by the accuracy of Hinton's delivery, one cross from him enabling me to head home, almost colliding with the far post.

I estimate Ally created 95 per cent of the goals I scored for Derby. He had two great feet and would deliver crosses with pace and accuracy into areas which made life difficult for defenders.

I would regularly take up a position at the back post for his corners and set-pieces. He only needed one stride to put the ball on my head.

12

Old Enemies

EARLIER in that winter of 1972, I returned to England duty in the World Cup qualifying competition. We had been drawn in Group Five with Wales and Poland for company, the winners alone progressing to the tournament in West Germany in 1974.

Facing only four matches, there was never going to be much room for manoeuvre if we started poorly or suffered a defeat along the way.

There was no sense within the camp that qualification would be a formality, although we were confident of topping the group and thought we were a better side than Poland.

In the Home Internationals, we expected to beat Wales home and away, year after year, but I had an inkling there might be a little bit of added pressure on us this time and that they might prove more resilient with the eyes of the world watching.

We certainly weren't going to take victory for granted against Wales when they could call on forwards of the calibre of Wyn Davies, John Toshack and Leighton James, defenders such as Mike England and our own Terry Hennessey, backed up by Gary Sprake in goal.

In short, if we weren't careful, the opening qualifier at Ninian Park had the potential to be a banana skin but it turned out to be a low-key affair, settled in our favour by a solitary goal from Colin Bell before the interval.

Meanwhile, John Robson, who won seven England Under-23 caps, had played his last match for Derby County. He left in the week before Christmas when Clough and Aston Villa manager Vic Crowe shook hands over a £90,000 transfer.

Robbo had effectively been in the departure lounge from the moment Nish settled into his No.3 shirt and while there was inevitably a little bit of sadness in saying goodbye to a key member of the team which won the Second and First Division titles, I was delighted he was going to a big club – and Robbo was looking forward to starting a new chapter in his career.

As Robbo made his Villa debut on Boxing Day, I was cursing a missed opportunity. I never scored a hat-trick in my professional career and I never got a better chance than I did when the new Manchester United manager Tommy Docherty brought the Red Devils to our place.

I scored with two headers in a 3-1 win, first from a Webster cross then via the underside of the bar when I connected with a free-kick from Hinton. I also had a marvellous opportunity to get a third goal, facing an inviting target from six yards.

Crucially, I forgot Frank Wignall's golden rule: "You haven't got time to fanny about ... just strike it first time." I took an extra touch to control the ball and toe-poked it straight at Alex Stepney.

There was serious disappointment at a missed chance in the new year when England's qualifying programme continued and we found the young Burnley winger James in thrilling form for Wales at Wembley.

His intelligent movement and cutting edge handed Toshack the opening goal on a plate and although Norman Hunter equalised with a thunderous drive, we weren't good enough to find a winner and the final whistle was accompanied by a cacophony of boos.

The England supporters were entitled to voice their disapproval, but I was sure there would be time to rectify matters against Poland.

My attention turned from the World Cup to the FA Cup, a competition which had provided encouragement and frustration in equal measure over the previous three seasons.

Each time we had gone out 1-0 in the fifth round – at QPR, Everton and Leicester's Filbert Street, where Arsenal pipped us in a second replay.

I had been fortunate enough to play at Wembley and I very much wanted to lead out Derby to experience that honour as a team, especially after missing an opportunity in the Charity Shield.

Clough had tweaked the attack, bringing in Roger Davies, who proved an awkward proposition for opposing defenders. While Liverpool and West Brom were still trying to work him out, he was away and scoring against them in successive matches.

We made a meal of our FA Cup third-round tie at Peterborough, where Davies scored the solitary goal, and he was on target again in the next round against Tottenham, stabbing home a late equaliser in the Baseball Ground mud.

The replay was upon us four days later, virtually before we had the chance to savour the prospect.

Spurs fans were captivated too and the game attracted a crowd of 52,736, the Londoners' biggest of the season.

I always fancied our chances against Bill Nicholson's side because they played an open game.

Equally, I knew Todd, Hennessey and myself needed to keep a close guard on my England colleague Martin Chivers and Scotland centre-forward Alan Gilzean.

Our plans were ruined when the twin strikers scored before half-time and our hopes sagged still further during an emotional exchange in the dressing room during the interval.

Terry Hennessey played a lot of matches in pain for Derby and this, he felt, was a match too far for his sore knees and nagging Achilles injury.

"I've had it, gaffer," he said to Clough, removing his yellow away shirt. "I've got to come off." Clough was having none of it and shouted: "Like fuck, you are. I've only got Durban on the bench, and I'm not putting him on."

Terry was 30, a big, brave man but he was very upset, almost in tears, as he slowly bent down to take off his boots and reiterated that the pain had become too much to bear.

He was under enormous psychological, almost physical, pressure from Clough to keep going but the manager was eventually forced to concede defeat, turning to Durban and telling him: "Get your stuff ready, you're going out."

It was a very difficult occasion for Terry, a sad experience for him. I knew a little about how he felt, having played many times in pain – often at the manager's instigation.

But I wouldn't call Brian Clough a bully, although he was frequently hammering Terry to play during that period in the premature twilight of his career.

Clough simply wanted his best players on the pitch and there was no escaping the fact that Hennessey was a very efficient performer. He never played for Derby again, retiring officially at the end of the season to go into coaching.

The half-time drama ended and Durban, wise to the ways of the manager and not perturbed in the slightest at being rubbished by him, came out smiling and rubbing his hands.

Derby might have been 2-0 down but Durbs, as usual, was just delighted to be playing.

He loved the game and played it his own way, almost as if it was chess. He was never the quickest but his understanding of what was required to create and score goals earned him 27 caps for Wales. On the training ground, when Clough told us to do something, he would quickly work out how to do it with fewer passes. He was intelligent that way and lived for matchday. Whether it was a game against Liverpool, Leeds United or, in Taylor's parlance, Doncaster Pork Butchers, Durbs was itching to get on the pitch.

Although Hector pulled a goal back with a hook shot, off the far post, similar to his effort against Benfica, it seemed we wouldn't even get as far as the fifth round this time.

An innocent McGovern was hit on the hand at point-blank range when Cyril Knowles struck a free-kick at him and the referee Don Biddle awarded a penalty.

I led heated protests because it was a wretched decision. John didn't stand a chance of getting out of the way.

If Mr Biddle thought he was in for an early night when Mike England scored from the spot to make it 3-1 with 12 minutes to go, however, he was out of luck.

So were some of our supporters, who started to leave White Hart Lane to beat the traffic jams and begin the trek home up the M1. They can only have tuned into radio coverage of the remainder of the match with increasing incredulity while the Derby faithful who stayed in the ground enjoyed a feast of football.

For what followed summed up the very essence and spirit of the romance of the FA Cup as we ripped the tie out of Tottenham's hands with a classic attacking performance and a tremendous fightback.

Davies drove home a low shot through a ruck of bodies before equalising in the 86th minute with the sort of goal for which Marco van Basten was later lauded.

There didn't seem much on when O'Hare threaded over a low cross but Davies, his back to goal, scooped the ball up with his right foot and turned in one movement to unleash a ferocious volley inside the near angle of bar and post.

Game on? It felt as if we had barely started getting our teeth into Tottenham when the whistle went after 90 minutes with the score 3-3, and I sensed we had virtually battered Spurs to a standstill.

Their backroom staff arrived to massage the tired legs of players lying and sitting on the ground. They looked 'gone', most of them flat out, shattered, and seeing them in that state gave us another lift.

Clough and Taylor would have regarded it as a sign of weakness, and unnecessary interference, to have emerged from their dugout to issue instructions.

Instead, they pushed out Jimmy Gordon, who did no more than congratulate and encourage us to keep going for another half an hour.

I played a significant role in the goal which gave Davies his hat-trick in the second period of extra-time – even though I never touched the ball.

Pat Jennings was an excellent, lively keeper on his way to being crowned Footballer of the Year and I decided that if we were going to get any joy from set-pieces it might be a good idea to 'stand on him'.

Jack Charlton, at Leeds, was the acknowledged master of placing himself directly in front of a keeper to obstruct his movement, and I took a leaf out of my England predecessor's book. When Hector sent over a deep corner from the right in the second period of extra-time, Jennings was imprisoned on his line, unable to get round me to the far post, and Davies took advantage to plant a header into the roof of the net.

We completed an amazing 5-3 scoreline in our favour when the honours were reversed, Davies heading on a massive clearance from Colin Boulton for Hector to race away and score.

Whenever the famous night at White Hart Lane is mentioned, the words of BBC commentator Barry Davies return to me: "Surely, one of the finest comebacks of all time in the FA Cup."

The fifth round brought QPR to the Baseball Ground and, just like their fellow Londoners, the Second Division promotion-chasers had no answer to the Hector-Davies partnership. Roger opened the scoring and Kevin scored a hat-trick before half-time in a 4-2 win.

When the draw for the quarter-finals was made, there was just one name I didn't want to hear. Luton, Arsenal, Coventry, Manchester City or Sunderland – who had to replay, Chelsea or Wolves I would have happily accepted, home or away.

Then the balls were juggled in the velvet bag at Lancaster Gate and out it came, Derby County will play ... Leeds United.

They were such a good, hard team packed with internationals who never conceded an inch.

Even with home advantage, I felt that quite apart from this being the toughest tie available, the build-up would be dominated by the loathing and distrust Clough and Revie had for each other. I was right on both scores, unfortunately, and Peter Lorimer's goal put us out of the competition.

There was no time to mope after Leeds had again turned their evil eye on us, because four days later we had to get our act together against Spartak Trnava in the European Cup or face elimination.

We had gone down in Czechoslovakia by a single goal, a defeat which wasn't the end of the world. Flying home, Taylor was upbeat and told me: "Roy, if I wasn't sure we could score twice, I wouldn't bother coming into work tomorrow."

With the quality we had in attack – Davies, Hector and Hinton – with John O'Hare in support from his temporary role in midfield, and the atmosphere generated by a vibrant, packed crowd making for one of those special European Cup nights at the Baseball Ground, I felt the overall package would be one Spartak had never experienced and all too much for them, and that they would crack under the pressure.

I was right, but only just, because the Czech champions were a well-organised bunch. Two goals from Hector did the trick in the end, taking his tally to 10 in six weeks, and reinforcing my impression of him as a supreme finisher.

In my opinion, Jimmy Greaves was the most natural goal-scorer of our generation but if you were looking for someone to put up alongside him, it would be Kevin.

He wasn't a powerhouse, battering-ram type of forward who dominated defenders in the air but more in the mould of a continental player. Kevin was prolific with a wonderful ability to glide past opponents at pace.

Frank McLintock described him as a "nightmare" opponent because the Arsenal captain could never be sure if Hector would take him on down his right or left side.

Kevin rarely seemed to score tap-ins, either, but goals of grace and beauty from the unlikeliest of angles.

Rich satisfaction at beating Spartak gave way to the bitter disappointment of both the Juventus ties, then it was back to the First Division.

We faced three remaining League matches, all at home, and a lesser team – or a team under lesser motivation – might have gone through the motions.

Victories against Everton, Ipswich and finally Wolves, on a Friday night when I scored, lifted us into seventh place, two points shy of qualifying for Europe again via the UEFA Cup.

England duty beckoned once more and I found myself back on familiar territory for the start of the Home International series.

Because of the Troubles in Ulster, Northern Ireland asked to switch their home match with us from Belfast to Merseyside and Everton hosted the contest, which we won 2-1 thanks to a pair of goals from Chivers.

The atmosphere was strange with so many Irishmen in the crowd and I think we frustrated our supporters because we certainly weren't at our most fluid.

It was a memorable occasion for me because I knew I would never get another opportunity to win an England cap in my home city and only political unrest had made it possible.

Several of the other England lads generously gave me some of their allocated tickets, so I could pass them on to friends and family and be assured of my own personal fan club.

Three days later, we faced Wales at Wembley, doing what we should have done four months earlier – putting them to the sword 3-0. Instead of the 62,273 crowd which saw us drop a point in the World Cup qualifier, only 38,000 bothered to turn up to see goals from Chivers, Mick Channon and Martin Peters.

The miserable attendance was down to a few factors. There was no novelty value whatsoever to a domestic tournament crammed in at the end of the season.

Most of Britain's top players were on show, but many were jaded after lengthy, tiring club campaigns and then there was the fact that England had been stuck in a rut at home.

In fact, this win over Wales was our first victory at Wembley for two years.

There is always one fixture, however, which guarantees a massive crowd and the Twin Towers were rocking at the end of the week with 95,950 packed in for the visit of Scotland.

Peters was on target again for the solitary goal of a game which featured a bizarre contribution by Celtic's Jimmy Johnstone on the right wing. He was such a good player, a European Cup winner in 1967, and on several occasions he gave Emlyn

Hughes a roasting only to constantly drag the ball back and try and beat Emlyn all over again with another trick. Kenny Dalglish and Lou Macari must have been in despair waiting for the crosses which never came from Jimmy, whose self-indulgence allowed Bobby Moore and myself crucial time to organise the defence.

With the Home Championship in the bag, we steeled ourselves for four more matches in Europe – three friendlies and a World Cup qualifier of paramount importance in Poland.

First came the warm-up match against Czechoslovakia in Prague where Allan Clarke spared us defeat with a last-minute equaliser.

The Czechs had been chosen as opponents specifically because Sir Alf and the FA felt they played in a similar style to the Poles and that conditions would be similar 200 miles away in Chorzow. Yet it was not an encouraging dress rehearsal on a very grassy pitch which made it difficult for us to move the ball quickly and create anything.

Poland was a disaster – pure and simple, especially for Sir Alf and Bobby Moore.

We combined to cobble together the worst England performance it was ever my misfortune to be a part of, going down 2-0 in a feverish atmosphere generated by a crowd of 73,714.

Chorzow was a mining town, a very dull, dour place but the Polish supporters turned the Slaski Stadium into a bear pit, producing the most powerful, intimidating backdrop I ever experienced, even taking a full house at Hampden Park into account.

We were constantly a yard off the pace although, to be fair, Poland were superb on the night.

England stayed in the only decent hotel in the place but it still didn't have a bar for us to drown our sorrows.

Afterwards, we did succeed in buying some bottles of beer from a little shop and we were all in Bally and Mooro's room when there was a knock at the door.

It was Sir Alf, asking: "Do you mind if I join you boys for a beer?"

There was absolutely no question that he was most welcome and my heart went out to him at that moment.

He must have been feeling extremely lonely and very vulnerable with his job on the line – through no fault of his own.

Fingers should have been pointed at the players. We were the ones who had performed so poorly.

I look at our line-up that Wednesday in June and can't believe we lost: Shilton, Madeley, Hughes, Storey, McFarland, Moore, Ball, Bell, Chivers, Clarke and Peters.

Bally took the top off a bottle of east European pilsner and handed it to Sir Alf, who was adamant that defeat was all his fault because we had been caught out by an early set-piece. He was unbelievably harsh on himself.

The situation was this – when the opposition had a free-kick or corner, Bell was detailed to fill the hole at the near post.

Only seven minutes had gone when the Poles won a free-kick deep on our right and Colin was already out there trying to stop them taking it quickly.

Robert Gadocha swung the ball in low and Jan Banas scored. How Sir Alf interpreted this in any way as being his fault was beyond all of us. We were caught out. In normal circumstances, the free-kick would have been dealt with.

Things went from bad to worse in the second half when I cushioned a header back to Bobby from the halfway line but he lost control and Wlodzimierz Lubanski robbed him before racing away to score off the inside of a post.

Ball was sent off 15 minutes from the end when he saw Peters being roughed up and decided to dish out a little retribution of his own.

I count myself fortunate that not too much rubbish has been written about me in my career, but I was irritated to read an article on the website, In Bed With Maradona, headlined How Roy McFarland Cost Poland The World Cup, which contained this nugget of dubious information:

"However just seven minutes after putting the game beyond England's reach, Poland were to suffer an injury blow that would see their star striker out for two years. After latching on to a ball forward, Lubanski skipped past England defender Roy McFarland – only to see a very late tackle from the Derby County man bring him down. Stretchered off the Chorzow turf, the 26-year-old would play no further part in helping his team successfully qualify for the 1974 World Cup, or take part in the competition itself. With a career spanning a total of 23 years, and a record that stands at 327 goals in 590 competitive games, Wlodzimierz Lubanski remains as one of Poland's greatest ever strikers. But Polish fans will forever wonder if it hadn't been for Roy McFarland's tackle back in 1973, could they really have overcome West Germany and lifted the World Cup."

I'm not going to claim that I wouldn't have been able to live with myself if I had been responsible for Lubanski missing the World Cup. I did what I did in the moment, the heat of battle. If I had tormented myself about the outcome of every challenge, I might as well have packed up professional football and joined the Derbyshire knitting circle.

That said, it was illuminating when Lubanski's memoirs were published to see that he exonerated me from blame for the cruciate ligament damage he suffered. He maintained the leg was injured without my involvement as a result of a previous knock and insufficient preparation for the big game.

Licking our wounds after Chorzow, we moved on to confront Russia in a friendly in Moscow's hot and humid Lenin Stadium, where Moore emphasised what a superb player he was with a top-class contribution to our 2-1 victory, courtesy of Chivers and an own goal.

Another huge crowd, around 85,000, turned out hoping to see England embarrassed but our squad was shot through with character and ability, and we gave those supporters precious little encouragement.

Turin was our final port of call and I thought there was little to choose between us and an Italian team half-comprised of Juventus players when Causio came on in the second half to join keeper Zoff, that thug of a centre-half Morini and forwards Capello and Anastasi, who both scored.

I wasn't tempted to confront Morini again, on account of his outrageous antics against Derby, in all honesty, because I had more than enough on my plate dealing with Italian football's golden boy Gianni Rivera spraying passes through our back four.

Italy were a very decent team in terms of ability and, although there was little to choose between the sides, the quality of their finishing proved decisive as they beat us 2-0.

I was proud to retain my place in the Rothmans Golden Boots XI for 1972-73 in this 4-3-3 formation: Pat Jennings (Tottenham and Northern Ireland); Paul Madeley (Leeds and England), Bobby Moore (West Ham and England), Roy McFarland (Derby and England), Emlyn Hughes (Liverpool and England); Billy Bremner (Leeds and Scotland), Alan Ball (Arsenal and England), Johnny Giles (Leeds and Republic of Ireland); Peter Lorimer (Leeds and Scotland), Mick Channon (Southampton and England), Allan Clarke (Leeds and England).

This is what the experts thought of my efforts: "For Roy McFarland, it was a season in which he consolidated his position as the most complete centre-half in England. His international experience proved central to Derby County's first run in European competition, and it was no coincidence that he was missing on the night that Juventus ended Derby's hopes of making the European Cup final. By lending his skills to the offensive, and nodding in vital goals, he often masks the magnitude of his defensive play. Always positive, always wanting to meet the ball, he possesses the determination to win challenges and the perception to finish the job with intelligent clearances. He becomes the first centre-half to retain the Golden Boots award for a second year."

That summer, I was sure England were capable of beating Poland at Wembley in October to qualify for the 1974 World Cup and equally convinced that Derby County would be better prepared the next time we were in the European Cup after Clough and Taylor had masterminded another championship triumph.

I was in my prime, and felt nothing could go wrong.

13

Broken Dreams, Broken Body

FAME has its rewards, and Lin and I have a teenage French football fan to thank for rescuing our honeymoon after our marriage in July, 1973.

A friend's chauffeur-driven Rolls-Royce whisked us away from the reception to Heathrow for an evening flight, but luxury turned to poverty.

Our hearts sank in Paris when the taxi dropped us off at this dirty, scruffy, third-rate, dive of a hotel.

An ancient lift and a landing covered in threadbare carpets led us to our room, where the door creaked open against the bed, allowing only one of us to squeeze in at a time.

When Lin saw tin ashtrays, more suited to a backstreet bar, on the bedside tables, she didn't know whether to laugh or cry at first. Budget didn't even come into it. She cried.

Although a popular local travel company had booked us into this establishment for four nights, within four minutes I was down at reception making the point that the room was wholly unacceptable, and requesting alternative accommodation.

In charge was a young chap, no more than 15, who told us the hotel was full, and so was everywhere else in Paris at 10pm on a Saturday night in the middle of summer.

I should have known demand would be at a premium, while all the joy and excitement of our wedding day was draining away from Lin, who was devastated and all for coming home immediately.

The lad seemed more interested in my passport photo than helping us, when he looked up shyly and asked if I was the same Roy McFarland he had seen on television playing for England against Italy in Turin three weeks earlier.

I said I was and his face broke into a broad smile. He may have been a kid but he certainly knew his stuff and after a few brief phone calls, he had negotiated us a decent price in a superb hotel.

There was one slight snag, however, this being before the advent of credit cards.

I hadn't bothered bringing a chequebook with me, having paid up front for bed and breakfast in the fleapit.

Having to stump up a hefty proportion of our spending money at our swanky new honeymoon venue meant we had to count the centimes visiting the Louvre, Notre Dame and the Eiffel Tower where, on the final day, we were so broke our lunch consisted of a shared sandwich and two beers.

Our wedding itself was a huge success, although I was a bit the worse for wear following a last-gasp stag night in my old quarters, the Midland Hotel, with family and friends from Liverpool.

My best man, John Wignall, suggested a swift pint of Bass in the Red Cow next to the church, St Edmund's, in Allestree, might possess restorative powers and he was right – although no one in the congregation needed a drink to appreciate Lin looked stunning.

We invited all my team-mates along with Brian and Barbara Clough, and Peter and Lilian Taylor, and headed off to the Riverside Hotel at Burton-on-Trent for the reception where, on my strict instructions, the boss and Barbara were treated to genuine champagne while the rest of the party were served sparkling Italian Prosecco for the toasts and speeches.

Clough informed me: "You've got a diamond there, Roy. Look after her."

He was always delighted when his players settled down and started to think about having a family because, in his words, it meant they weren't "out and about all hours using precious energy chasing girls".

Once upon a time, Sam Longson liked to think he had a cosy relationship with Brian Clough, but they were more like the principal members of a family at war when the 1973-74 season began, and there would be no fairy-tale ending.

The boss used his newspaper column in the Sunday Express to slaughter Leeds for their poor disciplinary record, claiming Don Revie's men should have been relegated, rather than slapped on the wrist with a suspended £3,000 fine, and adding:

"The men who run football have missed the most marvellous chance to clean up the game in one swoop".

Influential people in the game started to badger the chairman, demanding to know what he was going to do about the gaffer and how he was going to rein him in.

Then Clough antagonised Longson further by signing a contract with London Weekend Television to appear on both On the Ball and The Big Match, maintaining the job was only part-time and did not herald an increase in the volume of TV work he'd been doing for the previous three or four years without complaint.

But Longson started asking: "Why are we paying our manager a fortune when he spends so much of the club's time driving up and down the motorway?"

I feared that every time Derby had a poor result, the chairman was going to use Brian's television commitments as a stick to try and beat him over the head.

Brian's nose had been put out of joint because he was getting messages via our secretary Stuart Webb from Longson, rather than directly, although the chairman maintained that when it suited Clough he drove up to Chapel-en-le-Frith to visit him at home.

Longson was in his seventies, his health was suffering and his mood wasn't helped by sleepless nights, but he was well enough to dish out lectures to Clough, which further antagonised the manager.

The boss was frequently bursting into the dressing room, jerking a thumb towards the boardroom and complaining about "those bloody idiots up there". He was completely open about his contempt for Longson and the other directors, including

Jack Kirkland, a major shareholder who was becoming increasingly influential.

It shouldn't have been this way, it should have been Derby County – all together, wiser, more experienced for a fabulous run in the European Cup and seeking to win the Football League championship again.

We were perfectly capable of reclaiming the title and the management were thinking of replacing Terry Hennessey with another big-name signing.

The omens were encouraging as we beat both Chelsea and Manchester City at home 1-0 and kept another clean sheet in a 0-0 draw at Birmingham.

I was surprised after a 2-1 home win over Everton not to see Longson in our dressing room, for the first time in memory. I found out Brian had said something to offend him a few days earlier at Anfield and that he was demanding an apology as well as threatening to refuse to sign pay cheques for Brian and Peter Taylor.

Liverpool, the champions, had outplayed us 2-0 but we took our revenge the following week in the return fixture on a day of mixed emotions.

It started with the team bidding Alan Durban a fond farewell as he left for Shrewsbury in a £12,000 deal.

Our Welshman loved to play, anywhere, and worked like a Trojan to get back in favour whenever he was ousted.

He always managed to talk his way back in, but after completing a decade at the Baseball Ground his number was up.

Clough and Taylor worked their magic in the dressing room that Wednesday night, telling us that while Liverpool were good, we were better, and that they were not prepared to tolerate Bill Shankly doing the double over us with the season still in its infancy.

"Just go out there and play," said Taylor. "There's nothing to worry about."

We took him at his word and turned on the style, winning 3-1, a scoreline that didn't do us justice. I was at fault when Phil Boersma went past me to equalise against the run of play, but I had the satisfaction of shooting us back into the lead five minutes before the interval.

Durban's departure did not create any waves, unlike the management's next foray into the transfer market as they made what was, on the face of it, an outrageous attempt to prise the England captain Bobby Moore and Trevor Brooking away from West Ham for a combined fee of £400,000.

But that was the level Derby were operating at, and I know that Bobby fancied the move, having been approached by the gaffer through a journalist.

Forget notions of 'little old provincial Derby', Clough and Taylor considered the club major players in the transfer market.

We had come a long way with honest journeymen and bargain buys such as myself, Archie Gemmill, John O'Hare, Alan Hinton, John McGovern, John Robson and Jim Walker.

Serious money had been invested to bring in players of the calibre of Hennessey, Colin Todd, David Nish and, so very nearly, Ian Storey-Moore.

I know Clough envisaged Moore playing in midfield, acting as a defensive screen in front of Todd and myself.

If that didn't work, Plan B was for Bobby to play sweeper behind us.

Brian and Peter were full of tricks like that. It wasn't so much tactics they were interested in, though, but people, characters who could come in and improve the team.

Moore was 32 but he would have done that, as would Brooking – one of the most talented midfield players of his generation. He was being spoken of as a full England international and was clearly destined for greater things.

The West Ham directors agreed to accept £400,000, but their manager Ron Greenwood was having none of it.

Brian later admitted to the board that his approaches to Moore were illegal but said he only wanted the England skipper for one year, or two at most, to win the League.

Although Kirkland was uncomfortable with this revelation, he must have lapped it up as he compiled his dossier of Clough's 'misdemeanours'.

With Moore out of bounds, Clough and Taylor wasted little time in turning their attention instead to Henry Newton, who had been at the Baseball Ground earlier in the month, filling in at left-back for Everton.

Three years after identifying Newton, at Nottingham Forest, as a player they felt would improve the team, the management got their man for £100,000.

We duly celebrated another quality signing by thumping Southampton 6-2 at home with a Kevin Hector hat-trick to go second in the table.

Despite having sanctioned a £100,000 fee for Newton, the board could be fixated over trifling sums and I remember there were complaints when a chitty went in on behalf of Barry Clough, Brian's brother, for £13.10p to cover his expenses for chauffeuring Kevin and myself to Wembley in the manager's car for England's 7-0 demolition of Austria. It was a little kindness from the boss, his way of saying: "Well done". He asked me: "How are you getting down to London? Train? Car? Tell you what, put your feet up and I'll get our Barry to drive you."

Moore was rested for the friendly, Martin Peters captaining the side as I won my 19th cap, partnering Norman Hunter in the back four for only the second time.

It was strange not to glance over and see that familiar curly blond head next to me, but the Austrian threat was so minimal that either Norman or myself could have taken the evening off and watched from the terraces instead.

The contest was far too one-sided to be meaningful preparation for a vital World Cup qualifier against Poland.

Back home, Kirkland was 'busy'. Before the home match against Norwich, Brian ordered a bottle of champagne at the Midland Hotel which he drank with Sydney Bradley, the vice-chairman and a man who could be easily manipulated, and the club picked up the tab but it wasn't long before Kirkland kicked up a fuss and the bubbly was transferred to Clough's personal bill.

That same afternoon, Kirkland wound-up Taylor by asking why Burnley – in his opinion – had the best scouting system in the land.

Peter took that as a serious personal rebuke and hit back with chapter and verse on the quality of players he had brought to the club.

The ill-feeling became intense and I later learned the directors were already privately lining up a new manager.

They discussed the merits of Frank O'Farrell, who was out of work having being sacked by Manchester United the previous December. Gordon Milne, at Coventry, was another potential candidate. He had been a hero of mine, growing up watching him play for Liverpool. Milne had done well at Highfield Road and was beginning to be linked with other jobs. It was only natural that his name was suggested.

As far as Derby County were concerned, nothing was ever the same again after Saturday, October 13th, 1973, following our first away win of the season, courtesy of an early goal by Hector against a Manchester United side which Tommy Docherty couldn't prevent slipping into the Second Division.

We stood third in the table, but I felt very uneasy when word reached me there had almost been a scene in the Old Trafford boardroom when Kirkland beckoned over Taylor – like a headmaster might summon an errant schoolboy – and told our assistant manager to report to him first thing on Monday morning to explain precisely what it was he did at the club.

Brian had rid the club of one director, Bob Kirkland, and Jack was out to avenge his brother, calculating that Clough would explode with rage when he learned of Taylor's humiliation.

Inflaming proceedings was the relationship between Brian and Stuart Webb which had fractured beyond repair. From Webb's point of view, it was a case of: "Clough goes or I go".

One of the worst weeks of my life began when I travelled down to Hendon Hall, one of four Derby players along with Colin Todd, Kevin Hector and David Nish reporting for England duty on Sunday as Sir Alf Ramsey prepared a side to beat the Poles.

Kirkland versus Taylor very quickly escalated into Longson versus Clough over the weekend, the chairman demanding that Brian scale down his media work. That acted like a red rag to a bull, and Clough and Taylor reacted by resigning on Monday.

Emlyn Hughes and Alan Ball broke the news in the hotel at Hendon that they were gone.

The other Derby lads and myself didn't believe them at first – although unpleasantness had obviously been bubbling under the surface for a couple of months, so it was not a total shock.

Still, we thought it was a wind-up and joked about it, until we walked into the lounge and found Bally there brandishing the back page of the London Evening Standard.

Further confirmation arrived with the six o'clock news on the television and there was deep disappointment among our little group.

I have always prided myself on mental toughness, but suddenly my emotions were all over the place – frustration, anger at this incredibly stupid, unnecessary parting of the ways and fear that it might mean terrible upheaval at the club.

I could not get my head around the fact that this was the end.

Myself and other players had been with Brian and Peter at Derby for six years, but in so many respects it felt as if we had only started out on the path to all we could achieve at the club with the players we had.

Unfinished business barely came into it.

Quite apart from a shedload of trophies, it was said in jest that we could have won the Eurovision Song Contest, Crufts and the Boat Race under Clough and Taylor.

Perhaps that provides an indication of how far the team had bought into their ideals, the way they wanted things done, their winning mentality.

How I got to sleep that night I don't know, so much was whirling through my mind but I prayed that Longson and Co, in the sober light of day, would come to their senses and refuse to accept the letter of resignation. I feared the turmoil could destroy the club.

Clough was a great manager and had made Derby a great club. God knows what would happen without him.

If it hadn't been for him and Peter, I doubt whether I would have been playing for England at Wembley. He made me into an international player.

For now, I knew I had a job to do for England and a Polish attack to concentrate on. Before a game we had to win to reach the World Cup finals in West Germany, I walked out on the pitch and Brian, who was working for ITV, appeared and said: "Good luck tonight – don't worry about what has happened, just make sure you win."

Clough made some ill-judged utterances in front of millions of armchair football fans, denouncing Jan Tomaszewski as "a circus clown in gloves", and confidently predicted a 2-0 home win.

The Poland goalkeeper might have been eccentric, but he was effective and pulled off a succession of blinding saves as we rained in shot after shot.

Hunter suffered a moment which was to haunt him 10 minutes into the second half when he missed a tackle out on the left touchline and the Poles charged forward in a rare breakaway which ended with the ball being fed to an unmarked Jan Domarski, who shot under the diving Peter Shilton.

We equalised in the 63rd minute when Peters was fouled and Allan Clarke scored a penalty – and never for a single minute of the remainder of the match did I think we wouldn't score a winner.

The Poland goal led a charmed life however and there was

mounting concern then utter confusion on the sidelines when Moore's constant pleading with Sir Alf to bring on a substitute led to the manager eventually issuing the instruction: "Kevin, get stripped."

Ray Clemence tugged so hard on Kevin Keegan's tracksuit bottoms that his shorts came down as well, but it was Kevin Hector who was required for the last throw of the dice and Moore helped virtually chuck him on in the 85th minute with orders from Ramsey to "go through the middle".

Poor Kevin, he was literally inches away from becoming a national hero. Tony Currie sent over a corner from the left and Hector's close-range header bounced off the knees of a defender stationed on the line.

Time was our greatest enemy now. The final whistle sounded and England had failed.

The mood in the dressing room was one of devastation.

Sir Alf was numb, like the players, as he moved among us having a quiet word here and there.

It was never his scene to sit us all down and rant and rave, and on an occasion as sombre as this, what could he say?

He was a pragmatist and, as the nation had observed, we had battered Poland to the point of submission.

No one could understand why we hadn't won and the manager placed a sympathetic hand on a few slumped shoulders, saying: "Boys, you didn't deserve that result."

There was disbelief that we hadn't qualified, that the World Cup had bypassed us, a sense that it was all an illusion and that there had to be another chance. But there wasn't. It was game over.

Headlines such as "End of the World" and "Sir Alf's future in the balance" summed up the national black mood the following morning, by which time I was already back in Derby.

I couldn't face another night away when I knew it was my place to organise the players and make a stand to try and get Clough and Taylor back.

Frank Cholerton, a massive Rams fan, drove Hector and myself up the M1 and it was a desperately depressing journey, full of long awkward silences once Kevin and I had grilled Frank for every snippet of information he had about the shenanigans at the club.

Not going to the World Cup was horrific in itself. Not working for Clough and Taylor any longer compounded the misery.

Some of the stuff Longson came out with was truly disturbing.

Brian and the authorities had clashed several times, notably when Derby's shoddy accounting cost them a fine and a ban from Europe and also over the Storey-Moore debacle, but I could see nothing that merited the chairman's wild accusation that he feared the club might cease to exist with the gaffer at the helm.

Yet he insisted: "We will go into the Second Division with our heads in the air rather than win Division One wondering if the club will be expelled from the Football League."

I am convinced Longson was bullied by Jack Kirkland into hastily accepting the resignations, while other elements sweet-talked the chairman into standing firm against Brian and Peter, reinforcing his prejudices and warning him about what action the Football Association and Football League were considering – as if anyone had that inside information – if Clough didn't toe the line.

I discovered the team in a state of shock when I went into

the Baseball Ground for a jog on Thursday morning, and our coach Jimmy Gordon and trainer Gordon Guthrie had their hands full trying to rally some very depressed troops.

Still, it seemed, nobody could quite accept the enormity of what had happened.

The place seemed empty – the massive personalities of Clough and Taylor conspicuous by their absence.

It all felt wrong. Very wrong.

Bobby Robson swiftly became the front-runner after the resignations. He was offered the job and fancied it a great deal but the Ipswich chairman John Cobbold did his best to sabotage matters, claiming Robson was subject to a 10-year contract at Portman Road, although Derby knew that was inaccurate.

Friday dawned and Jimmy took a full training session to prepare for the visit of Leicester, exhorting us: "Come on, boys, we've got a game tomorrow."

There was a great deal of emotion and opinion being aired, even talk of whether we should boycott the match.

But that notion was quashed almost as soon as it arose.

Instinctively, we knew it wasn't the right thing to do. Our fans paid hard-earned money to watch us. For many of them it was the absolute highlight of a week spent grafting in factories, and Clough had always reminded us how important they were.

Meanwhile, under local playwright Don Shaw, supporters formed a protest movement which marched two miles from Derby market place to the ground before the match to demand the reinstatement of Clough and Taylor.

Robson phoned the Baseball Ground from Highbury, where Ipswich were about to face Arsenal, and relayed a message that he would call again at 8pm to give Longson a decision. But when Robson made contact it was to say he was meeting Cobbold on Monday morning at 10.30am and he would give a definitive answer that lunchtime.

Meanwhile, Clough had smuggled himself into the main stand, right next to the directors' box, to take the acclaim of the crowd minutes before the kick-off and then he was off, leaving a managerless, rudderless side to beat Leicester 2-1.

Monday arrived and Cobbold must have been delighted to tell Longson that Robson was staying in Suffolk. Within minutes, I know Derby were using Cholerton as an intermediary to phone Dave Mackay to see if he was interested. A posse of directors drove to Northampton where Dave was watching a youth match and got permission from Forest chairman Jim Willmer there to speak to his manager.

Despite having left the club in the summer, Hennessey was still our representative at the Professional Footballers' Association and he drove over from his home in Birmingham to help us draft a letter to the directors, formally asking them to meet us to discuss the situation.

I have seen it suggested that the tone of the letter was more strident than that, demanding the reinstatement of Clough and Taylor – but that's not my recollection.

We knew our place as employees and we weren't in a position to demand anything. Just a fair hearing, that's all we wanted.

But yes, there was a belief we could get Brian and Peter back while nobody else was running the show in their place.

I led the players into the Baseball Ground in mid-afternoon, asking to see the chairman and deliver the letter personally only to be told that Longson was not on the premises.

Kirkland and Webb were there, however. That was clear because their cars were parked outside, yet we were told they had accepted lifts home.

We could hear someone in the boardroom, so decided to stage a sit-in. It was becoming farcical now. All we wanted to do was express our feelings but Kirkland and Webb were refusing to talk to us. I found that incredible.

Our actions were based solely on speaking to the board, not demanding anything, yet two of the club's figureheads were hiding from us.

What did they think we were going to do? Bash them, belt them, kick them? We wanted to express our feelings regarding Clough and Taylor, we couldn't do anything else. Not having the courage to listen to us really choked us.

I suspect that Brian informed the press because around 6pm when most of us left, we had to shove our way through a knot of reporters and television cameras.

We split up into five or six groups and drove our separate ways to meet again at Archie Gemmill's house and formulate a plan of action. Ronnie Webster and Colin Boulton stayed behind and did manage a token confrontation when Kirkland and Webb seized their chance to break out of the boardroom and escape to their cars.

The vice-chairman and secretary had used a champagne bucket to have a pee, while the team felt bitter and in a militant mood now.

Escalating news of the Baseball Ground siege and consequent publicity excited Brian while the team became increasingly agitated, but I was very aware we had to play things by the book.

Many phone calls were made to take advice on how far we could push things legally without stepping out of line.

The board had acted very quickly to diffuse an explosive situation and Clough was tipped off that his job had been offered to Dave Mackay. That evening the Derby contingent went to the Albany Hotel in Nottingham and shook hands on a contract for four years with Dave and his assistant Des Anderson to take charge. Forest were at Blackpool the following night and it was agreed to keep the appointment a secret until after the match had kicked off at Bloomfield Road.

Brian was with us when I phoned my old team-mate to say: "Listen, Dave, we're trying to get Brian and Peter back and that's not just me talking, it's the whole staff. If you are approached by Derby County, we would respectfully ask you not to take the job."

I was shocked when Dave replied: "I've accepted the job, Roy. Simple as that. Brian's not coming back and, if you don't get me, you'll end up with someone else."

He sensed the mood of rebellion and added: "Des and I will be arriving on Thursday to take over and if there's any trouble whatsoever, you won't be playing at West Ham. I'll send out the reserves instead, report you to the FA and they will suspend you."

It was a masterly appointment from the club's point of view and one which bore all the hallmarks of Stuart Webb.

He would have been the prime mover – suggesting, convincing and telling the board that Dave was the answer to their prayers, the only logical choice to appease supporters who had still been idolising him in a Derby shirt a little over two years earlier, and he was just down the road in charge of Nottingham Forest.

With Mackay installed, there was never a chance that the directors would have to explain anything to us. The burden for dealing with anything messy had been dumped in Dave's lap. It would be up to him to quell any remaining revolt. The quicker the new manager got his feet under the table, the sooner the directors could breathe a little easier.

Still, several of them felt under immense pressure from the TV, newspapers and irate Derby supporters in the hours leading up to the Mackay announcement.

One director, Bob Innes, was in tears and another, Bill Rudd, told Longson he would even have Clough back if he signed an undertaking to "behave himself".

Mike Keeling, who had been one of Brian's staunchest supporters on the board, tried to persuade Innes and Rudd to help him get Clough and Taylor back, telling them Brian was prepared to abandon a 30-week contract with the Daily Mirror and his TV contract if he could return.

Longson was shattered at the prospect of being undermined and left the Baseball Ground for home, leaving Kirkland to act as his enforcer and talk Innes and Rudd into standing firm, despite their fears of a libel writ from Clough.

Kirkland and his gang drove over to the City Ground, where Mackay was watching Forest reserves, and had a drink before watching the last 20 minutes of the match.

The drama shifted to a hotel at Newton Solney, near Burton-on-Trent, for a farewell get-together.

Brian and Barbara Clough were there with their children, so too Peter Taylor and Lilian, and the players were encouraged to bring their wives and girlfriends. But far from being a chance to say our goodbyes, the occasion was dominated by Brian's desire for the players to organise things to get him back as manager.

He introduced the potential for industrial action into the debate when he suggested: "Why don't you lot go on strike?" and someone piped up: "Why don't we all fly off to Majorca?" A frisson of excitement swept through the party. Although these guys were quite intelligent, it was more than a half-thought. We said: "Yeah" as a group, we thought; "We can do this, we can go on strike."

It sounded quite romantic, standing strong together on the continent and all flying back together as heroes with Clough our leader again. Kicking back in the Spanish sun would certainly mean we wouldn't be playing at West Ham a few days later.

When word of our proposed mutiny became common knowledge, I had a telephone conversation with Cliff Lloyd, secretary of the PFA, and he warned me of the catastrophic consequences of going on strike.

Basically, Cliff said, we didn't have a leg to stand on. He told me: "If you lot fly to Spain and are unavailable for selection at West Ham, you will probably never play English football again. There's a fair chance you will be banned. Your job is to play football, Roy, and you know that."

Coming from the guy who represented our union, who supported us in any grievance, Cliff's warning carried great clout.

It was all well and good for Brian to pack his bags and head for the sun, but we had jobs to go to. It was a crazy time. Brian would have given virtually anything to get back in at Derby, but he had made the crucial error of resigning and he would not go down and beg on his knees for his job.

He realised the only way back was through the influence of the players on the board.

There was one highly charged moment in the dressing room when Longson came in to effectively give us a telling-off – and must have departed feeling as if he had been stabbed in the back.

Longson insisted the situation was stupid, silly and that we should simply get on with playing football.

Now Sam idolised Hector, having sanctioned his £40,000 signing from Bradford Park Avenue in the pre-Clough era.

In fact, he doted on Kevin to such an extent, he referred to the striker as "my son" and we sometimes teased Kevin, asking him: "Have you seen your dad lately?"

Kevin was a very quiet, unassuming guy, so there was a stunned silence when he, of all people, stood up and had a right go at the chairman.

"Stop there, Mr Longson," he said. "I think you're wrong. You are the person who is out of order – not us. We are employees here and when we wanted to talk to somebody about what was happening, nobody had the decency to face us, there was no response from the board, so don't tell us that we have been stupid."

Coming from 'his son', rather than a member of our militant tendency, that speech hit home and put Longson in his place.

He mumbled half an apology, acknowledging: "Yes, it should have been handled better, but we do need to move on."

I knew for sure that the game was up when we all went to the Clough household in Allestree – and the man who told me was Peter Taylor.

The wives headed the few miles into town to be paraded on stage at the protest movement's rally in the King's Hall, something that sat uncomfortably with me.

What I did was one thing, but I didn't like Lin being used in any stunt.

While Brian was holding court in one corner of his lounge, I found Alan Hinton. We had a chat and agreed matters were going too far and getting out of hand.

The phone rang. Brian answered it and after a few moments, he shouted over to me: "Roy, can you come over here for a second?" He handed me the receiver and said: "It's Peter."

I took a deep breath and spoke to our assistant manager, whose first question was: "Is he still there?"

With Clough virtually perched on my shoulder, giving me a quizzical look, I replied: "Yes." And what followed was a brief, yet extremely awkward conversation, as Peter spoke and I responded mostly in monosyllables.

Peter told me: "It's over. It's finished. It's gone. It's not going to happen. You've got yourself a manager in Dave Mackay and he deserves your full support. Get yourself out of that house as soon as you can, Roy."

I put the phone down and Brian asked: "What did he say?"

Although Brian knew perfectly well what his right-hand man had said, I very much suspect he'd been hoping my response would have been along the lines of: "Well, you might think that, Peter, but we don't agree. The fight goes on."

I could see it in Brian's eyes that he was a beaten man, he just didn't want to accept the fact.

Peter was always very astute, grounded in reality, while Brian was grasping at straws now.

It was as if he simply couldn't let go and admit defeat.

He had made things happen before purely by dint of his own charisma and personality. He bent people to his will.

Still, I didn't dare tell Brian what Peter had said because he wanted his job back so badly you could almost see a physical yearning.

It was rather a sad cameo, Peter acknowledging the truth while Brian prayed for a miracle.

I told the team what Peter had said, and they agreed. It was the definitive turning point in the saga.

I had mixed emotions. Relief because the situation had threatened to get out of hand, yet massive disappointment that it wasn't going to happen.

We had to get on with life under Mackay and, to be fair, he handled us with respect, giving us time and space to come round to the new order. It was like going through the grieving process.

Dave's first match ended in a 0-0 draw at Upton Park after which Longson made another risible statement: "I could manage this lot!" Not a statement we wanted to hear from our chairman.

Shaftesbury Crescent still resembled a scene from a spy thriller, with scarcely a day going by without talk of plots and dark acts.

There was also a sense that things were unravelling at a rate of knots on the international scene.

Mackay had little to celebrate on his 39th birthday on November 14, falling as it did between two dreadful 3-0 thumpings we suffered at Ipswich and Sheffield United, and there was no cheer for England that evening at Wembley, where Italy won 1-0 in a friendly.

Four weeks after our World Cup hopes were destroyed, we found ourselves up against the runners-up in Mexico and one of the favourites for 1974.

The match had nil-nil written all over it entering the final five minutes, neither side in the remotest danger of conceding a goal, although Tony Currie had forced a couple of notable saves from Dino Zoff.

Then Giorgio Chinaglia broke on the right and got round Moore to fire in a powerful cross. Shilton could only parry the ball a few yards beyond me and Fabio Capello, a mobile midfield player, knocked in the rebound.

Capello's goal was overshadowed by the end of a remarkable England playing career – and calls from the press for Sir Alf to follow Bobby Moore into international retirement.

I never had an inkling that Moore was poised to call it a day after captaining England for a 90th time to equal Billy Wright's record.

It wouldn't have been Bob's way to say anything. He had come in for criticism in the run-up to the match, I remember that vividly. He would have been aware of the criticism and maybe he discussed it with others, but the camp was normal.

I don't know if he had been told anything. If he did he never let it affect the way he approached the match. Bobby Moore didn't need to prove himself to the public, the press or anyone else and certainly not to the players. He was the ultimate professional, the ultimate captain. He never bragged or was demonstrative. He was asked to lead the team and that's what he did.

There was a dilemma and it was Sir Alf's. The pressure was on him to make changes and that, quite naturally, was hard for him to do. Alf had created a tremendous atmosphere and the criticism was that he was being too loyal. The squad I joined included a number of the players who had won the World Cup and there was frustration among players, such as Toddy, that they were not getting the chances.

Bobby had been caught in our first World Cup qualifier in Poland, the centre-forward fired it in – game over. There was the gutting return at Wembley, the failure there and then the Italy friendly. The pressure was on. But as far as the players were concerned, Bobby Moore was untouchable.

The pressure on Sir Alf to go was cranked up to fever pitch, headlines screaming "Alf's final humiliation" and "L-plate England" among a more restrained "Whole-hearted England are no match for Italian finesse".

Back at Derby it took time for things to settle down with Dave in charge and we went eight matches without a win, including two League Cup replays against Sunderland.

Mackay handled it the best of all of us. He knew there was deep unrest but got on with the job of managing the football club and managing us.

As defeat followed defeat, we were accused of "not trying" and "not putting it in for Dave" but the truth of the matter was that we were still in a state of shock.

We had enjoyed six years of virtually unbroken success. We had gone from playing Oxford and Bury to taking on Benfica and Juventus, and it had all ended. Just like that.

Much as the directors and Dave yearned for the spectre of Clough to disappear, it didn't, even though by now he and Taylor had taken over at Brighton. Dave had been in charge for a full month when unrest surfaced again.

It was a very emotional time, we were raw, we were hurting. And no, we didn't get over it too well, either as individuals or as a group. The bond between that set of players and Brian and Peter was unbelievably strong. We were grieving because it was almost as if there had been a death in the family.

Yet towards the end of the bleak run there were encouraging signs in a 0-0 draw with Leeds and a 1-1 home draw against Arsenal, in which I scored.

Dave's luck definitely improved on December 15 when he finally tasted victory as Derby boss, Alan Hinton and Roger Davies scoring against the run of play in a 2-0 win at Newcastle.

Mackay felt relaxed enough to try his luck in the transfer market and paid £100,000 for Swindon's Welsh international right-back Rod Thomas.

We were deeply indebted to Rod for his diligence in warding off humiliation at the hands of non-league Boston United in the FA Cup.

Dave claimed before the third-round tie at the Baseball Ground that the difference in class between the sides was so enormous, that anything other than a Derby win was inconceivable, but it proved to be a tremendously difficult and hard game. We made the cardinal error of believing it would be a stroll.

How you start a match frequently sets the tone for your performance – and we began sloppily.

Boston were immense that muddy afternoon under grey January skies, which matched my mood when a hamstring injury forced me off after half an hour.

Encouraged by player-coach Howard Wilkinson, the future Leeds and England manager, Boston came frighteningly close to an upset when a diving header struck the inside of a post and came to a standstill on the goal-line before Thomas hooked the ball away.

There were no such alarms in the replay as Archie Gemmill scored a hat-trick in a 6-1 win but we went out in the next round at home to Coventry following a draw at Highfield Road.

Rod was a lanky six-footer with a few inches over Ronnie Webster and his height enabled him to play centre-half on a handful of occasions. He was also deceptively quick, an important asset for a full-back.

Dave had worked with Rod at Swindon, knew there were no weaknesses in his game and the manager was right on that score.

While Rod was a solid player, Dave's next signing epitomised the buccaneering spirit he was intent on bringing to the team and, with that in mind, he paid Aston Villa £200,000 for Bruce Rioch.

It was an inspired piece of work for Rioch developed into the complete midfield player, a talent good enough to captain Scotland at the World Cup in Argentina in 1978, a wonderful passer of the ball and a regular scorer of goals – some of them spectacular and struck with venom.

There was also a darker side to Bruce, who could 'put himself about'. It was inadvisable for opponents to attempt to rough up Bruce, because reprisals could be brutal.

Although he didn't mark his debut at Norwich with a goal, Bruce helped pull the Canaries apart as we won 4-2.

Much to my disappointment, I was no use to Sir Alf in his hour of need in Lisbon. Injury forced me to miss three League matches and, just as importantly, the opportunity to help the England manager, who must have thought everything was conspiring against him for a friendly against Portugal which finished 0-0.

Sir Alf was distraught because an FA Cup semi-final replay involving Liverpool and Leicester on the same evening and assorted injuries – some genuine like mine, others no doubt induced by the clubs – meant he had to make nine changes to his original squad.

Four weeks later, Ramsey was sacked and I felt sorrow.

When I first joined the England squad, I was struck by the huge admiration and respect felt towards him by the men who had won the World Cup.

He created a warm, homely feeling and was like a father figure, seeking me out to discuss certain aspects of my game. I was always happy to see him approach me on the training ground for a chat because he always spoke sense.

He was a very, very good manager who got the best out of his players. If there was one criticism of Sir Alf, it was that he maybe stayed loyal too long to several players who had served him so loyally.

That reluctance to change drove Toddy to despair and he picked up an international ban when he refused to turn up for England duty once because he felt he would be chained to the substitutes bench in his role as Moore's understudy.

Publicly, Sir Alf may have come across as a cold fish, sitting implacably as the rest of the England bench jumped in joy to celebrate a World Cup final goal in 1966, but he was very far from cutting an aloof figure with his players.

He had been a distinguished right-back himself with Southampton, Tottenham and England, so he knew there was a time to laugh and how necessary it was to relax to break the tension. He could certainly be humorous and amusing at times.

I have a very fond memory of Sir Alf before a European

Championship qualifier against Greece when the England squad were smartly turned out at an official dinner in a restaurant down by the port in Athens.

After the salad and moussaka, speeches and presentation of mementos, we got up to leave just as a very well-endowed belly dancer appeared on the dance floor and proceeded to start her show to much clapping, stamping of feet and verbal encouragement from the Greeks.

The signal went round the players that we could stay and have another beer, which went down well on both scores.

Eye-popping entertainment concluded, Shilton, Nish and myself were first to reach the coach.

Sir Alf was next to arrive, taking up his customary place at the front, from where he suddenly wheeled round, face beaming, to declare: "Boys, what a magnificent pair of fucking tits!"

A combination of hearing our noble leader swear for the first time and his enthusiasm for the dancer's physical attributes had the three of us almost rolling in the aisle with laughter when the rest of the lads turned up.

Back on the domestic front, three home wins in our last four matches over Sheffield United, Coventry and Wolves saw Derby finish in a highly respectable third place in the 1973-74 season and qualify for the UEFA Cup.

Despite the chaos and turmoil at Derby, I was satisfied with my contribution on the pitch and completed a hat-trick of personal honours, the Rothmans Football Yearbook acknowledging: "A third successive Golden Boots award is a tribute to the class and consistency of Derby's Roy McFarland, sadly injured at the end of the season. Often lending vital assistance to the attack, he is probably the most complete centre-half in the country."

The press pack generously voted me among these top 11 players in Britain in a 4-3-3 formation: Pat Jennings (Tottenham and Northern Ireland); Paul Madeley (Leeds and England), Roy McFarland (Derby and England), Norman Hunter (Leeds and England), Alec Lindsay (Liverpool and England); Billy Bremner (Leeds and Scotland), Emlyn Hughes (Liverpool and England), David Hay (Celtic and Scotland); Kevin Keegan (Liverpool and England), Mick Channon (Southampton and England), Tommy Hutchison (Coventry and Scotland).

Joe Mercer was released from his role as Coventry's general manager to become England's caretaker for the Home Internationals and summer tour of Eastern Europe, while the FA waited for the man they really wanted – Don Revie.

Although I would have played for Sir Alf for ever and a day, 'Uncle' Joe was like a breath of fresh air and gave the England squad a good spring clean by introducing flair players and renegades such as Stan Bowles, Frank Worthington and Keith Weller.

I can never recall seeing Joe without a smile on his face. He wanted to make the game fun, a laugh, and told us: "Listen you lot, I'm not going to tell you how to play. You can play so just go out and play."

His approach was as simplistic as that, and it was refreshing in a sense that reputations counted for nothing, otherwise two or three extremely gifted characters who were deemed to be 'awkward' would never have got the England caps they deserved.

I only partnered Colin Todd in central defence for England on five occasions, the first coming in Cardiff where we won 2-0, courtesy of goals from Bowles and Kevin Keegan on a pitch as hard as iron.

My ankle felt wrong at the end of the game, the Achilles was sore and tender.

Training was out of the question for at least a few days. Hunter, who wasn't picked for that match, was similarly afflicted and said he was in no fit state to deputise for me four days later against Northern Ireland at Wembley.

It wasn't the first time Norman had suffered with his Achilles and, crucially, he knew how to manage his condition.

The other candidate to play centre-half was Sunderland's Dave Watson but he made a call which led to a quirk of fate.

Had Dave requested leave of absence on the Monday night to attend a business meeting with colleagues under the previous regime, Sir Alf might have ordered him to clear off home instead.

Yet in the relaxed environment fostered by Mercer, Dave was granted a free pass for the evening – only to be laid low by food poisoning.

My ankle felt a little improved after two days' rest and a little training, and when Joe asked me if I was fit to play, I foolishly said I was.

I suppose bravado and a sense of duty got the better of me. With Norman less than 100 per cent and Dave sick, Joe was struggling to find a partner for Toddy.

I had never suffered a dodgy ankle like this before, so I had no way of telling how serious it was. For all I knew, I would be able to grit my teeth and bear the pain throughout 90 minutes and there would be no lasting damage.

I was apprehensive before the kick-off only to the extent the ankle was sore, but then after 36 minutes I jumped with Sammy Morgan near the halfway line to dispute the ball and, on landing, something suddenly snapped in my left ankle – and nothing was ever quite the same again.

14

Crock Of Gold

A SHARP pain shot through my ankle before everything went numb in my left leg. I knew instinctively that something was wrong but had no idea what it might be.

Les Cocker rushed on, got me to stand, and my immediate reaction was, "Oh, it's all right" because I couldn't feel anything at all in my foot, but when I tried to walk I collapsed again and the England coach said: "Roy, don't worry, we'll get you off."

Between them, Les and the physio carried me away, my arms draped around their shoulders to sit on the bench for the rest of the first half. I was still sitting there, in a trance-like state, when Joe Mercer, the substitutes and backroom staff departed for their half-time cup of tea.

Fortunately, Les and the physio spotted my plight and returned to complete their salvage job, supporting me to the dressing room.

The pair couldn't be more specific in their diagnosis than Achilles damage, so I showered, dressed and hobbled up to the mouth of the tunnel to watch Keith Weller's goal give England a win.

Lin was in the crowd, five months pregnant, and I hoped she wouldn't worry too much. After the final whistle, a car was organised to transport me to Stanmore Hospital where I was met by three young doctors who had watched the match on television and witnessed my injury.

A top surgeon, Mr Tricky asked me to lie on my stomach. He simply squeezed my calf muscle and told a nurse: "Yes, lovely. Get this patient ready for theatre in 30 minutes." I was anaesthetised around midnight and Mr Tricky went to work.

After lunch the following day, I saw him again and he broke the shattering news: "Roy, you realise you won't be able to play football again for six months. You need three months in plaster and three months in rehabilitation," and that's when the severity of my torn Achilles hit home with a vengeance.

I struggled to accept the fact that I would be out of action for what seemed like an eternity.

The longest I had been missing previously was a month – and, hell, how time dragged then.

A torn Achilles is dreaded in all sports, but particularly football, where it was regarded as more serious than a broken leg.

It was in the back of my mind that I might never play again. I just had to prevent that notion dominating my thoughts, and convince myself that worrying to that extent would only make things worse. So I concentrated on the medical advice and doing precisely as I was told in the rehabilitation process.

My foot heavily bandaged and walking with the aid of crutches, Lin and I went over to Nottingham with David and Carol Nish in the build-up to Wimbledon to watch tennis stars such as Bjorn Borg, Stan Smith, Jan Kodes and Ilie Nastase, the George Best of tennis, in the John Player tournament. I was determined to try and avoid spending the entire summer moping indoors.

Yet after the operation and during the weeks that the leg was in plaster I suffered spells of depression.

Hobbling around on crutches, time weighed very heavily with nothing physical to keep me occupied – no training, tennis, jogging, swimming, golf or even going for a walk.

Dave Mackay was fantastic to me when my contract was due for renewal and I was seeking a rise from £300 a week to £350 for the following two years, a reasonable request in my view considering all I had achieved for Derby County.

I went into the manager's office to discuss the matter with Dave, who supported me completely, only to find the chairman, Sam Longson, unprepared to play ball. He said: "Roy, we would rather not improve your terms, but get back playing for the club and you can not only have your rise, we will double your money!"

I was taken aback, both by the prospect of earning £700 a week and the thought that Longson maybe knew something about my condition that I wasn't aware of. Was someone keeping something from me? I composed myself and replied: "No, Mr Longson, I'm not a player worth £700 a week, I don't deserve that, but I have asked for what I think I'm worth."

With that, I left Mackay and Longson to it, and when I was

called back, we all shook hands on £350 a week over two years. Dave had clearly won that argument. I felt let down by the chairman yet deeply indebted to the man I had pleaded with not to take the manager's job.

Days before the season kicked off, Mackay demonstrated his bravery, charisma and nous by signing Francis Lee from Manchester City for £100,000 – a fee which left both clubs feeling they had got the better of the deal.

Franny was 30 and City manager Tony Book believed his best days were behind him, glorious days which had seen the stocky striker represent England in the 1970 World Cup in Mexico and help bring the First Division title, FA Cup, League Cup and European Cup Winners' Cup to Maine Road.

He was busting a gut to show City they had been premature to write him off as a has-been and Mackay charmed him down from his considerable business interests in Cheshire with the promise of a suite at the Midland Hotel whenever he needed to stay with us away from his home among the millionaires of Wilmslow.

We maybe needed a bit of swagger up front and Franny undeniably provided it.

An inspirational signing, you always knew what you were getting when he played – 100 per cent effort and commitment. He loved his football, gave everything and never held anything back. That, to me, was the mark of a true professional.

Off the pitch, Franny was different, calm and cool-headed yet direct as a person in terms of his opinions.

He took a practical view of matters after weighing things up. He saw both sides to every story and delivered his considered opinion: "I think we should do this." It was no surprise that

Franny became such a hugely successful businessman with diverse interests.

My No.5 shirt went to 27-year-old Peter Daniel, an honest, dedicated lad. He wanted to make me adapt an old folk rhyme into: "Derbyshire-born, Derbyshire-bred, strong in the arm, strong in the head."

Ripley's finest arrived at the Baseball Ground as an apprentice in 1963, but was regarded as a stop-gap full-back.

He had to be mentally strong to go seasons on end playing just a handful of matches – and none whatsoever when we won the First Division in 1971-72. I could never have been as patient as Peter. I would have left the club years before then.

I doubt Mackay realised Peter had it in him to perform to such outstanding effect at centre-half because there was speculation that the manager would buy a replacement for me.

Socially, Peter was a lovely, likeable guy with a surprisingly dry sense of humour. He could be amusing with some of his observations in the dressing room and we'd stop, look at each other and ask: "Did Peter really say that?"

I was determined to see the opening match at Everton and was pleased the lads – captained by Archie Gemmill – gained a creditable 0-0 draw, Daniel keeping Joe Royle and Bob Latchford off the scoresheet.

The day became memorable before the kick-off when we pulled up in the official Everton club car park alongside Bill Shankly, one of my all-time heroes. The iconic Liverpool manager had ended his reign the previous week, leading out the Reds at Wembley against Brian Clough's Leeds in the distasteful Charity Shield scarred by Kevin Keegan and Billy Bremner ripping off their shirts after being sent off.

But nothing could ever dilute Shanks' love of the game and with Liverpool safe in the hands of Bob Paisley and playing away at Luton, here he was, the great man helping me out of the car and onto my crutches before escorting me painfully slowly around the perimeter of Goodison Park to the main entrance.

It was a long and hilarious journey, delayed by banter and backchat with Everton fans and a constant stream of requests for autographs – Bill's rather than mine.

I thought our conversation might turn to the question of me leaving Tranmere for Derby rather than Liverpool, but Bill was concerned about my injury, or rather how he felt I had been partially to blame.

"You should never have headed that ball, son," he admonished. "There was no need." He thought I had been impetuous, over-stretching myself trying to beat Sammy Morgan in the centre circle where Northern Ireland posed not the slightest threat, when in fact the damage was down to my impact on landing.

To soften the blow, Bill assured me: "You'll be back because you were born here, and this city puts steel in the souls of men. I wouldn't fret, son."

Watching Derby occupied my time, but it wasn't the greatest therapy because it brought home in stark terms how far I was from being fit. My mood picked up when the tortuous ordeal of three months in plaster was over.

When Mr Tricky originally told me I faced six months out, a voice inside me said: "Yeah, sure. But you don't know me. I'll be back quicker than that, just you wait and see." But he was correct and there was a tremendous amount of treatment and physiotherapy involved in my rehab. I learned the hard way that time is the greatest healer.

The minutes ticked away slowly one Saturday in September when I had the privilege and pleasure of becoming a father to our beautiful Beth, who weighed in at a healthy 7lb 13oz – giving me enough time to nip down to the Baseball Ground and cheer the lads on in a 2-2 draw against Newcastle!

Lin had been admitted to Holbrook Maternity Hospital on Thursday morning and two days later our family doctor Hugh Price decided the baby needed to be induced. We had, of course, been hoping for a normal, natural birth but it became a stressful, traumatic long delivery in the operating theatre with forceps brought into play. But eventually, at 12.30pm, there was relief and delight all round as Beth was safely delivered by Dr Price.

I kissed Lin and Beth goodbye after waiting for Lin's family to arrive, and hot-footed it to the match. I felt really chuffed and proud to be a father and the news spread rapidly, directors and their wives congratulating me. I don't know why. Lin deserved all the credit and praise for putting in such a monumental shift at Holbrook.

Although it would be ages before I would be on international duty again, England occupied my thoughts when news broke that Derby were seeking £400,000 from the Football Association for my injury.

While the top brass at Lancaster Gate acknowledged that compensation was due, secretary Ted Croker was alarmed by the size of the claim. I never discovered the compromise figure – but there was a deal of some sort because Longson stopped threatening to sue the FA if he didn't get satisfaction.

Although I could be of no immediate help to Don Revie, I was pleased when the new England manager kept me in the loop for a rallying talk. I was surprised when he selected 80 or so players for his first squad meeting, however, and a large proportion of them piled into a hotel lounge in Manchester to listen to him one Sunday morning.

I drove up the previous evening with David Nish and Kevin Hector after Derby had beaten Burnley 3-2, with Colin Todd travelling independently. The four of us were in the mood for a celebratory meal in Manchester and maybe going on to a nightclub.

Fortunately, Norman Hunter marked my card. My friend said: "Whatever you do, don't leave the hotel tonight. If you lot go out for a drink until the early hours and Don discovers it, he will wipe your name off the slate, and I'm not joking."

Duly warned that Revie intended to run England as a 'club side', as he had done at Leeds so successfully, we settled for a game of cards and a few beers in the hotel lounge.

Don told us all we had a chance of playing for England, and that we had to look after ourselves properly at our clubs, keep on our toes, work hard and then we would not escape his notice.

It was fairly predictable stuff but while I felt very happy in the company of so many seasoned internationals, I couldn't help wondering about the fringe players Don had invited.

Many of them must have felt uncomfortable, wondering: "Am I really good enough to play international football?"

This sounds brutal, but obviously the answer was 'no'. Players aren't stupid, they know there's only 11 who can start, yet here was the England manager preaching to virtually four full squads, promising them this and that.

I felt like a kid again when I found myself able to kick a ball in November. Then came the excitement of playing in three A team matches before a setback. I had weakened the right ankle by placing extra pressure on it to protect the one damaged at Wembley. It was a severe blow to my hopes of returning in the new year.

A niggling pain and twinges meant another trip to Stanmore Hospital and a second operation under Mr Tricky, this time to repair a partial tear in the right Achilles. Even before I plucked up the courage to ask him how long it would be before I would be playing again, I knew the answer. Six months was the prognosis, three of them in plaster, three in rehab. Again.

I wasn't depressed this time, however. I had a belief that I would be playing again at the top level before the end of the season. Naturally, I was also anxious to regain my place in the England squad but that seemed a long way off. Before I could really think about that, I had to re-establish myself in the Derby side.

If the lads were to win anything, I thought it might be the UEFA Cup, and hopes were high after eliminating Servette Geneva 6-2 on aggregate, then Atletico Madrid in a dramatic penalty shoot-out in Spain with the teams having drawn both legs 2-2.

The significance of taking each game a step at a time was brought sharply into focus when the team, having beaten Velez Mostar 3-1 at home, got carried away by the prospect of pulling out a plum in the quarter-final draw.

Would there be the chance of revenge against Juventus?

Maybe it would be Ajax in the last eight, or perhaps Borussia Moenchengladbach.

And if it wasn't one of those three, well, the others didn't look as if they would provide much of a barrier to our path to the semi-finals.

All the speculation should have waited until the 'job done' sign went up in our dressing room in Yugoslavia because the European adventure ended in the huge disappointment and anti-climax of a 4-1 defeat.

A hangover saw the lads suffer successive 1-0 defeats, at home to Everton, who went top of the table as a result, and away at Luton on a bitterly cold afternoon – the last Saturday before Christmas.

It was wretched stuff at Kenilworth Road. The Hatters were bottom of the table and had lost six matches on the spin before we turned up.

There had been encouraging signs the previous month, a rare away victory at Leeds, Kevin Hector's hat-trick in a 5-2 mauling of QPR and a 2-0 win to knock Bobby Robson's Ipswich Town off pole position.

But the events at Luton left us down in 10th place, still a side full of bristling attacking intent and capable of beating the best yet, equally, just as likely to get stuffed 3-0 at Carlisle.

No side, to my knowledge, had ever won the title from so far back at Christmas.

From the moment we beat Birmingham 2-1 on Boxing Day, however, what followed was staggering.

Franny Lee went back to Manchester City to plunder a glorious winner, cutting in from the left wing to crash his shot into the far top corner and young Steve Powell scored both goals in a 2-1 victory over Arsenal.

Easter saw Roger Davies score all five as Luton were dispatched 5-0, while Burnley were beaten 5-2 at Turf Moor.

No one was running away with the title and approaching the final month of the campaign, I calculated that no fewer than seven clubs were in with a shout – ourselves, Liverpool, Ipswich, Everton, Stoke, Sheffield United and Middlesbrough. It was going to be nail-biting stuff on the run-in.

Jack Charlton's Boro were on the verge of beating us at Ayresome Park when Hector broke clear in the final minute to grab an unlikely equaliser. Coolness under pressure was one of Kevin's major virtues and that goal was priceless, keeping Derby in the race and effectively ending Boro's hopes.

My training with the first team increased step by step as my strength and confidence returned. I came through a few reserve games unscathed and suddenly I was fit for the last four matches – 329 days by my estimation from the date of the injury.

I was apprehensive because I didn't want my presence to spoil our chances, and I considered Mackay very brave to bring me back at such a critical stage. Yet, equally, I relished the prospect of helping us get over the finishing line.

I eased myself back into the side alongside Colin Todd for 1-0 home wins over Wolves and West Ham, witnessing top scorer Bruce Rioch score his 15th goal, a handsome return for a midfield player.

They were both very, very tough games, Wolves expectedly because they were always difficult opponents, West Ham less so because they didn't tend to travel well out of London. And they were both difficult games for me personally. Was I really 100 per cent? Maybe not. I was probably 10-20 per cent short, although I was not unduly concerned and thought things would improve.

For Derby supporters on the penultimate Saturday of the season, all roads led to Filbert Street and we were greeted by an amazing roar from around 15,000 of our fans, who swelled the gate to 38,943.

We fancied the job, confident we would beat Leicester, but we didn't perform particularly well and the game was a non-event, a 0-0 draw on a dry, bobbly surface – but results elsewhere suited us perfectly.

For a long time, I feared Everton would end up top, but Billy Bingham's team drew too many matches and now they suffered a catastrophic second 45 minutes at home to Sheffield United, who came from 2-0 down to win 3-2.

For once, Leeds did us a favour, beating Ipswich 2-1, and when the news came through that Liverpool had lost 1-0 at Middlesbrough, Filbert Street was invaded by thousands of Derby supporters who had clearly decided it was all over.

It wasn't, not quite, but now our second First Division title in four years was in the bag if we beat relegated Carlisle at the Baseball Ground, or simply if Ipswich failed to win at Manchester City in midweek.

That Wednesday evening was epic with Bailey's nightclub in the centre of Derby the hottest ticket in town for our awards night.

Todd had won the PFA Player of the Year award and there could be no greater fitting tribute to Peter Daniel than to see the supporters crown him as their Player of the Year.

When the news came through from Maine Road that Bryan Hamilton's second-half equaliser was all that Ipswich could muster in reply to a goal from Colin Bell, the balloons went up at Baileys and the place went berserk.

The champagne was flowing and we danced to disco hits.

There was a fabulous meal with the supporters, and I was almost a supporter too because I had brought crumbs to the feast, featuring in such a tiny proportion of the season.

An overwhelming sense of relief washed over the players that we'd made it and wouldn't have to go out against Carlisle needing anything from our final game.

It was party time, the players could let their hair down and I was delighted for my team-mates – especially Archie Gemmill, who did a magnificent job as captain; the immaculate Colin Todd; Franny Lee, who still looked every inch an England forward; Bruce Rioch, for an endless supply of goals; David Nish, who had settled down to become the most cultured left-back in English football; two reliable right-backs in Ronnie Webster and Rod Thomas; Alan Hinton, who came in to create a stack of goals from March onwards, and Steve Powell, a championship winner again at 19.

Lin and I got in at three the following morning, while some of the other players arrived home to find their paper delivery boys on the doorstep.

A few of them were still a little the worse for wear as we sweated our way to a stalemate against Carlisle before the Football League championship trophy was presented on the pitch to Archie.

My four matches fell way short of the criteria required for a winner's medal but the club pleaded with the Football League, who granted special dispensation, and I was both surprised and delighted to be presented with my medal.

It was a strange nine months, bizarre even when I leaf back through the statistics of the 1974-75 season.

The lads won only one of their opening seven games and suffered away defeats at five of the bottom seven clubs – Carlisle, Luton, Tottenham, Birmingham and Arsenal.

Ipswich won two more matches; Everton suffered two fewer defeats; 10th-placed Burnley scored one more goal than our 67, while five teams conceded fewer goals – led by Liverpool, who let in 10 fewer.

So how the hell did Derby County win the League?

As in life, timing is everything in football, and when push came to shove at the business end of the season, nobody was prepared to push harder than us, feet hard down on the accelerator as the lads seized 17 points out of a possible 20 from 10 matches before easing off against Leicester and Carlisle when the job was virtually done.

And while it doesn't look too clever to get beaten by struggling teams, those defeats came before the turn of the year and did not benefit our rivals, who were busy cutting each others' throats.

When we really needed a goal, we invariably found one and it was a huge advantage to find four players who got into double figures in Rioch, Kevin Hector, Lee and Roger Davies, who had been transformed from the big, awkward, bumbling softie with potential spotted by Peter Taylor into a very effective centre-forward.

He still played with a smile on his face but his physical presence had developed and a streak of selfishness, a will to win and never-say-die attitude had been instilled. Part of the journey in Davies realising his potential had involved learning when to be greedy. Scoring goals must go with the territory if you wear No.9 on your back.

Colin Boulton completed a second title-winning season as an ever-present in goal, emphasising his talents as a solid, dependable keeper. I had huge respect for the way Colin had shown such patience, waiting for his chance to arrive when Reg Matthews, then Les Green, barred his path. Once he had that green jersey, no one was going to take it from him easily. He was never going to let it go.

And then there was Henry Newton. When Alan Hinton and Terry Hennessey had joined us from Nottingham Forest, and ex-Forest forward Frank Wignall arrived via Wolves, they talked about Henry as a great team player with immense defensive qualities – and they weren't wrong.

It was Newton's misfortune to play just a handful of matches for the man who bought him, Brian Clough, after years of trying, and that was a major disappointment for Henry.

He didn't chase the limelight, he didn't want the glory, he was content to stand in the background and get on with his job, breaking up opponents' attacks.

For everything Gemmill and John McGovern brought to the table, Newton gave Derby that steel and venom which we'd been missing, and which all the great sides need.

Leeds had Billy Bremner and Johnny Giles, who both put it about when it mattered, while Graeme Souness developed into an expert in the field at Liverpool.

My missing season gave me ample opportunity to consider the rival merits of Derby's two championship-winning sides.

Clough's team was more solid than Mackay's – less likely to concede goals. Hinton was a great provider who could also score goals, while in Hector we had a guy who could pull something out from any angle. I can't believe Kevin beat keepers so often at their near post but he was a clean striker of the ball and his pace meant he was always on the end of things. He seemed to glide over the Baseball Ground mud. He was a gambler on the pitch. To be a good striker, you have to gamble. Strikers cannot stand still. The boys of 1971-72 were more methodical. You knew what you were going to get and Clough was always content to win 1-0 or 2-1.

Mackay's side had more flair and thanks to Rioch scored more goals from midfield. He and Lee gave us something different and Dave wouldn't mind winning 5-4, and Hector was still there up front, of course, weighing in with 13 goals.

Watching so much football as I was nursed back to fitness gave me a taste for management.

I studied how, and tried to understand why, managers changed players and used substitutes. I would dissect the Derby team and our opponents, wondering what I would do differently if I was in the shoes of Dave Mackay, or Bobby Robson, or Bob Paisley, or Bertie Mee at Arsenal.

I knew I fancied having a crack at being a boss in my own right when the time came – but I didn't come to any earth-shattering conclusions about the game.

However much you care to dress things up, football has always basically been about stopping goals at one end and scoring them at the other. And it helps no end if you have a strong spine – a quality goalkeeper, centre-half, central midfield player and centre-forward.

15

Real Mad World

FRANNY LEE, wild-eyed and breathing heavily, had the strength of a mad man as he jumped off the treatment table, bleeding from a split lip and shouted: "Get out of my way, Roy – I'm going to kill that bastard Hunter."

The consequences of our striker escaping and finding the Leeds defender didn't bear thinking about, and I had no intention of finding out what might happen in the cramped corridors of the Baseball Ground in November, 1975.

Fortunately, I was playing 'stopper' with my back to the door, so I fronted up, looked him straight in the eyes and said: "Franny, you'll have to knock me out first because I'm not going anywhere."

It was a disturbing moment fraught with tension ended only

when our physio Gordon Guthrie grabbed Lee in a bear hug.

The infamous fight shamed football and led to a cruel suspension which impacted badly on Derby County's European Cup chances.

Before the match against Leeds, it seemed as if Lee could do no wrong – but then everything went wrong.

Don Revie had left Elland Road, Brian Clough too after 44 days, and the genial Jimmy Armfield was now their manager.

Sadly, Armfield's appointment had done nothing to defuse the antagonism between the clubs. A lot of hate and nastiness remained. I was injured and sat alongside Dave Mackay and his assistant Des Anderson.

Trevor Cherry and Archie Gemmill exchanged goals, then I chuckled when Lee tore into the penalty area and went flying as Norman Hunter placed little more than a hand on his back.

My England room-mate protested his innocence to no avail, arms waving in the air. Charlie George scored from the spot to give us a 2-1 half-time lead and I thought to myself: "Norman is going to be spitting feathers after that."

The flashpoint came in the second half after Franny had a shot saved by David Harvey and turned to find Norman waiting for him on the edge of the box.

There was a spat and the next thing I noticed was Norman catching Franny in the mouth with a right hook.

I don't think the referee Derek Nippard had any option but to send them both off. Mackay turned to me and said: "Roy, go and see what's happening. Make sure there's no problem."

Franny felt his tongue go through the roof of his upper lip, the hole made by Norman's punch, and it was all off again, Franny going at Norman like a windmill with his arms, desperate to land a blow, and Norman falling over as he backpedalled.

Both sets of players piled in, Billy Bremner jumping like a Jack Russell terrier, but to their credit, most of the lads had only one aim and that was to separate the warring factions.

They succeeded and Guthrie came on the pitch to lead Franny away, Mackay meeting them on the touchline, while the Leeds trainer Les Cocker took care of Norman.

The bile was still spewing in the tunnel with Franny raging at Norman, who was equally aggressive.

I kept them apart as Franny jabbed a finger, vowing to see Norman later and being told: "I'm looking forward to it."

Guthrie and I managed to shepherd Franny into the treatment room where the club doctor, George Cochrane, was already preparing to stitch his split lip.

Seething with anger, Franny was acting like a man possessed, his breathing very pronounced and out of synch.

The red mist had descended. There was a demented look in his eyes and I feared this wasn't the end of the matter.

The three of us tried to calm him down with soothing words and sympathy but nothing was registering one iota.

It was then Franny jumped up, hurled Guthrie against a wall and sent Dr Cochrane stumbling in a rush for the door, where he almost literally ran into me.

When Guthrie grabbed him, there was no resistance. Using boxing terminology, Franny had punched himself to a standstill and he sensed the futility of trying to continue the fight.

Calming down, his breathing returned to normal. Dr Cochrane had been shaken by the eruption of violence but pulled himself together to say: "Francis, I have to stitch that lip."

Although he and Hunter had roomed together at the 1970

World Cup in Mexico, there was 'previous' inevitably.

Franny was no shrinking violet. He gave as good as he got and antagonised defenders, who despised the fact he needed no encouragement to fall over in the 18-yard box.

As for Hunter, he was a vicious and nasty person on the pitch, a Jekyll and Hyde character, make no mistake.

The man who made me tea and biscuits, and was great company laughing and joking when we were on England duty, once swiped me over at Elland Road when I brought the ball into what he considered his domain.

He managed to belt me over both my shins and concede a free-kick on the edge of the Leeds penalty area. I was lying on my back in agony, gazing up at him, as I said: "Steady on, Norman." He hadn't moved yet since the foul but now he bent down towards my face to warn me quietly: "If you come back, there will be plenty fucking more of that."

That behaviour was part and parcel of football in the 1970s. Players could be daggers drawn for 90 minutes yet happily sharing a few pints by five o'clock on a Saturday.

Mixing after work was the rule, rather than the exception. Under Clough, there were a few occasions when we made our apologies and left Leeds on the coach sharpish due to poor results and Brian's desire to put as many miles between himself and Revie as quickly as possible.

Equally, I have fond memories of putting one foot inside the players' lounge there and hearing Bremner call out to me: "Big man, it's here for you," and going over to find the tough Scot handing me a beer, a wide grin on his face.

It was obvious that Lee and Hunter weren't going to be sharing drinks any time soon after their set-to.

I chaperoned Franny into our players' lounge, having been designated his minder for the evening. Norman walked in and Franny tensed visibly as he growled: "Roy, go and tell Hunter to get out of my sight or I'll come over and sort him out."

I wandered over to Hunter as inconspicuously as possible and, choosing my words carefully, warned him that the glowering Lee was still out for blood. Norman was never going to back down in a million years. Unimpressed, he sneered: "We're only stopping for a quick one, but make sure Lee gets the message – he doesn't frighten me."

Ten minutes later, the Leeds crew were on their way home that November afternoon and I could relax and remember there was something to celebrate. Derby had won 3-2. The aggro overshadowed a magnificent winning goal by Roger Davies two minutes from time, following Duncan McKenzie's equaliser. Cutting in from the right, our substitute struck a belter into the far corner of the net with his left foot.

The carrot of European Cup football had brought Lee a new partner in attack for the 1975-76 season.

I knew Clough and Peter Taylor were exceptional operators in the transfer market and it seemed as if Mackay had inherited their Midas touch in early July when he stepped in at the 11th hour to persuade Charlie George to come to Derby.

Charlie was Arsenal through and through but had become so disillusioned with life at Highbury he had demanded a transfer.

More than that, he was on the verge of crossing one of football's great divides and moving to Tottenham.

Charlie had passed his medical and agreed terms with Spurs manager Terry Neill when Mackay drove down to hijack that deal and bring Charlie to us instead for £100,000.

Three years earlier, most Derby supporters would happily have strangled Charlie had they got their hands on him following that FA Cup tie where he ran amok, flicking V-signs at all and sundry, but it took them less than 90 minutes to appreciate the breadth of vision he possessed and what a tremendous asset he was going to be.

Those 90 minutes were spent at Wembley in the FA Charity Shield, eagerly awaited after we were denied the opportunity to compete in the annual curtain-raiser in 1972.

FA Cup winners West Ham were soundly beaten 2-0 on one of the hottest afternoons of the summer. Kevin Hector opened the scoring in the 20th minute and I increased our lead two minutes before half-time, smashing the ball in from close range in a scramble following a corner.

That goal was a moment to treasure, the only one I ever scored at Wembley, and struck with my weaker right foot.

It was bloody hot out there, players taking advantage of any stoppages to leave the pitch and take on water on the touchline. The conditions probably helped West Ham because the heat was so intense we settled into a pattern of possession football, such was our superiority.

Charlie impressed himself on our dressing room as another strong, opinionated character, which we welcomed, and he struck us just as much on the training ground with a breathtaking array of skills. Quite apart from a hammer of a shot with minimal backlift, Charlie brought the ball down from virtually any angle and pinged perfect passes 40-50 yards.

All this and he was only 25, the finished article, coming into his prime.

He and I were on target when we launched our title defence

in low-key fashion with 1-1 draws against Sheffield United and Coventry before QPR delivered a jolt to the system.

Dave Sexton was piecing together a talented, exciting team and they absolutely murdered us 5-1 on our new pitch, Stan Bowles scoring a hat-trick before half-time. I pulled a goal back but we were chasing shadows.

Like the Charity Shield, it was another extremely warm afternoon and this time it was our turn to feel hot under the collar as QPR moved us about. Credit to them because we had a very solid, experienced defence. We didn't play very well though and they took full advantage.

Bowles was the typical cocky Londoner, or adopted Londoner I should say, and virtually everything he tried came off. There was always a touch of arrogance to Stan, the man from Manchester, and on this occasion it was not misplaced.

Personally, I received a huge psychological lift from simply getting through matches and enjoying football again after all the trouble, niggles and ankle operations.

But it still crossed my mind that I might have to leave Derby because I could no longer cut it at the highest level – something was wrong. I had been performing at my absolute peak in May 1974 when disaster struck. Now, as autumn beckoned in 1975, I didn't feel back to how I felt before the injury. Crucially, I had lost my edge, that little bit of sharpness. Before, when I thought about a situation I would be there in a flash, instinctively. Now I was a little bit short, my timing was not as good. I thought my reactions would sharpen up, given time. I was wrong.

We were soon into our stride, however, George and Lee sparking off each other, and our attention turned to the European Cup and a trip to Czechoslovakia to tackle Slovan Bratislava, a club with a decent pedigree on the continent.

I was very interested to discover the strength of our opponents because England were drawn against Czechoslovakia in a European Championship Qualifying group alongside Portugal and Cyprus, and only one nation would progress to the quarter-finals.

No fewer than six Slovan players had appeared at Wembley the previous year, losing 3-0 in Revie's first match as England manager.

The return was scheduled for October and I was keeping my fingers and everything else crossed that my form and fitness would hold up, and that Revie would bring me back after an international absence of 17 months.

Slovan's Czech striker Marian Masny scored the only goal in a tight match and we were confident, sensing they would not present a hell of a lot to beat in the second leg. We won that 3-0 with two goals from Lee, who might have had at least a hat-trick. He saw a penalty stopped by their overworked keeper Alex Vencel, who frustrated him on several other occasions with last-ditch saves.

The sense of anticipation was intense when the draw for the second round of the European Cup matched us with Real Madrid – THE top name in the history of the competition, winners of the tournament the first five years it was staged, champions again in 1966 and runners-up on another two occasions.

And did we fancy it? Did we fancy our chances against Miljan Miljanic's all stars? Just a little bit!

Real were a byword for the elite, any European Cup draw which didn't feature their name looked empty. It still does.

Miljanic was a canny Serb, whose reputation for excellence

had been founded on huge success with Red Star Belgrade, and he was in playful mood with the press in Derby's Pennine Hotel, half-expecting to lose the first leg.

He said he was confident that players of the calibre of Spain captain Pirri, midfielder Vicente del Bosque, later to manage Spain to World Cup and European Championship success, German thoroughbreds Gunter Netzer and Paul Breitner, winger Amancio and strikers Santillana and Roberto Martinez would have enough left in the locker to overturn a deficit back at the Bernabeu.

He laughed when asked to think of a scoreline which might be irretrievable, as if he couldn't imagine one, but he wasn't laughing on the plane back to Madrid.

Derby were absolutely magnificent, another tightly-packed crowd of 34,839 helping to create a magical night under the Baseball Ground floodlights.

George was at his irrepressible best, swooping when Archie Gemmill threaded over a low cross to open the scoring left-footed with a scorching first-time shot and continuing his run to blow kisses to the crowd. Then George sent a penalty high past Miguel Angel and into the roof of the net, after Lee was felled.

Real held their nerve impressively, indeed they attacked at every opportunity which made it such an absorbing, epic match. Amancio crossed to the far post for Pirri to control on his chest before stabbing the ball past Colin Boulton, yet the two-goal advantage was restored before half-time when Angel bent down like a man with lumbago twice his age and allowed a long shot from David Nish to creep inside a post.

Back came Real, all in blue, only to be cheated out of a second goal. There was no argument, and television replays showed clearly, that Pirri was a yard or so onside when he drove the ball into the net. Yet Tofik Bakhramov, the Russian linesman who played a major role in the 1966 World Cup final, waved his flag to disallow the effort. Real were angry and then disconsolate when Netzer tripped Kevin Hector and George did the honours with a second successful penalty to complete his hat-trick.

They should have left for home with a better outcome than a 4-1 defeat while we got away with a great result from a super match in which we outshone Real with the quality of our football, although we had no doubt about the threat they carried.

Quite apart from his dapper moustache, Pirri stood out as a magnificent central midfield player.

Real were excellent passers, neat and accurate in possession and their fitness levels were impressive.

Lee was in his element, a man at the top of his game, relishing every match, and in a rich vein of scoring form.

Then came his meltdown with Hunter, four days before the little matter of the European Cup return.

Our confidence at going over to Spain with the insurance of a three-goal advantage was tempered by the knowledge that Franny was banned, Bruce Rioch was carrying an injury which had forced him off against Leeds while I was suffering from a slight thigh strain.

The Football Association imposed on Franny an automatic one-match ban, the last one of its kind, for his sending-off, after which they changed their policy and domestic offences had no bearing on European matches. For us, the damage was done.

At full strength, we would have had enough in our locker to go through – of that I have no doubt.

But on the Wednesday morning of the match, Rioch was a

definite non-starter after failing a fitness test while I was struggling.

Dr Cochrane suggested I might have a cortisone injection but after a discussion between him, Dave Mackay and myself, we decided against it.

The danger with a jab like that is that while it reduces the inflammation, it can also mask the discomfort and you can end up doing more damage. Because you can't feel the pain, you don't worry so much about the injury and the repercussions can be serious.

I probably shouldn't have played in Madrid but I feared my absence, with Lee and Rioch also missing, would have given our illustrious opponents a psychological lift with Miljanic claiming: "Nothing is impossible for us at home, although we face a formidable task."

We were on the back foot after three minutes, Martinez glancing in a header, but reached the interval in optimistic mood having not conceded again. However, the opening 10 minutes of the second half proved disastrous as Martinez scored his second and Santillana pounced to make it all square on aggregate.

It was clear we required something special, certainly an away goal, and George provided it, evading three tackles to strike a 25-yarder that curved and dipped, going in off the bar. Advantage Derby, and that's the way it stayed until the 84th minute with a crowd of 120,000 becoming increasingly agitated.

We had been the beneficiaries of good fortune at home and now the tables turned when the agile veteran Amancio threw himself at Rod Thomas in the area and hit the deck.

Even Miljanic was gracious enough to admit: "It was certainly not a penalty, but that, unfortunately, is football."

Pirri was accurate with the spot-kick and, after identical 4-1 home wins, both sets of players prepared for extra-time. Somehow, I had got through 90 minutes in a large degree of pain and told the manager: "You'd better get that injection ready now, Dave. There's no way I can keep going feeling like this."

Dr Cochrane did the business with a syringe in our dugout and for the remaining 30 minutes I felt like a totally different player, running much more freely and now cursing the fact I hadn't taken the plunge and gambled on the cortisone before the kick-off.

But I was shattered physically and mentally when Real broke away and Santillana scored the winner to make it 5-1 on the night.

Joy from that memorable first leg was replaced by misery in an instant when the whistle sounded after 120 minutes.

It was devastating for us as a team. Yes, 5-1 does look fairly damning, but we didn't feel we had played that badly.

Charlie had scored a cracking goal from distance and we had been six minutes away from going through to the quarter-finals when a dodgy penalty decision had gone against us. The more we consoled ourselves, the worse we felt because we had been close, so very close to putting out Real Madrid. We didn't feel embarrassed by our failure to defend a 4-1 lead, just bitterly disappointed to be out. It was a massive blow.

Lee was a big loss in Madrid. The bigger the stage, the more he relished the occasion and he possessed a wealth of invaluable experience at the highest level gained with England and Manchester City in a World Cup and European competitions.

Our immediate response to exiting the European Cup was to win 1-0 at Arsenal then beat West Ham 2-1 to go top of the table for the remainder of the month. We had lost our biggest match of the season – but there was still a lot of football to be played.

On the international front, Revie came to check on me personally to assess my fitness and was sufficiently impressed to bring me back for the crunch European Championship qualifier in Bratislava.

The Czechs were better than originally suspected and had a 5-0 victory over Portugal in Prague to their credit, which should have sounded alarm bells in the England ranks because we had been held 0-0 by the Portuguese at Wembley.

Don was very much a hands-on manager, eager to talk and chat to me. He asked about my injuries, wanting to know if I felt stronger, and said he wanted me in his team.

Although I didn't agree with the way he constantly chopped and changed the squad, I warmed to Don as a man because he looked after his players, did his best to create a family atmosphere and tried desperately to get me back in an international shirt, playing to my previous standard.

A draw in Bratislava would ultimately have taken us through, but England's destiny was cloaked in uncertainty, rather like the fog which forced the original game to be called off inside 20 minutes.

When we tried again on Thursday, Mick Channon shot us into the lead only for the Czechs to recover and win 2-1 with goals from Zdenek Nehoda and Peter Gallis, both created by Masny either side of half-time.

I wasn't much use in the second half after suffering a pull at the top of my thigh, and Dave Watson replaced me. I watched England get dragged down and involved in some rough stuff as the Czechs were in our faces, challenging us with a what-we-have-we-hold mentality.

England were far from fluent, and this was my criticism for most of Revie's reign – England didn't flow as a team or knit together as well as they should have done given his resources. Don's England teams rarely seemed to click.

My injury jinx returned to keep me out of England's next game, a 1-1 draw with Portugal in Lisbon which virtually stamped the Czechs' passport into the last eight. They only needed a point now from a trip to Cyprus and won 3-0 in Limassol, while Revie was left to repeat the age-old mantra of England managers: "We need more time to prepare for these important games."

England weren't improving, but the Czechs were and they went on to beat Russia, Holland and, in a penalty shoot-out, West Germany to be crowned European champions.

There was a surprise at Derby too with Mackay splashing out a club record £300,000 on Burnley's dashing 22-year-old winger Leighton James. He watched us come from behind to beat Middlesbrough 3-2 at home and stay top in a thrilling game which had Dave's ever-cheerful No.2 Anderson, always ready with a quip and a pithy one-liner, exclaiming: "That was like riding pillion to Evel Knievel!"

Alan Hinton was approaching the end of his career and we had been operating, fairly successfully in my view, with a front three of Hector, George and Lee with Davies more than adequate back-up on the bench, but Mackay thought we needed greater pace and width, and that Leighton would provide it. He was wrong.

Our new Welsh international was full of himself, a bubbly

type of guy who received as much help as anybody in the dressing room.

He was very fast and could produce, in terms of crosses and goals for himself, as he had shown for club and country.

I really thought – we all thought – he would be successful but his career with us never really took off. He never settled into the team and was never as consistently effective as he had been at Burnley.

It was a major disappointment for everybody that he didn't click. Mackay's other major signings all improved the team. Leighton James didn't.

When you played Liverpool, Leeds and Arsenal, you accepted you would be facing 11 players who were at it, lathered in sweat and who knew what their jobs were. We were at a similar stage of our development. Maybe James thought it would be easy – but you have to work extremely hard to make football look easy.

We stumbled and Mackay made another surprise decision following a 3-2 home defeat by Tottenham in January. Out went Boulton and in came Graham Moseley, a 22-year-old keeper whose potential had been spotted by Taylor while he was playing as an apprentice for Blackburn and who had been at the club for several years.

Boulton was the only ever-present in both championship-winning seasons but Mackay decided it was time for a change, a switch which did not strengthen the team, it must be said.

Moseley was certainly not without talent as a shot-stopper but he made mistakes and was a totally different sort of keeper to the type Colin Todd and myself were used to playing in front of. He was forever coming for crosses in the 18-yard area, the centres which we routinely expected to mop up. We had to adapt to his expansive displays and he didn't help himself by dropping too many balls in the box.

Still, we had plenty of goals in us at the other end and, after the setback against Spurs, we lost just once again in a dozen matches – 4-3 at Newcastle in a thriller – while also making steady progress in the FA Cup with a succession of home wins.

The heavyweights of Everton and Liverpool were beaten 2-1 and 1-0 respectively before a very game Southend team, mired in relegation trouble at the foot of the Third Division, proved surprisingly awkward opponents, Rioch scoring the only goal to take us into the last eight.

There we took full revenge on Newcastle by beating Gordon Lee's men 4-2. It was never that close on a glorious May afternoon in Derby where some of our attacking football was irresistible. George cushioned a cross for the first goal by Rioch, who almost took out the roof of the net from a ferocious free-kick for our second. Not to be outdone, Henry Newton hammered in a spectacular long-range effort after the interval and it got even better when George headed on a long clearance and scored from Hector's impudent backheel into his path.

Bearing in mind how strongly we had finished the previous season to win the title, there was a mounting sense of excitement and anticipation now.

Was the League and FA Cup Double really on? It was a possibility, certainly. We were in with a shout but that historic feat was never mentioned, we never talked about it. The First Division was so highly competitive, it was virtually impossible to predict who would fill the top four places with any degree of certainty.

The FA Cup semi-final draw pitted Lawrie McMenemy's Second Division Southampton against Crystal Palace, of the Third Division, managed by the flamboyant fedora-wearing Malcolm Allison at Stamford Bridge.

We were matched with Wolves or Manchester United, and only had to wait a few days to learn that it would be Tommy Docherty's young thrusters at Hillsborough for us after they beat Wolves in a replay.

The Doc was full of himself, claiming: "This is the first time that the Cup Final will be played at Hillsborough – for what else can you call our semi-final with Derby? The other semi-final is a bit of a joke, really."

We had struck a rich seam of goals, even without the injured Lee, and kept the pressure on QPR, United and Liverpool above us by beating Norwich 3-1 at home and Middlesbrough 2-0 at Ayresome Park.

Then came a rearranged home fixture with Stoke – and disaster. It was difficult to assess just how influential George was until he wasn't there any more and Charlie's season ended abruptly when he suffered a dislocated shoulder and damaged his elbow in a challenge with Dennis Smith. As he was led off the pitch in very obvious discomfort, it felt like something else was departing with him, and there was a subdued feeling as Stoke held out for a 1-1 draw and a point we could scarcely afford to drop.

The cracks were papered over sufficiently three days later as Birmingham were seen off 4-2 and we moved up to third place.

All eyes turned towards Sheffield and the FA Cup, a competition which had provided Derby with painfully little to shout about since the Cup Final victory over Charlton in 1946.

That team had been paraded on the Baseball Ground pitch on several occasions, immortalised by our supporters, and the old boys were justifiably proud of their achievement. I envied them.

Despite George's absence, I was confident we would have too much all-round experience and ability for Tommy Doc's boys.

A month or so earlier we had drawn 1-1 at Old Trafford where they didn't make us break sweat. It was a remarkably comfortable evening's work and we returned home disappointed because we should certainly have won.

That night was possibly the worst thing that could have happened as I believe it bred a little bit of over-confidence.

The bald facts are that Gordon Hill scored early and late for United and we had an equaliser by David Nish chalked off because another player in a white shirt was deemed to be offside when our left-back pulled off an audacious chip and charge before going on to roll the ball past Alex Stepney.

If over-confidence was a factor in a gut-wrenching 2-0 defeat, I was as culpable as anyone.

I thought we were already there at Wembley. In fact I thought our name was on the trophy because, surely, neither Southampton nor Palace were equipped to humble one of the best sides in the land, were they?

And when you fall into that trap of getting ahead of yourself in football, the game has this terrible habit of dishing out your come-uppance.

We were simply inept, we didn't really perform to anything remotely like the level we were capable of while United did turn up on the day – sharper, quicker and bang up for it. They were very definitely not the team we had almost toyed with at Old Trafford.

Maybe Mackay missed a trick by not starting the semi-final

with a fit-again Lee, who began on the substitutes' bench.

Franny was a big-match player and the fact he was up against United, having spent the vast proportion of his career in City's sky blue, might have inspired him still further.

Recovering from our European Cup exit had demonstrated our character, but losing an FA Cup semi-final knocked the stuffing out of us and we were strangely listless and error-prone the following Saturday at Maine Road, where we gifted City a three-goal start before eventually going down 4-3. Leighton James succeeded in stoking up the home crowd against himself after getting involved in some silliness which led to Mike Doyle being sent off.

We were no longer functioning properly as a team and a 2-2 home draw with Leicester effectively killed off our fading title chances. The end of the season could not come quickly enough, a point emphasised by defeats against Aston Villa and Everton, after which Franny announced he was retiring.

He went out in some style too, scoring twice in the final two minutes as we roused ourselves to sign off with a 6-2 victory over Ipswich at Portman Road.

Franny had earned the right to go at a moment of his own choosing. He was brilliant for the club but was finding it difficult to marry professional football with his business interests. He was an extremely intelligent man, who knew he was at the back-end of his career and it was probably a bit of a strain keeping fit for Saturdays.

We also said a fond farewell to Alan Hinton, who didn't start a match all season.

He had far more serious matters to worry about and, as a close-knit team, we felt some of his pain in April when his son,

Matthew, died of cancer at the tragically early age of nine.

That rather put any tears we'd shed at Hillsborough into perspective.

Alan decided on a complete change of scenery with his wife Joy, and I was delighted for him when he went on to enjoy a couple of productive seasons in Dallas and Vancouver before going into management in the North American Soccer League.

Mackay allowed Alan to join us for training whenever he felt up to it.

At first, I took issue with Alan when I saw him arrive and questioned whether he had got his priorities right. "What are you doing here, Ally?" I asked. "Surely, your place is at home giving Joy and Matthew your full attention."

I didn't feel too clever when I learned that my old friend was, in fact, doing the right thing as he spelled it out for me like this: "Coming training and seeing you lot is my only bit of enjoyment and release. This is good for me. It makes me stronger and means I can do more, cope with more, when I get back home."

Liverpool took 17 points from a possible 18 to deprive QPR of the title, finishing seven points above us.

We had to be content with fourth place, and the consolation prize of a UEFA Cup spot, but there was no real sense of having thrown the League away. We were never that close and there had never been any margin for error on the run-in.

Meanwhile, Docherty's dismissal of Southampton and Crystal Palace as "joke" clubs came back to haunt him with a vengeance in the FA Cup Final when Bobby Stokes scored the Saints' winner at Wembley.

My season eventually ended on a low note with England as

we lost 2-1 in Glasgow to hand a Scotland team, skippered by Archie Gemmill and including Bruce Rioch, their first outright Home Championship since 1967.

The afternoon started encouragingly when I went marauding forward from inside our half and played a one-two with Crystal Palace's Peter Taylor. I found myself pushed out into uncharted territory on the left wing and curled over a right-foot centre, which Hinton would have been proud of, for Channon to head in.

Don Masson soon equalised however, and at the start of the second half I was caught out of position on the right touchline near the halfway line. Joe Jordan went steaming past me to deliver a low cross which found Kenny Dalglish.

Kenny's angled shot was meat and drink to any goalkeeper but, to the horror of Ray Clemence and every Englishman at Hampden Park, the ball nutmegged him. Things didn't improve because I had to come off with 20 minutes to go, Mike Doyle replacing me. Although Ray had to carry the can, I have always felt partly responsible for Scotland's winner.

Days later, I was in Don Revie's England party which crossed the Atlantic for the 1976 USA Bicentennial Cup Tournament.

Sadly, my hamstring was too sore to allow me to face Brazil, Italy or Team America in a friendly round-robin event that May to celebrate the 200th anniversary of the USA's Declaration of Independence.

There was, however, the compensation of meeting Pele for the first time – and perhaps gaining a little insight into one of the reasons he played well over 1,300 matches until he retired approaching 37.

After watching England lose 1-0 to Brazil in Los Angeles then

PRECIOUS THINGS: With wife Lin, daughter Beth and the championship trophy in 1975

CHAMPIONS AGAIN: I'm hanging back in this photo as David Nish and Kevin Hector parade the championship trophy at our game against Carlisle United in April 1975

SWEET CHARITY: Commiserating with West Ham keeper Mervyn Day after Derby's Charity Shield win at Wembley in 1975 when I scored our second goal. Then I collected the trophy on behalf of the lads

TOPLESS TWOSOME: Colin Todd and I were team-mates for Derby and England. This picture was taken before England's game against Czechoslovakia in 1975

CLEM CLANGER: Ray Clemence, Mick Mills and I can barely believe Kenny Dalglish's shot found the net as Scotland claimed a 2-1 win at Hampden Park

INTERNATIONAL WILDERNESS: Bidding to extend my England career in 1976 on a solitary training run at Arsenal in an effort to prove my fitness

SHARK ATTACK: Close encounter with Joe 'Jaws' Jordan who proved a handful in Scotland's victory over England in May, 1976

MANAGER, HERE: First day as Bradford City player-boss in 1981

ME AND MY GIRLS: With Lin and Beth at Valley Parade following promotion in 1982

HAPPY TO MUCK IN: Light relief with the Bradford lads as popular defender Cec Podd gets ragged in 1981 ... with Yorkshire cricketer David Bairstow (centre) 'punching' his weight

RIGHT-HAND MAN: With manager Arthur Cox and director Stuart Webb after being installed as Cox's assistant manager at Derby in 1984

WE HAVE LIFT OFF: Promotion from Division Three is in the bag following Derby's victory over Rotherham in 1986

CRYING GAME: Consoling Craig Short after Derby's Division One play-off final defeat by Leicester at Wembley in 1994

SUCCESS ON A PLATE: Arthur Cox and I show off our silver salvers at the Baseball Ground for winning the Second Division championship in 1987

HAPPY HOLIDAY: With daughter Beth while on holiday in Cyprus in 1990

IIXED BLESSINGS: My joint-managership with ld pal Colin Todd at Bolton didn't work out in 995

CUP HOLDERS: Striker Martin Butler and I hold the FA Cup ahead of Cambridge's fourth-round clash with Bolton

OME ON LINESMAN!: The passion was till there as I remonstrated with a referee's ssistant during my time as Torquay manager

SPECIAL GUEST: Dave Mackay paid me a visit at Chesterfield

AGING ROAR: Fury as Chesterfield concede a last-gasp goal after failing) make a substitution. My assistant Lee Richardson is frozen in horror

ALBION ARE UP: A hug from goalkeeper Saul Deeney as Burton celebrated promotion to League Two in 2009

CHEERS: Golf day with close Derby colleagues John O'Hare, Alan Durban and Alan Hinton

SPIRITUAL HOME: Derby County will always be special to me

beat Italy 3-2 in New York City's Yankee Stadium, we pitched up in Philadelphia to meet an odd assortment of players parading their talents under the star spangled banner.

The official USA national team was considered too weak to offer any of the visiting international teams a decent game, so Team America was created out of old stars plying their trade in the North American Soccer League, one of which was my great England colleague Bobby Moore.

Kevin Keegan scored twice and Trevor Francis hit the target in a 3-1 win before I was invited by Mooro into the home dressing room, where he introduced me to Pele.

I didn't think anything of it as we sat down on a bench for a chat and saw the legendary Brazilian disappear for a shower, then a 10-minute massage. But then he had another shower followed by a second massage lasting 20 minutes.

That was a radical departure from the cup of a tea and a fag that some Derby players used to unwind with when I was starting out at the Baseball Ground.

Pele obviously knew how to look after his body while I was happy for the opportunity to talk football with him as he lay on a slab near Mooro and myself, having his aches and strains soothed. I quizzed Bobby and he told me it was apparently Pele's set routine after every match.

I think about Maradona, Best, Eusebio, Cruyff, Messi ... but the greatest of them all was Pele in terms of what he produced and what he won for Brazil. He was, and remains to this day, the best player in the world I ever saw.

I envied Phil Thompson and my Derby team-mate Colin Todd the chance they had just experienced to face the great man on a football pitch.

16

Mack, The Knife

A BAD taste had lingered in my mouth throughout the long, sweaty summer of 1976 as a heatwave brought widespread drought and hose pipe bans to Britain. Rivers and reservoirs dried up, forcing the unlucky to collect water from standpipes.

Every night the weather forecast seemed to be: "Hot, dry and sunny – again".

Whenever Lin and I found a babysitter for Beth, we ventured to our village local in Quarndon, the Joiners Arms.

I had a hangover from our failure to reach the FA Cup Final and other stuff to worry about. I kept asking myself: "When will the spark come back? How long before I'm 100 per cent?" My fitness wasn't an issue. I'd played 37 of our 42 League matches but the zip which had taken me to the top was missing.

It's a worry. I'm a fighter looking forward to a new campaign, relieved to be playing football after major surgery, loving the game but the spark's not there any more – and I desperately want to re-light it.

I looked at what we had, Dave Mackay's excellent record in the transfer market and thought: "We'll be there or thereabouts when the honours are handed out."

Banged out to Bruges for £135,000, Roger Davies followed Franny Lee and Alan Hinton to pastures new and I felt sure that meant another forward was arriving, but either Dave couldn't find what he was looking for or the board wouldn't stump up the cash.

As a portent of stormy times, Charlie George got himself sent off in the opening match, an otherwise acceptable 2-2 draw at Newcastle. He left Arsenal saddled with the reputation of being a maverick, a loose cannon, but his disciplinary record with us was exemplary until now.

I was uneasy when we failed to score in the next three matches – Charlie getting booked for chasing and haranguing the referee at Leeds – and struggled past Fourth Division Doncaster Rovers in the League Cup.

Charlie's misdemeanours did not stop Don Revie picking him for his England debut in a 1-1 draw against the Republic of Ireland alongside Colin Todd and myself.

The three of us combined down the right for a super goal, Charlie nonchalantly flicking the ball with the outside of his right foot for Kevin Keegan to cross and set up Stuart Pearson to score.

If only Charlie could have engaged his brain sometimes instead of shooting from the lip, he might have gone on to play 50 times for England instead of going down in history as a one-cap wonder in a Wembley friendly.

Even that solitary cap was the result of only an hour's play. As contrary and finicky as ever, Revie told Charlie at half-time to go and play on the left wing. It was plain to everybody in the dressing room that Charlie was disenchanted with the idea.

Charlie's international career lasted only another 15 minutes before Revie introduced a natural left-winger from the bench, Manchester United's Gordon Hill.

I was gutted for Charlie, even if he didn't do himself any favours by giving Revie a mouthful as he walked off the pitch, upset at what he judged to be a humiliating substitution, with the manager holding out a hand to console him.

I asked myself: "Is this the end for you, Charlie?" Only getting an hour on your debut does not augur well for your future prospects.

It was not even a competitive match and, with respect, neither were the Eire lads' scalps worth a great deal unlike, say, the Germans or the Italians. It wasn't imperative that Revie had to win or change the shape of the team.

Later, I tried to talk Charlie into seeing sense and thinking a bit more before acting impulsively, but he was his own man and acted on his feelings straightaway. Once he felt one way there was no turning back.

Sometimes I marvelled at his sheer nerve as much as his God-given skills. He was as opinionated as he was talented, and that talent was exceptional.

There's nothing wrong with being outspoken in football providing you back it up on the pitch – and he very rarely failed to deliver in that respect.

Charlie signed for Derby to win more titles and silverware. It didn't work out that way, but he was very professional whenever he crossed that white line to go to work – even if he frequently spent the preceding minutes being sick through nerves in the dressing-room toilet. Charlie should have been among the last people in the world to be uptight and fearful because he had every tool in the trade at his disposal.

Relief at the club arrived in the UEFA Cup in the shape of a visit from Donegal of Finn Harps, and football's equivalent of men against boys resulted in a 12-0 win.

The return leg in the north-west corner of Ireland was virtually a 'jolly up'. After flying to Belfast, we broke the drive across Ulster, by stopping for tea and biscuits in a small village, where we were engulfed enthusiastically by a wedding party.

They pressed us to stay and have a proper drink with them, but Mackay insisted any drinking had to wait until after the match, and the bride, groom, hordes of friends and relatives had to settle for having their photographs taken with us.

As we boarded the bus to resume our journey to Ballybofey for a 4-1 win, the entire party waved us on our way. Such a touching scene and the bride was so thrilled by our appearance she looked ready to toss her bouquet in our direction.

Divorce was in the air back at the Baseball Ground and it would be a grim affair.

Adding to the insult of my own goal at Finn Harps, I picked up an injury that meant I had to watch with mounting discomfort three days later as Kenny Burns, at his brutal best, scored four goals when Birmingham thrashed us 5-1.

Ill-feeling bubbled over, accusations flew and angry fingers were pointed. The management took the view that two of our most senior players either weren't trying or hadn't tried hard enough.

Colin Todd was so unsettled he asked for a transfer and swiftly got the security of an improved contract instead. Whoever might be leaving, the board decided that it wouldn't be one of the best central defenders in Europe.

Eight games down, we still hadn't won a First Division fixture and the five points we'd scratched together meant we languished down in 20th place with only West Ham and Sunderland beneath us.

Several directors were unhappy with Mackay, which I thought was ridiculous considering that he was probably the only man in the country who could have stepped into the turmoil created by the resignation of the previous regime, and quelled the mutiny. Not only that, Dave could point to successive finishes of third, first and fourth place.

Instead of listening to half-baked rumours and silly accusations, chairman George Hardy and his henchmen should have pressed Mackay to sign the new striker we needed and another player or two to freshen up the side.

But no. The word on the street had it that discipline was a problem, certain individuals were taking advantage of Dave's preference to treat them like adults rather than schoolboys, and one or two players were spending too much time at the bar.

The £300,000 Dave spent on Leighton James became a running sore and even the manager's weight became an issue for a couple of directors who complained he enjoyed himself too much in the evening. If any member of the first-team squad abused himself through booze I would have known – but one player on the payroll performed disgracefully.

Eric Carruthers looked like Goldilocks with his mop of long, blond curly hair but rampaged around town more like a big, bad wolf.

He arrived for £15,000 from Hearts as an immature 22-year-old, sourced by Mackay and Des Anderson as 'one for the future'.

The size of fee meant he couldn't be classified as a costly flop, but his attitude was so poor he never gave himself a chance.

When word of his carousing reached the boardroom, Carruthers was used as another stick with which to beat Mackay.

From the ridiculous to the sublime, a fortnight after the shambles at Birmingham, we broke our duck by beating Tottenham 8-2.

Bruce Rioch, pressed into service as an emergency striker, scored four of the goals past Pat Jennings as Spurs suffered their record League defeat. I fully accept it was a one-off but we were so good that day, it was difficult not to sense we had turned a corner.

If we had, it was only to discover a juggernaut coming the other way at pace. The vehicle in question was driven by a bunch of Greeks in the colours of AEK Athens on UEFA Cup duty. Despite losing the first leg 2-0, we were equipped to turn the tie around but made a string of poor decisions, and Graham Moseley had a sloppy game in goal, as we lost the return match 3-2.

Another revenue stream for the club had unexpectedly been turned off, the players had failed to perform, yet Mackay was blamed. And he also needed to find someone to fill in at left-back because David Nish suffered a knee injury which ruled him out for the remainder of the season.

Despite a stormy shareholders' meeting when he was criticised, I'm sure Dave didn't know how close he was to the end.

Neither did I appreciate that my international career was on the verge of closure.

Injury prevented me from playing in a World Cup qualifier against Finland the previous month, but Revie brought me back for the big one – Italy away.

Even at this early stage, the stakes were immense with only one nation progressing to the tournament in Argentina in 1978. Several astute judges thought that if England and Italy cancelled each other out in London and Rome, the decisive factor would be who scored most heavily against the Finns and Luxembourg, the minnows in Group Two.

England's qualifying bid had started with a 4-1 win in Helsinki but anxiety crept in when the Finns were only beaten 2-1 at Wembley, both because of the narrow margin of victory and the fact England played poorly. Italy, for their part, had kicked off with a 4-1 win in Luxembourg.

We started well enough in Rome with Emlyn Hughes, recalled after 18 months in place of the injured Paul Madeley, slotting in alongside me in central defence.

But the tide turned in the 37th minute when the Italians won a free-kick a few yards outside our box. The set-piece was tapped sideways, Giancarlo Antognoni's shot changed direction when it struck Keegan, who was on the end of the wall, and Ray Clemence was left helpless.

If there was an element of good fortune about Italy's first goal, nobody could doubt the quality of the second and final goal of the afternoon. Franco Causio, my nemesis from Derby's European Cup defeat by Juventus, pulled off a confident flicked pass between his legs to free Romeo Benetti down the left and his accurate centre was headed in emphatically by Roberto Bettega.

The mercurial Stan Bowles was one of Revie's six changes. Causio's trick was just the sort of audacity we needed from Stan but the miserly Italian defence, marshalled by Marco Tardelli and Claudio Gentile, never gave him a sniff.

Italy were better than us by quite a wide margin and beat Luxembourg 3-0 the following month to finish top of the group by dint of a superior goal difference – a factor which did come into play, as many of us feared.

The opportunity to extend my England career came when Revie selected his squad to tackle Holland in a friendly at Wembley.

I was carrying another injury and arrived at the team hotel, as demanded by the Football Association, to go through the formality of the doctor confirming that I was unfit.

I stayed to see England torn apart by the genius of Johan Cruyff as the Dutch did pretty much whatever they fancied before settling for a 2-0 win thanks to a couple of first-half goals from Jan Peters.

Cruyff was untouchable, far too good for Paul Madeley, who was recalled to play in midfield and found himself dragged from pillar to post by the Barcelona star. With Johan Neeskens, Johnny Rep and Rob Rensenbrink also at the top of their game, this was Dutch football of the highest order and ringmaster Cruyff ran the show.

The curtain came down on Mackay following a 2-0 defeat at Everton, which left Derby in 19th place, and I phoned to commiserate.

"Dave, I can't believe how badly they've treated you," I said to the man who had always looked after me unbelievably well, especially when the treadmill days of recovering from surgery turned into sombre months.

"Ah well, what's done is done now, Roy," he replied. "I was so angry when I read in a paper that my job was on the line, I stormed into the board meeting and told them to stick it up their arses."

I heard hoarse laughter on the other end of the line, as Dave went on: "But I quickly regained my senses. I thought about the compensation, went back in, withdrew my resignation and demanded that they did sack me!"

Our conversation turned to general chat about other managerial jobs and what might crop up soon. Dave was anxious not to spend too long out of work because he and his wife Isobel were having a magnificent new house built in Derby, a costly project they had to abandon.

For a second time in four years, there was major upheaval at the club as reserve team coach Colin Murphy was appointed caretaker manager while the team waited for Hardy to go to Nottingham and come back with Brian Clough and Peter Taylor in his Rolls-Royce.

Instead, he got led up the garden path.

It was ridiculous not to have a top-class replacement guaranteed in the wings – and they didn't come better than Clough.

Murphy had only been in the job a week before our rivals started gathering, wondering which players they could pick up while chaos and confusion reigned.

Everton boss Billy Bingham tried his luck with a bid for Rioch, one of Mackay's earliest signings, calculating that he was ripe for a move. Bruce said "no" but then had a change of heart and went to Goodison Park.

Derby recouped £200,000 for him but it was a highly questionable piece of business. Bruce was 29, a thoroughbred regular in the Scotland team when the competition for midfield places was intense, and he had scored 28 League goals in the previous two seasons. Where Murphy or Hardy thought they could find an adequate replacement or, perhaps more pertinently, attract a player of similar standing, was beyond me.

As for Murph. I didn't dislike him as a bloke. You could share a laugh and a joke with him, he treated us well but he was what he was – the reserve-team coach. After Clough and Mackay, he had massive shoes to fill. Put bluntly, he was out of his depth.

We were a mature team, full of experienced internationals, which had won two titles in four years. Murph had spent his formative years in football kicking around at Gravesend, Folkestone and Hastings, and wasn't equipped for the job.

He had enthusiasm and loved his football but I don't think Murph ever had it in mind that he would manage us, and neither did we.

Hardy wanted to demonstrate that he was a mover and shaker in football circles, and also that he was prepared to back his man in the transfer market.

With Rioch at Everton, the need for an alternative source of goals had grown and the club paid £330,000 to make Derek Hales the costliest player to emerge from the Second Division. The big, bearded centre-forward was on fire at the time, having scored 16 times in as many matches for Charlton after making his mark with a shed-load of goals in Division Three.

I'll give Hales two things: he was exceptionally quick and he was self-confident, with an attitude screaming, "take me as I am or leave me".

The problem was he wasn't a particularly good footballer, or at least we never saw the best of him consistently. He didn't remotely compare to the class of Kevin Hector, John O'Hare or Charlie George.

Maybe I'm being harsh. At Charlton, Hales thrived on a steady diet of crosses from the wings, but we didn't play like that and weren't about to change our successful style simply to accommodate him. Football at the highest level involved more passing, more build-up play, linking more team-mates – the sort of stuff that was meat and drink to O'Hare.

James was a languid starter out on the flanks with a tendency to take possession and slow things down before lengthening his stride and often cutting inside to try his luck with a shot himself.

Murph made a dreadful prediction when he said: "Whatever happens about the managerial situation, I am certain that Hales will be a great asset to Derby." He wasn't. He wasn't a success by any stretch of the imagination.

Dario Gradi came up from London as assistant manager when the caretaker part of Murph's title was dropped in early January, Hardy insisting nobody else had been approached about the job and that, in his opinion, Murph had done well.

The intrigue, plotting and planning continued and six weeks after permanently promoting Murphy, Hardy changed his tune entirely following three successive defeats by Manchester United, Leeds and Liverpool – and made a concrete play for Clough and Taylor.

When word reached me that Brian Appleby, the Forest chairman, had given permission for Derby to formally open negotiations, I was delighted and relieved at the prospect of the club returning to normality, but the euphoria quickly subsided.

Hardy was confident he had got his man, but Clough was dubious about working again with figures he held responsible for plotting his downfall in 1973 – Sam Longson, now club president, and secretary Stuart Webb.

Still, Brian relished being asked to come back, and for the right salary he may well have done so.

Something went drastically wrong with Hardy's calculations. It seems he didn't value Clough to the extent of offering him an increase on his salary at Forest and after sleeping on Derby's offer, Brian turned up in Shaftesbury Crescent, fighting his way through a mob of supporters, reporters and TV cameramen to deliver this verdict: "I'm sorry, I don't want the job."

He enjoyed that moment of retribution against certain individuals within the club. Make no mistake, Brian was hurt by what happened to him at the end of his first spell at Derby.

I felt a huge sense of anti-climax and disappointment, players moped around with hangdog expressions as if to say "where do we go from here?", and Hardy had to eat humble pie, asking Murphy and Gradi to effectively 'carry on the good work'.

Murph celebrated his new-found security, if you could call it that, by splashing out £175,000 on Manchester United's Republic of Ireland international Gerry Daly as a replacement for Rioch.

James, Hales and now Daly – we were making a habit of spending big money on characters I could honestly describe as "not Derby County players".

Daly's introduction was to watch alongside me, injured again, as the team slumped to the foot of the table with a 2-0 defeat at

West Brom which had Longson rattling the sabres and calling for Mackay to be reinstated.

While Daly, who had fallen out with Tommy Docherty, was quite effective, he was not a great team player. He gave the impression he was perfectly content to weigh in with 10 goals a season and that defending, running about – those jobs were for other players.

A different type of player was starting to arrive, characters who were not improving us. The unselfish team ethic which had carried us to those two epic Football League championships was eroding.

Instead of asking themselves, "what can I do for the team?" certain individuals wanted to know "what can the team do for my benefit?"

To give Daly his due, he scored a few – including the infamous spot-kick in a 4-0 win over Manchester City when the penalty spot disappeared in the mud and dust, and was painted anew after our groundsman came out with a tape measure and bucket of whitewash.

That was a very decent victory over a City side in second place and pushing for the title.

We were solely concerned with getting over the finishing line to safety and avoiding relegation and when another turbulent campaign ended, we found ourselves in 15th place. It was one of the tightest relegation scrambles for years.

Four points fewer and we would have gone down.

On the Home International front, I wanted to contribute but although the spirit was willing, the flesh was weak.

Recurring injuries were dragging down my level of performance, and there was no way I was prepared to cheat England.

The pulls and strains to thighs and hamstrings were catching up with me, my displays were drifting downwards.

I never felt completely right or fully fit these days and experience had taught me that you needed to be at the very top of your game to play for England – otherwise you ran the risk of being made to look a mug, or worse, letting down your country.

There was no great drama, no fuss, no tears when Don Revie and I met in the England hotel. He told me: "Roy, I still want you to play if you're up to it."

That was pleasing and I was grateful but the game was up, it was time to withdraw gracefully. I owed it to him to hear the truth. "Thanks, Don. But I don't think I can hack it any longer, I don't think I can do this any more."

As much as I wanted to play for England we had come to the same conclusion: It was time to call it a day.

And so my international career was laid to rest at Wembley as I watched from a seat near the royal box as Scotland were crowned British champions after winning 2-1 and thousands of the Tartan Army's foot soldiers celebrated like crazy on the pitch, digging up lumps of turf and snapping a crossbar.

I drove home to Derby, thinking how fixtures against the Scots had provided my best memories when I was wearing the Three Lions on a white shirt.

That domestic international week in May raised the pulse when England played the Old Enemy in the final fixture, frequently as a championship decider and the matches in front of full houses were extremely competitive and vicious.

Scotland had produced great footballers and characters such as Mackay, Jim Baxter and Denis Law and my era saw Kenny Dalglish emerge as a world-class attacking talent.

It was imperative you were up for a scrap against Scotland, switched on mentally and physically from the word go and 'at it'. The Scots were quality, nearly all plying their trade at leading First Division clubs or with Celtic and Rangers.

By far my worst experience with England was our failure to beat Poland on that dreadful Wembley night and blow the chance of going to the 1974 World Cup tournament.

When the opportunity came to help England possibly qualify for the 1978 World Cup, I was past it.

I was fortunate to come into the team after Jack and Bobby Charlton retired, yet still containing half the boys who won the World Cup. It was magical, I felt very honoured, and the team made my transition from club to international football an easy one. They were so homely and welcoming.

The team was settled, even the substitutes seemed to acknowledge their place in the pecking order under Sir Alf Ramsey.

I was grateful to Revie for giving me four caps after the debilitating Achilles injury, probably four more than I deserved.

Years later, I was proud to be selected in a Best All-Time England XI on Sky Sports TV by presenter Richard Keys, Alan Ball, Alan Mullery and Frank McLintock, my old Arsenal adversary who argued forcibly for my inclusion.

As you can imagine, I was up against opposition of the highest order as the panel considered Billy Wright, Jack Charlton, Norman Hunter, Emlyn Hughes, Colin Todd, Phil Thompson, Kevin Beattie, Dave Watson, Terry Butcher and Tony Adams.

McLintock said: "Taking nothing away from Big Jack, but Roy McFarland was possibly the best centre-half I saw when he was with Colin Todd under Cloughie at Derby. And McFarland, to us, was an absolute nightmare at corner kicks."

I was even more honoured when I saw the panel's England dream team in full: Gordon Banks; Roger Byrne, Bobby Moore (captain), Roy McFarland, Ray Wilson; Stanley Matthews, Bobby Charlton, Duncan Edwards, Tom Finney; Jimmy Greaves, Alan Shearer.

I would dearly loved to have called it a day with England at a time of my own choosing after playing a final international, like Bobby Moore, but football can be an unforgiving business.

Between that fateful evening at Wembley in May, 1974, and the 2-0 World Cup defeat in Rome's Olympic Stadium in November, 1976, I missed 22 of England's 26 internationals and had to be content with earning 28 caps.

Yet I did not feel cheated, I accepted what happened – and moved on.

17

Doc's Medicine

IF Tommy Docherty had his way, I was to be crated up and shipped off to the USA to see out my playing days with the Fort Lauderdale Strikers.

The Doc breezed into the Baseball Ground in September 1977 full of wisecracks and one-liners and proceeded to go through the dressing room like a whirlwind, seemingly hellbent on getting rid of all the senior professionals, and buying younger, more impressionable players prepared to hang on his every word and laugh at his jokes.

Half a dozen competent operators, including Archie Gemmill and Charlie George, were missing from the side when the season began with a dismal 3-1 defeat at Coventry and Colin Murphy's fate was sealed the following Saturday at the City

Ground where Brian Clough's newly-promoted Nottingham Forest beat us 3-0 – a result which inevitably provoked another bout of weeping, wailing and gnashing of teeth among the Derby County directors.

Murph and his assistant Dario Gradi were dead men walking, their imminent departures and potential candidates to replace them the talk of the sports pages.

While Murph had not risen to the challenge of succeeding Dave Mackay, there is a right way and a wrong way to relieve people of their jobs, and it was to nobody's credit in the boardroom that Docherty had been anointed as the next incumbent, and was already in the Baseball Ground while Murph oversaw a 2-2 draw against Leeds.

Docherty hadn't got his feet under the table before my teammates were expressing grave misgivings.

Various Scottish lads didn't think he was the best in the world from working with him at international level, and he had a reputation for scorning loyalty. Several Scots who felt they helped him get the job at Old Trafford were subsequently shown the exit, Denis Law and Pat Crerard among those he fell out with.

The word was that Docherty wasn't what he portrayed, that he was insubstantial with a reputation built on image, embellished by smoke and mirrors.

Gemmill, for one, greeted his arrival with something less than enthusiasm having been humiliated by Docherty in May 1972 on duty for Scotland against England in a match I played in. Held responsible by the manager for Alan Ball's first-half winner, Archie started the second half, only to be hauled off in the 50th minute as Docherty chose to publicly apportion blame for the goal on him.

Clough was under no illusions that Gemmill and Docherty were at loggerheads and revealed: "I'll tell you what Tommy Docherty was quoted as saying about him when he was full-time Scotland manager. Archie played in an international on the Wednesday for Scotland and we played on the Saturday. Docherty was in conversation with a pal of mine from Manchester and he turned round and said, 'I knew Derby would have trouble on Saturday. I got every little thing out of that little shit on Wednesday night, he couldn't walk when he left us.' In fact, Archie couldn't bloody walk and we either got a none-none or we got beat."

Our Welsh internationals, Rod Thomas and Leighton James, were convinced they would be the first casualties but Gemmill was immediately sacrificed on the altar of Docherty's pride and self-importance.

Archie was on international duty in midweek in a World Cup qualifier against Czechoslovakia in Glasgow and returned to play a lead role in the Leeds match, scoring a goal and impressing sound judges.

He was as fit and strong as anybody on the playing staff, yet Docherty summoned him to the Midland Hotel to tell him he was finished at Derby, a has-been, too old at 30, his legs had gone and that he was being sold to Forest as a makeweight in a transfer bringing young goalkeeper John Middleton in the other direction.

Clough had his own take on the second time he signed Gemmill, telling friends: "It was the biggest con in the game, biggest con in the game that was. I'd heard that Tommy Docherty wanted a goalkeeper. Now John Middleton was, supposedly, the up and coming goalkeeper. And I thought, well, he's not as good as people say he is, because I worked with him. He was as soft as my backside for a start and I'd got three or four goalkeepers. Docherty was absolutely ... his bloody tongue was hanging out for a goalkeeper, so Docherty came in for him. I went, 'Hello, Tom, what do you want?' and he was all this, 'Da,di,da,di,di,da,' trying to browbeat me. I thought about it and thought about it and eventually I said, 'Go on then, I'll take cash'. Then I said, 'Do you want to get rid of Gemmill,' just as a daft thing. 'Yes' he says, 'you can have Gemmill' just like that. He's on the telephone. Well, I thought he's either had a bloody drink or when I see him face to face, like, he'll say, 'Fuck off, you're not getting him,' ... and it was as simple as that. And I said, 'I'll take him' and added 'You get John Middleton,' and Tommy Doc thought he got the best of the deal, simple as that. In fact, he went round telling everybody as much."

If Gemmill's services could be dispensed with so readily, before Docherty had seen him to make a considered opinion, it meant none of us were safe.

Frank Blunstone followed him from Old Trafford and the head coach wore his Manchester United training kit for his first session. The first thing you get when changing clubs is new training gear. I could fully accept that his Derby kit was maybe not ready for him immediately. What I could not accept, however, was that his flaunting of the United training kit went on for at least a month. I found that grossly insulting. United were obviously the biggest club in England but, really, what was Blunstone trying to do? Impress us? He merely succeeded in making himself look stupid.

To your face, Docherty radiated all the confidence in the world, always cracking jokes, having a bit of fun. I never saw him in a serious mood, never sat down with him to talk football. Everything had to be a wisecrack, jovial, jolly banter – he craved an audience. And at 10 to three on a Saturday afternoon when you wanted guidance, a steer and a little inspiration, the best he could manage was: "Come on, lads, let's get on with it, let's get the job done!" The programme seller could have done that.

With Gemmill gone, the rest of us knew what was coming. Other established faces left the club swiftly and younger replacements arrived, the vast majority of them lacking the class and authority we needed. The speed with which it happened was bewildering. Derby needed a makeover, not major surgery, but Docherty ripped the heart out of the club.

Leighton James went to QPR in exchange for Don Masson, a Scottish international who was past his best and destined to join Notts County on a free transfer. Rod Thomas was packed off to Cardiff, Derek Hales to West Ham at a huge loss. Colin Boulton and Kevin Hector were written out of the plans.

I was pleased to see Bruce Rioch return from Everton but his signing, and that of Masson, was strange. Neither player had a decent word between them to say about Docherty.

Neither did left-back Steve Buckley, one purchase which did pay off very successfully. Anyone who witnessed Docherty rib Bucko unmercifully about his looks would never have believed our new defender had signed for his tormentor.

Years before, there had been gentle humour in Clough's little digs about Gemmill's pact of silence, but Docherty went way beyond the bounds of acceptable behaviour with his comments to Bucko.

A dour character, Bucko grew to hate Docherty and, when the

manager kept going on remorselessly about his features during a meal on a foreign trip, he rose from the dining table, told Docherty to: "Piss off" and walked out of the restaurant.

For once, Docherty appeared embarrassed and didn't have a smart-arse reply. He often targeted the weak and vulnerable to make them the butt of his so-called humour.

Buckley was far from being alone among Docherty's signings in quickly wising up to what he was – unpleasant, in it strictly for himself and there are lots of players with lots of stories which don't show him in a very favourable light.

My testimonial match provided a moment of light relief when I popped into a converted drying room, which resembled a cramped school gym, to thank David Hamilton's Celebrity XI and a team of Derby old boys for providing the entertainment before the main event – a match against FC Bruges.

The home and away team dressing rooms being already occupied, I found Bobby Charlton roaring his head off in laughter as he got stripped on an old bench next to the actor Robert Powell, who made his name playing Jesus of Nazareth in a film on telly. Robert was gingerly removing his immaculate suit and folding it carefully. I think he was a bit star-struck, being a lifelong Manchester United fan.

I had good reason to thank each and every Derby supporter who made the effort to get out that Wednesday night, because I benefited initially to the tune of £25,000.

The only slight disappointment was that the club had made Bruges certain financial guarantees and I ended up paying them £10,000 appearance money plus a £2,000 hotel bill.

I should have invited Clough and Taylor to bring Forest over. They would have been only too happy to oblige for £2,000, job done. But Kevin Hector had booked them for his testimonial six months earlier and I wanted something a little different. It proved a costly lesson.

Bruges were a very useful outfit who reached the European Cup quarter-finals, and would go all the way to the final at Wembley where I enjoyed watching Liverpool beat them 1-0. But they could not be described as big box office in the Midlands, unlike Forest.

We rounded off Docherty's first season with a 3-0 home win against Arsenal to finish in 12th place but, inevitably, the suicidal revolving-door policy could never bring a sustained recovery and in September 1978, the manager celebrated a year at Derby by concluding his 30th transfer deal – 16 players out, 14 players in – which took Colin Todd to Everton for £330,000.

Days later, it might easily have been deal No.31 had Docherty got wind of Peter Taylor's bid to tap me up to go to Nottingham Forest but the terms weren't right and in any case I wasn't about to do the dirty on Derby County and leave them in the lurch.

Docherty enjoyed telling an audience that before a match he came into our dressing room to ask: "Who's playing today?" and quip: "Good luck, whoever you are" but he deluded himself if he thought we bought into his flippant attitude.

He claimed he had to buy at Derby because the likes of Toddy were moving on, but Docherty was selling senior, established players who had formed the bedrock of two title-winning teams – or at least oiling the wheels to encourage their movement.

Vic Moreland arrived from Glentoran, via a spell with Tulsa Roughnecks, with fellow Irishman Billy Caskey, a forward, in a double package valued at £90,000.

He was the chosen replacement for Todd when my partner was sold to Everton.

Now Vic was a very competitive player, better suited to operating in midfield, yet Docherty admitted: "He will never be a Toddy."

That £330,000 should have been invested more wisely because Vic had never previously been anywhere near the First Division.

I could not get my head around it. If you don't at least buy like for like, but gamble on trading down, your chances of success in management are going to be in jeopardy.

Shortly before Christmas in 1978, a disillusioned Charlie George signed for Southampton for £350,000 on the same day Docherty paid £12,000, relative peanuts, to bring in defender Dave Webb from Second Division strugglers Leicester, to play alongside me at the back in Toddy's old position. Webby had given years of top-class service to Chelsea and QPR, but he was pushing 33 and his best days were well in the past. Dave was an excellent professional who became a very good friend, and remains so to this day.

A deal, any deal, appeared to be like oxygen to Docherty, that he couldn't exist without leading a transfer merry-go-round. It was crazy.

And now it was my turn to leave, or so I was led to believe.

Word reached me that the manager wanted to see me in his office.

"Come in, come in," said a smiling Docherty, "and help yourself to a seat."

There was no preamble as he leant across his desk, continuing: "There's someone who's interested in you, Roy. Ron Newman at Fort Lauderdale Strikers has been on and he's interested, very interested. He's going to phone again tomorrow afternoon. If you want to hear what he's offering, speak to him then. If you don't, then don't."

Images of all those tried and trusted team-mates booted out of the Baseball Ground flashed through my mind.

I suppressed my rising anger, replying: "You're telling me you want me to go?"

He said: "Well, I think it's time. There needs to be changes here and things are really opening up in America. A lot of the British lads are going there and they love it – the environment, the challenge, the climate – the whole package."

I pressed him: "What you're saying is that I have no future here?"

He spelled it out: "Yes, that's about the size of it. But think of America, Roy. It's a fabulous chance and Ron Newman is really keen to talk to you."

I got up and left with this parting shot: "I've got a lot of thinking to do – and a lot of talking to Lin."

And there was a great deal of talking done at home, not to mention a few awkward silences as the enormity of what was on the horizon dawned, especially for Lin. Leaving the club after 10 years would be a wrench for me. Leaving her home town and big, close-knit family was going to be considerably harder for Lin.

Newman painted a vivid picture of life with long, hot summers on the Florida coast in the Sunshine State where the Strikers would pay for medical insurance, find us lovely accommodation, an excellent school for Beth and help with things we couldn't even begin to worry about. The money on offer was decent, too. "Ron," I said, "it all sounds almost too good to be true. I've got to be very interested because my career is finished here."

Lin took some convincing, she really didn't want to leave Derby, but I talked her round, keeping in constant contact with Newman and assuring him we were up for it.

For a week at least, I was coming to terms with walking away from a special club before Docherty approached me after training one morning. He always was insensitive and said bluntly: "By the way, Roy, that deal is off."

I replied: "What do you mean 'off'? I've just spent the week selling the idea to Lin and we've agreed everything with Ron Newman."

Docherty bristled and looked very put out as he explained: "Well, the board have said you can't go. They won't allow me to let you leave. I want you to go, but apparently you can't, so that's it. End of story."

I found it very strange that Docherty had mentioned nothing to the chairman and directors of Fort Lauderdale's approach to sign me before allowing me to start negotiations.

The chaos and lack of understanding on the pitch manifested itself as we plunged towards a relegation battle, winning only three of our last 25 matches to finish one place and six points above the three doomed clubs – Chelsea, Birmingham and QPR.

Five days after I watched Docherty's final Derby selection lose 3-0 at home to Middlesbrough in 1979, relief flooded through the club as he left for QPR where he embraced Stan Bowles, telling him: "You can trust me, Stan," to which the quick-witted Bowles said: "I'd rather trust my chickens to Colonel Sanders."

Docherty inherited this Derby team: Colin Boulton, David Langan, David Nish, Gerry Daly, Roy McFarland, Colin Todd, Steve Powell, Archie Gemmill, Billy Hughes, Charlie George, David Hunt – and signed off selecting this side: David McKellar, Langan, Steve Buckley, Daly, Steve Wicks, Vic Moreland, Jonathan Clark, Billy Caskey, John Duncan, Paul Bartlett, Paul Emson. Nearly all my team-mates, internationals and men who had won League titles, had moved on.

18

Down And Out

LAWRIE McMENEMY went up in my estimation the day he called to discover if I could be persuaded to join him at Southampton – and I was tempted.

Florida had been off limits, but my contract was up and there was no shortage of clubs keen to take me away.

McMenemy told me bluntly: "Roy, I'd love you here at The Dell. Wages will not be a problem, there won't be any haggling. You know what we're about at Southampton but I won't muck around. I'm not going to sell this football club to you. The question is this, Roy, 'Do you want to leave Derby County?' That's what you have to ask yourself. Take as long as you need and just promise me one thing ... when you phone back, be honest about it."

Lawrie had suffered a bad experience with Colin Todd, physically shaking hands on a transfer before Toddy changed his mind, opting for Everton instead. He wasn't going to risk a repetition.

I put the phone down and wondered: "Why can't everybody in football be like that?" No bull, straight to the point, down the line, and I admired the fact he appreciated the massive pull Derby had on me.

I felt he was a man I could do business with at a club going places. Three years earlier, Southampton had won the FA Cup then gained promotion to the First Division, and they were clearly looking to push on with players such as Alan Ball, Mick Channon and Charlie George in their ranks.

Lawrie was earning a reputation for signing players towards the end of their careers and getting the best out of them. I knew Peter Osgood had enjoyed his time down on the south coast after leaving Chelsea.

Derby had no manager, Stuart Webb resigned, there was yet another split in the boardroom, police seized documents and launched an investigation into alleged corruption.

So many changes had left no structure in the team. Whoever took over was going to find it a Herculean rebuilding job.

The Southampton project tickled me. Maybe a fresh start in a different part of the country and the challenge would suit me.

Three days later, I told Lawrie: "I'm going to stay at Derby County, thank you very much, Mr McMenemy. I appreciate the offer but there's unfinished business for me here. I want to get back as fit as possible and play more matches for the club. I have been here a long time and it would break my heart to walk away with the place in such a mess. I hope you understand."

He said: "I understand entirely, Roy. Thanks for being so open about it. Good luck this season." Then he went out and paid Werder Bremen £200,000 for Dave Watson, my successor in the England team.

Still the offers came, with Alan Dicks at Bristol City keen for me to bolster a defence which had seen Norman Hunter and Terry Cooper move on. John Barnwell, the Wolves manager, wanted to take me to Molineux where Richie Barker, a familiar face from my early Derby days, was his assistant.

Dicks and Barnwell received the same polite "thanks, but no thanks" reply while I sat tight and waited and waited for George Hardy to unveil the next Derby manager.

After two months with nobody officially steering the ship, compensation was paid to West Brom to appoint Ron Atkinson's assistant Colin Addison, who recruited John Newman from Grimsby as his number two.

I felt a knot in my stomach arranging to meet them for the first time after receiving a dinner invitation. What if I had made a gross miscalculation by rejecting those overtures from Southampton, Bristol City and Wolves? What if the gaffers wanted a brief chat to say "cheerio" over the mints and coffee?

We met in the restaurant at eight o'clock and were still going strong at one in the morning. A new two-year contract was on the table as I learned I was very much in demand as a figurehead, around which fresh young players would gel. I was sold on the idea. After the way Docherty had tried to casually discard me like an empty wrapper, it was reassuring to be wanted and I was very grateful.

When we parted company in the early hours of a July morning, I wished Addison and Newman well and the three of us shook hands on what we accepted was going to be an enormous task.

I was desperate for them to succeed because they were such good football people, two of the most genuine guys in the game.

Addison had just one drawback – he couldn't stop bloody talking. Twenty-minute team talks to deliver everything and more we needed to know invariably stretched to 45 minutes and ended with players yawning, staring into space and examining their fingernails intently.

Newman was one of the most honest men I ever met. He didn't pull any punches, and you could always trust what he said and believe him. Just like the role Peter Taylor fulfilled for Brian Clough, Newman added something potent to the mix.

McMenemy welcomed me at The Dell in September, where I was forced off with an injury and had to sit and suffer. Phil Boyer, a former Derby apprentice, scored a hat-trick as the Saints marched to a 4-0 win which consigned us to the foot of the table. It would be February before I was fit enough to return.

November brought a glimmer of hope, three wins out of four – including a notable 4-1 thrashing of Nottingham Forest, which left Clough incandescent with rage – but the rot set in quickly and the lads picked up a paltry three points from draws in the following dozen matches, nine of which ended in defeat.

With me in no fit state to render any assistance, the lads went to Bristol City in the FA Cup and suffered a humiliating 6-2 defeat, after which I managed a wry smile. How ironic, getting stuffed by the Saints and Bristol City, two of the sides I might have joined. Needless to say, we also lost 1-0 at home to Wolves. It felt as if I was being punished for staying at the club.

Addison's answer to our shortcomings in attack was to spend

a club record £410,000 on Crystal Palace striker Dave Swindlehurst then £300,000 on spiky, blond-haired Rod Stewart lookalike Alan Biley from Cambridge United. One wag noted that given the club's recent record in the transfer market, Derby were more likely to get a Swindle than a Hurst, but Dave put in some decent shifts while Biley emerged with great credit and nine goals in the last 13 fixtures.

Despite beating Manchester City 3-1 on the penultimate Saturday of the season, results elsewhere ensured there was no Houdini-like escape from relegation. We were three wins short of survival, yet miles away in terms of the quality and consistency required to stay in the First Division.

Docherty saddled his successors with a load of unwelcome baggage, unwanted players on big wages and, of course, he got rid of perfectly adequate performers who would have stood the team in good stead. Addison and Newman inherited a backlog of characters who were difficult to shift and it proved too big a job.

Addison was hit and miss with signings as he struggled desperately to find a blend capable of halting the slide and erosion of confidence. Barry Powell was a huge investment at £340,000, and one which must have left Coventry laughing all the way to the bank. For that money, we expected more of an attacking midfielder than a nervous boy who never settled. In time, he drifted away to play for Bulova in Hong Kong.

Promising young right-back David Langan and Gerry Daly would have been handy in a promotion campaign but before a ball could be kicked at the start of the 1980-81 campaign they left, to Birmingham for £350,000 and Coventry for £300,000 respectively.

Still, hopes were high that Derby could bounce back at the first time of asking when we kicked off at Cambridge. Those hopes burst like the balloons among 3,000 travelling fans because 90 minutes later Cambridge, sharper and hungrier, were celebrating a 3-0 win, and I was distraught after picking up an injury.

Just to prove it was no fluke, Cambridge came to our place and repeated the scoreline. Five years earlier, while Derby had been taking on Real Madrid in the European Cup, Cambridge had been scuffling around in the Fourth Division against the likes of Workington, Southport and Newport County. Those 3-0 defeats demonstrated what can happen when the rot sets in at one club and another sets sail on a successful course.

Our supporters received a boost when the 'King' returned, following a spell at Vancouver Whitecaps.

Kevin Hector was pushing 36 and it was unrealistic to expect him to be as sharp as in his prime when he was one of the most natural finishers in the game. But Hector, who never suffered major injuries, could still perform regularly – which is more than could be said of me.

Addison and Newman wanted me out there, playing and leading by example but it was a very difficult period because even getting on the pitch was a struggle and when I did manage it, I was constantly worried about which part of my body was going to betray me next – groin, calf or hamstring.

With that nagging fear lodged in my brain, it became a nightmare whenever I played. At 32 age was against me, and it didn't help that I had not been fit, fully fit, due to niggling injuries.

Both playing and watching, I found much of the football bland now, certainly compared to the adrenaline-filled romps along the way to titles and facing Benfica, Juventus and Real Madrid in the European Cup.

Derby were on the way to finishing in sixth place, suffering a few jibes along the way as neighbours Notts County won promotion, when Addison called me into his office soon after my 33rd birthday.

I didn't need to be psychic to know what was on the cards as I walked down the narrow corridor.

I was totally at ease, completely prepared to accept that my life as a Derby player was about to finish.

It was time to go and I was ready to go.

I couldn't sustain my career any longer in the face of mounting injuries.

I tried as hard as anybody, but my mind and body could no longer cope with the stresses and strains.

I couldn't have reproached Addison or Newman for anything they had done, I just regretted not having been of more use to them in their hours of need.

Colin smiled weakly as he said: "I am sorry, Roy, you know how it is – but we don't feel able to extend your contract."

I replied: "There's no need at all to apologise, Colin. All good things come to an end."

I did feel a twinge of disappointment, but perked up when he revealed he had good news – his friend Bob Martin, chairman of Bradford City, wondered if I was interested in becoming the next manager at Valley Parade.

I had been preparing for this moment for years, having spent a ridiculous amount of time out injured, fretting over the future.

My full Football Association coaching badge was in the bag and I had roomed with George Graham on a course for aspiring managers in Manchester, where assorted chairmen and secretaries from leading clubs came and warned us of the perils and pitfalls of our intended profession.

Graham's success at Arsenal came as no surprise for he had a great sense of presence, which impressed people, and a deep interest in football. I studied Graham and came to the conclusion that here was one guy destined to become a leading manager who would be around for a long time. He was serious about winning, deadly serious.

Howard Wilkinson was in charge of the full badge boys and the great thing about him was that he encouraged us all to talk – and argue. He said: "I can tell you how to set up a defence for a corner or a free-kick, but it doesn't necessarily mean I'm right. You have to find a way of working which suits you, a framework you're happy with."

I made contact with Bob Martin the following day and drove my Saab on the 45-minute journey north to a rendezvous at Woodhall Services on the M1, near Sheffield, where he made his pitch over coffee and biscuits. I was immediately impressed by a smartly-dressed, curly-haired dapper young man, oozing confidence.

He might have been mistaken for an executive in the music industry, but had in fact made his money out of buckets, mops and cleaning products in a haberdashery, and he also owned a small supermarket.

Martin's enthusiasm and plans sold Bradford to me within 10 minutes. He didn't try and pull any wool over my eyes. We both knew they were a struggling Fourth Division outfit, but he assured me the potential and fan base was there to win promotion, despite gates of under 3,000.

We agreed a two-year contract for me to take over as player-manager in May and I drove to York to see 'my' new team turn on a super show in the second half, winning 3-0 with the impressive Bobby Campbell scoring twice.

I was back at the Baseball Ground for the final Saturday of the season to sign off in a 2-1 home defeat by Preston. I survived to play the full 90 minutes in what I expected to be my final match in a Derby shirt.

I had made my debut for the Rams at Rotherham in August 1967 in the Second Division, and was leaving them there in May 1981 after 14 seasons.

With the exception of Kevin Hector, I was the last man standing from the early days under Clough and Taylor, and this was the right time to go.

The club had changed, I had to move on too.

We had reached for the stars, been champions of the Football League twice, brought the mighty to their knees and rattled the cages of several of the most famous clubs in Europe, while I was the proud owner of 28 England caps.

Maybe it should have been a tear-stained moment, but I wasn't quite ready to shuffle off into retirement with my memories, pipe and slippers.

I'd had plenty of time to prepare for this parting of the ways and my overriding emotion was one of excitement.

In fact, I felt energised by the challenge lying ahead of me in West Yorkshire.

Even now, with all the money available in football, I wouldn't exchange starting out again for what I achieved at Derby County, the memories, the friends, the fun.

We were well looked after financially when we played, certainly compared to the workers at Rolls-Royce, the British Celanese chemical works and on the railway, the blokes and women who helped form the bedrock of the club's support.

19

Sweet Valley High

A MAD Ulsterman with a thirst for beer and a hunger for goals, the gift of a case-load of fine champagne from the Ipswich Town chairman, and preserving the Lady Mayoress's dignity when her wig slipped as we got drunk together celebrating Bradford City's promotion ... my debut season as a rookie manager contains a fund of fond memories.

First of all, there was a phone call from Nottingham on my first morning at Valley Parade.

The tone was familiar: "Good luck. You'll need it," said Brian Clough. "There's only one thing you've got to do, young man, and that's win football matches. Ta-ra."

I was determined to hit the ground running at Bradford and knew it would be impossible unless I appointed the best assistant I could find, someone I could trust implicitly to guard my back.

I had been warned: "Unless you get it right early on, Roy, clubs at this level have a nasty habit of sacking you – and they don't pay you either. Then it takes forever to take them to court for compensation, and that's a costly business in itself. So there you are, stuck in limbo. Another job comes up, you take it because you're broke, and because you're working again your case folds against the club that owes you, as they always intended."

And I thought football was a ruthless business in the First Division.

There was only one man for the job: Mick Jones – a close friend I first encountered limping around the Baseball Ground with a broken leg in 1967. By rights, he had good reason to be sick of the sight of me because I was on the pitch with Clough and Peter Taylor, waiting to be introduced to the Derby County directors as their new hot shot centre-half.

Mick played in the same position and must have known his chances of graduating from the reserves were remote when he paused briefly to see me, suited and booted for official photographs. After struggling through a couple of laps alongside physio Gordon Guthrie, he introduced himself and I asked: "Why are you limping, Mick?" only to be informed: "I'm not limping, I'm coming back from a bloody broken leg!" I blushed, feeling very insensitive, but it was an honest enquiry. I thought he just had a sore hip.

As I quickly grew in stature as a player, Mick was pushed further down the pecking order until he upped sticks and enjoyed a decent career at Notts County and Peterborough. But it was what he achieved in a handful of seasons as a manager, leading

Kettering to the 1979 FA Trophy final, allied to his personality, that made him such a catch.

I wasn't the only one who thought so, as I discovered when I phoned Mick to enquire: "What are you doing?"

Mansfield had sacked him – with indecent haste – but the wind was taken out of my sales pitch as Mick informed me I had been lucky to catch him at home because he was on his way for an interview at Plymouth, where Bobby Moncur had been given the top job. I pressed on regardless: "Mick, I don't care what Plymouth promise you, I want you at Bradford with me."

He was offered the role as Moncur's No.2 at Home Park but we went back to the Sixties, knocking around together as carefree bachelors in Derby. I was confident that our enduring friendship and a northern environment in Yorkshire would swing it for me, and I was right.

Mick had all the relevant coaching badges, knew the game, read the game well and, more than that, he could give me something I'd never had since my teenage years – an insight into football in the lower divisions, the dangerous opponents, the shysters, the con men.

His judgement of people was to prove uncannily accurate. After away matches, we were assured of a welcome in the boardroom whatever the result and Mick spared me any embarrassment by introducing me to a great many chairmen, directors and secretaries I had never previously clapped eyes on.

He knew the ropes down here, the structure of all the clubs. Mick was never a 'yes man' but spoke his mind and always ventured an opinion, which I valued.

We took it in turns to play good cop, bad cop with the Bradford lads to keep them fully motivated and on their toes. I learned from the masters and would have been stupid not to have picked up certain things from working with Clough and Taylor and putting them into practice.

My salary as Bradford player-manager was less than I had been earning at Derby. But there was the incentive of a promotion bonus and the chairman had a leasing arrangement with the local Ford garage on Manningham Lane which provided me with a new saloon car.

Lin and I kept our home in Quarndon and rented at Rawdon where a boys' private school had been converted into houses. Mick moved in next door, we had a nine-hole golf course virtually on our doorstep and Beth was soon happily installed at a private school, Rossefield. In many respects, it was the perfect set-up.

Things weren't so comfortable at Valley Parade, where money was so tight that the club secretary Terry Newman disappeared for two hours in the middle of the day to avoid the string of creditors who turned up at lunchtime seeking money owed them.

The whole future of the club might have changed the day Bob Martin invited me along to meet Ken Morrison, a local-born businessman and Bradford Grammar School old boy.

Martin was at his most persuasive attempting to get Morrison on board in some capacity or other – main sponsor, board member, anything – but Ken told him: "I'm sorry, Bob, I've got too many things to do to think about becoming a director."

And he was right, he did have a lot on his plate. The last time I looked, Morrisons were the fourth largest supermarket group in the UK with an estimated family fortune of £1,595million.

I felt refreshed during pre-season working with a new set of players and it was immediately apparent that centre-forward Bobby Campbell, a 24-year-old bruiser from Belfast, was a bit of a hero after rattling in 19 goals the previous season.

And it was also evident that he loved his drink. Bobby lived in Huddersfield, where I found out he got tanked up every Thursday night at the local working men's club.

A few of the lads tiptoed around Campbell before training on Friday morning because he was in such a delicate state. I thought about tackling him over his prodigious drinking and then dismissed the notion.

Bobby was as rough and tough as old boots and a prolific marksman at this level. Providing he continued to do the business for Bradford, I wasn't going to interfere with his lifestyle. I think I made the right call because he went on to become our top scorer with 24 League goals.

Campbell's partner up front was David 'Daisy' McNiven, sharp and quick, a great little player who got me 19 goals over the course of the campaign. He had been at Leeds and maintained he should still have been playing at a higher level.

Our other major threat to opposing defences was local boy Barry Gallagher, a midfielder with real ability who was just coming through, and he chipped in with 16 goals.

Next to Gallagher in the engine room was Les Chapman, an old head and a massive plus, not only in terms of what he brought to the team with experience and teaching the younger players a thing or two, but for his ability to act as a calming influence on the hot-headed Campbell whenever he threatened to explode.

Chapman's legs were beginning to run out by May, coinciding with the end of his contract, and it would have been easy to pat him on the back, thank him for his efforts and send him on his way, but I decided to keep him on because of the influence he brought to bear on and off the pitch.

David Staniforth, another forward, was useful at this level, although he was a strange mixture. A touch nervous and unsure of himself, he was also a hard grafter. While Campbell and McNiven were an ideal partnership, I tended to deploy Staniforth in some away matches.

Young winger Mark Ellis showed bags of promise. Lightning quick, nobody could catch him when he got away, and he could also cross a decent ball.

My skipper, midfield player Billy Ingham gave us everything. The 'Ginger Pele' was a diamond, an excellent professional who was never once late for training despite living over the Pennines in Burnley. Unfortunately, he was injured towards the end of the season, his legs weren't getting any younger, and it was a sad day when I had to let him go. I couldn't afford to keep both him and Chapman.

You would struggle to find a lovelier guy in the game than our West Indian right-back Cec Podd, from St Kitts and Nevis. Full of humour, he lapped up all the banter – even when he was the butt of some good-natured jokes. Cec got on well with one Bradford old boy who asked if he could join us for training. David Bairstow played a handful of matches for the juniors in the early Seventies and was keen to keep in trim for his job now as the Yorkshire wicketkeeper.

One of my first signings was Mike Lester, a man who put his foot on the ball in the middle of the park and orchestrated attacks. I identified him as a player we needed during the summer when he left Barnsley, but Exeter manager Brian Godfrey beat us to the punch. Then in the new year, my phone rang and it was Godfrey, asking: "Are you still interested, Roy?" I confirmed that I was, as Godfrey went on to explain that Lester was homesick and hankered after a move back to Yorkshire. I was delighted to accommodate him.

Another local lad, Peter Jackson, was a promising centre-half who needed guidance and, recalling how much Dave Mackay had helped me, I decided that I was fit enough to hack it in the jungle of the Fourth Division and give Jacko the benefit of my wisdom.

I started 30 League fixtures, more than in any of the previous four seasons with Derby, and much of this was due to the fact I could dictate entirely when I played, and I quite enjoyed it when I did. Maybe there was something in the Yorkshire air, but my injuries were few and far between. My pace had declined, but the first two yards were in my head and experience had heightened my positional sense.

After drawing a thriller with Wigan 3-3 and losing 2-1 at Hull, we embarked on a club record streak of nine straight wins, plundering 29 goals – I even got in on the act with one against Aldershot when we triumphed 4-1 after going behind.

Interest in Bradford soared and when Sheffield United came calling in October, backed by a sizeable away following, we packed in a crowd of 13,711. I picked up a strain in that one, a 2-0 defeat, decided I needed a rest, and went looking for another central defender. I chose to bring Joe Cooke back to the club from Exeter and he did a magnificent job stiffening the back four and putting himself about.

Although Fourth Division points were our priority, the League Cup provided a delightful diversion when we travelled to Ipswich in the third round, having seen off Blackpool and Mansfield.

Several reporters wrote that Bradford "had nothing to lose" but I have never been comfortable with that phrase.

It wouldn't be a major disappointment if we were beaten by one of the most accomplished teams in the country, but a heavy defeat might have a detrimental knock-on effect on our form, and I wanted to avoid that at all costs.

The League Cup was still serious stuff then and eyebrows would be raised if managers did not field their best teams.

The competition was held in high regard and Ipswich felt they were well-equipped to win it to add to the UEFA Cup they had lifted against AZ '67 in Amsterdam six months earlier, shortly after finishing First Division runners-up.

Even the biggest names were keen to play in every match because they wanted the appearance money, so I was not unduly surprised when teamsheets were exchanged and I glanced down at my counterpart Bobby Robson's selection, noting we were poised to pit our wits against the odd international... or 10: Cooper, Burley (Scotland), Mills (England), Thijssen (Holland), Osman (England), Butcher (England), Wark (Scotland), Muhren (Holland), Mariner (England), Brazil (Scotland), Gates (England).

John Wark gave Ipswich a first-half lead before our left-back Gary Watson equalised to force a replay, and the quality of our performance was matched by the grace and class on show afterwards in the Portman Road boardroom.

I nudged Bob Martin to ask if we might buy some champagne for the players to celebrate on the long bus trip home. Patrick Cobbold, the Ipswich chairman, overheard me and said promptly: "Oh no, we can't be having that, chaps" before asking a director to open a cupboard, from which he produced a dozen bottles of very fine champagne. "Please consider this to be a gift from us," he said warmly. "You played extremely well this evening."

The replay was eventful and, in anticipation of a bumper gate and to reciprocate the generosity, Bob happily pushed the boat out a bit for the Bradford board to take their Ipswich counterparts out to dinner and then for a nightcap on the eve of the match.

We pushed Ipswich all the way, in front of a 13,518 crowd, drawing 2-2 after 90 minutes before falling to a goal in extra-time to a side eventually eliminated in the semi-finals by Liverpool.

A good team spirit, application, a sprinkling of talent, youthful zest and touches of experience on the tiller kept us on course for promotion.

It was impossible to stop the team dreaming of going up, of course, but as far as possible I tried to get us thinking the Liverpool way, the Bill Shankly way.

Shanks always preached: "Let's get to Easter, then see where we are," and I told the lads: "You just concentrate on winning until Easter, then we can maybe talk about gaining promotion, winning the League, whatever."

Easter Sunday arrived, sandwiched between a 5-2 home win over Halifax Town and a 1-1 draw at Bury, one of two extremely difficult contests provided by Lancashire clubs in the run-in. Rochdale also gave us a huge test, and again we were pinned on the back foot and happy to emerge from Spotland with a point.

This was the first season that the system changed to three points for a win, and for a while it was difficult to gauge how you were doing. There were no play-offs, the top four went up automatically and five clubs were in the running when it came to the crunch – Sheffield United, Wigan, Bournemouth, ourselves and Peterborough.

I extended a warm welcome to my pal and fellow manager David Webb when the Bournemouth team coach rolled up on the penultimate Saturday. At Derby, we struck up a firm friendship and often dined with our wives at each others' houses. Webby grinned as he warned: "Don't expect any favours, Roy, we're still going for the title." Knowing him as the ferocious competitor he was, I laughed as I replied: "The last thing in the world I'd expect is a favour from you, Dave."

Campbell was pumped up to the limit, having just won his first cap for Northern Ireland in a 1-1 draw with Scotland, and he equalised twice – his second goal coming in the dying seconds.

Moments later, the referee blew for a 2-2 draw, and when we discovered that Peterborough had collapsed to a 4-0 defeat at Sheffield United, the champagne started fizzing. Dave and I would be meeting again in the Third Division in the 1982-83 season – we were both up.

There was one more match to go, Mansfield away, and I drummed it into the team that it meant a lot to Mick Jones and how it was important we played like a team which had just won promotion.

The lads signed off with a quality display and following our 2-0 victory Mick rose above any temptation to rub the Field Mill directors' noses in it for sacking him. He never held grudges, and wasn't abrasive, loud or vindictive. When we went for a drink in the boardroom, he just basked in the reflection of another job well done.

The square in front of Bradford's magnificent City Hall was packed with our jubilant supporters decked out in claret and amber colours to salute us after a short journey from the ground for a drinks reception to celebrate our success – and drink we certainly did.

The Lady Mayoress, Joan Lightband, proceeded to get exceedingly merry in my company. She was a wonderful woman, so jovial, full of it and got carried away by the emotion of the moment – not to mention all the bubbly and gin and tonics we downed together, both ending up totally blotto.

Joan was oblivious to the fact her wig kept slipping, threatening to fall off the back of her head and I was kept busy preserving her decorum by gently pushing the misbehaving hairpiece back into place and trying not to collapse in a fit of giggles.

20

For Pete's Sake

WE met on a damp winter's night, the three of us in his Mercedes, at Woodhall Services on the M1 – the very place where I jumped at the chance to manage Bradford City.

Only this time I found myself in the car park with Mick Jones on the southbound side.

The driver was no stranger to drama, a touch of cloak and dagger. Part of his success was founded on mastering the art of disguise, dressing as a punter in flat cap and muffler to stand, unnoticed, on the terraces at windswept outposts and run his expert, critical eye over a likely lad.

So there was no possibility of a cosy chat in the full public glare of the busy motorway cafe and the chance we might be spotted, our plotting and planning exposed.

This secrecy was typical of the man. He looked older than I expected, but the fire within him burned as brightly as ever while rain dribbled down the outside of the car windows.

Turning round to face me, his mind was in overdrive as he asked urgently: "Who do you recommend, who are we going to sign from the Fourth Division?"

He was working me already, and that was part of the genius of the man, always seeking an angle, a clue, an answer. On he went: "You and Mick know the score. Who's it to be, Roy?"

And that started the ball rolling for Peter Taylor to pay £80,000 to make Halifax centre-forward Bobby Davison, a player I had tried and failed to take to Bradford, his first cash signing as the new manager of Derby County.

My controversial return as Pete's assistant, or team manager as I was officially called, was the biggest mistake I made in football – and the circumstances behind it do not fill me with pride. It was too early. I should have stayed and learned my trade at Bradford. But the excitement, the emotional pull, clouded my judgement.

I was still employed by the Bantams when I met Pete and agreed to join him that November evening in 1982, and Derby jumped the gun by hiring me before officially asking for permission to engage in talks. Breaking the rules led to one hell of a row.

Stuart Webb, who was as shrewd as they come, was back as a director. Few people caught Webb with his proverbial trousers down but Bob Martin trapped him, thanks to a tape recorder hidden in a vase of flowers, into admitting that he knew I was keen to rejoin Derby before Bradford had a clue about the extent of developments. That cost Derby a £10,000 fine and sent the chairman Mike Watterson, a snooker promoter, ballistic.

Few things were further from my mind than changing clubs when the 1982-83 campaign began with Bradford winning four of the opening six fixtures to sit third in Division Three.

I refreshed and strengthened the side by signing goalkeeper Eric McManus from Stoke, experienced winger Ian Mellor from Sheffield Wednesday and a promising teenage defender Greg Abbott, released by Coventry. And then there was Stuart McCall, a feisty young Scot who was absolutely determined that nobody was going to overlook his claims for a place in midfield.

I was painfully aware that things had gone from bad to worse at the Baseball Ground where Colin Addison had been sacked, and it looked very much as if John Newman, promoted to manager, would be following him out of the door as the defeats mounted and boardroom politics dominated events, Watterson taking over with a stark warning that he might have to make some "unpopular decisions".

Years of failure and outbreaks of hooliganism had left their mark on Derby, where gates had slumped to below 10,000 and the club, once so tidily turned out, was beginning to look like a tramp.

Family and friends who were diehard supporters regaled me with tales of woe, complaining how poor the team had become. I was lucky to be out of it now, they told me.

I discovered for myself the poverty of Newman's team when I went to watch them lose 2-1 to Halifax in a Milk Cup tie at the ramshackle Shay in front of a crowd of 2,820. Davison scored that night and got two more goals to make the Rams suffer in the second leg before the Fourth Division side were squeezed out in extra-time.

In contrast, Bradford were lapping up the Milk Cup, eliminating Mansfield and Rochdale 3-0 and 5-0 respectively on aggregate. We had developed into a very decent outfit and our reward was to pull the cream of the crop in the third round – a home tie against Ron Atkinson's Manchester United, to the undisguised delight of Bob Martin.

The chairman, one of Big Ron's best buddies, was always off to Old Trafford for midweek matches whenever they didn't clash with our fixtures.

Newman was put out of his misery and Derby was agog with the news that Taylor was back in business, much to the disgust of Brian Clough at Nottingham Forest, where Pete had ended their partnership six months earlier and apparently retired for good.

I knew before it became common knowledge because Pete phoned me at home to declare bluntly: "I'm taking the Derby job and I want you with me. Where and when can we meet? I've got to see you. Mick's coming too, bring him with you. You're coming, I want you there." It wasn't so much the start of a debate as a demand, but I needed time to think. I couldn't say "yes" there and then, so did my best to stall. Hang on just a minute, I thought. I do have a choice in the matter, my opinion is valid.

Progress could hardly be better at Bradford. Of course it was early days, but a second successive promotion wasn't beyond the realms of possibility, the place was bouncing at the prospect of Big Ron and Man United coming over the Pennines, and there would be a few quid coming our way from the gate receipts.

Ironically, Derby were in a far worse financial state than City and I knew they weren't ready yet to take off. Far from it, I feared things might have to get worse before they got better. The club needed extensive surgery because the quality in the dressing room was dire, by and large, the job required a huge influx of better players, and I was not at all convinced that the money was available to enter the transfer market with any degree of confidence.

But dealing with Taylor was like fighting the incoming tide, and Pete was on the phone the following morning, a tidal wave of persuasion drowning any semblance of resistance.

Once he had set his mind on a course of action, it was very hard to deflect Taylor from his goal. He had found me, helped shape me into an England international player. And I knew that he needed me now.

Mick was thrilled at the prospect of returning to Derby, due to the size of the club, after years working in the lower divisions.

The phone went again. It was Pete. I said: "yes". The temptation was too great. Anyone else but Taylor or Clough, and I would have said "no". Any other club but Derby would have got the thumbs down.

And so Mick and I spent 30 minutes with Pete in his Mercedes, where we shook hands on a deal, as the man who first spotted me at Tranmere busily pumped me for information. Pete's enthusiasm was matched by his confidence that he could pull Derby out of the doldrums and he said: "No time to mess around, let's sort it."

Mick was 100 per cent happy, and I was suddenly happy and relieved too because I had made a tough decision.

Life is all about choices and suddenly I had no nagging doubts. Lin was thrilled to be returning to her home town, where we knew Beth would be going back to her old school and school friends.

Mick and I returned to Bradford to prepare for the United match, knowing that we'd soon be saying goodbye to all and sundry.

Big Ron has his detractors, but I have always liked him, admired his bravado, the way he spoke and set up his teams. I was in my prime as a player when he developed West Brom into a fine side, with Cyrille Regis scoring goals and Bryan Robson emerging as the most complete English midfield player of his generation.

I took all Ron's flashness with a pinch of salt because at heart he was no flamboyant fool, but very serious about his football. He knew the game intimately and he also knew what he wanted to drink after I had played my final match for Bradford and helped subdue young Frank Stapleton in a 0-0 draw.

Ron wanted a glass of champagne, while I settled for a beer and thought that's the way it should be. He was at the top of his trade and I was still a novice.

United were relieved to avoid a giant-killing, while Bradford looked forward to another decent pay-day from the replay after putting in a superb effort. We could not have played very much better and were even fairly comfortable, although it wasn't a typical United gung-ho performance. They respected us, Paul McGrath and Gordon McQueen determined not to give Bobby Campbell and 'Daisy' McNiven the slightest early encouragement or concede a silly goal.

Word leaked out that I was on my way back to Derby and, understandably, Bob Martin was not happy when we met. He told me bluntly that I was making the wrong decision, and that there was every chance Bradford would exchange places in the Football League with Derby.

I said: "I'm sorry, Bob, but I want to go and I've made my mind up. I'm going to resign." Knowing Bob, he would have improved my contract had I stayed, but anything he offered would not have been enough.

This was about more than money, it was all down to raw emotion.

We had our rows and disagreements, almost always over players and how much I wanted to spend, but we enjoyed an excellent working relationship and conversations often ended with one of us saying: "Come on, are we going to have a beer or what?"

Bob loved Bradford City Football Club and tried his level best to keep me there. We were good for each other. In hindsight, he was 100 per cent right. I wasn't ready to leave. We had a good thing going and I destroyed it.

Mick and I resigned three days before the Milk Cup replay, which United won 4-0, and Bob came out fighting publicly.

He claimed, with good reason, that we had been illegally approached and said he would seek justice by way of an order for compensation.

Satisfaction at a job well done was replaced by sadness as Mick and I said our goodbyes to a team we had developed and coached into a very capable unit, one it had been a pleasure to play a part in, and we left behind players equipped to go forward under Trevor Cherry and Terry Yorath, two Leeds old boys.

Within days, the Football League reacted to Bradford's complaints and staged a hearing at which evidence emerged that in

Martin's office, with that hidden tape recorder running, Webb said words to the effect: "I'd like to talk about taking Roy back to Derby. I get the feeling he might want to come back." Martin then asked Webb directly if I had been approached, to which there was an admission along the lines of: "Yes, I believe we have spoken to Roy already."

The authorities came down heavily on Derby, fining the club £10,000 for poaching Mick and myself, before fixing compensation to Bradford at a further £55,000, money which Watterson could ill-afford to lose. He went berserk, threatening to drag the League through every court in the country, but the club solicitor calmed him down, saying: "You can appeal, but it will cost you money. And if you lose that appeal, who knows how much you will end up paying out. I suggest you pay up."

So Watterson, a nervous, edgy character, took it on the chin against a backdrop of bitterness and recriminations, and I started work again at the Baseball Ground under Taylor with Derby marooned at the bottom of the Second Division, having won just one of their opening 15 matches.

Pete's first reaction was to recruit much-needed experience in the shape of a character we both knew extremely well.

Archie Gemmill was 35 and playing out the remainder of his career for Wigan in the Third Division under Larry Lloyd when he got a call to meet Pete in the car park of the Dog & Partridge at Tutbury to shake hands on a contract which would be very lucrative for Archie should we avoid relegation.

Gemmill's energy and enthusiasm was undimmed. You knew precisely what you'd get from him – a player prepared to run all over the park for 90 minutes and stick his heart and soul into the cause. Signing Archie gave the place a huge lift, he still lived in Derby and was happy to go to work on his own doorstep rather than commute to Wigan.

Striker John Richards provided another wise old head when he swapped life in Wolves' reserves for a 10-game spell on loan, but that was a stop-gap measure, and the forward the team was crying out for arrived when Taylor twisted a few arms to buy Bobby Davison, who was to become a prolific scorer and cult figure with the fans.

Meanwhile, I was in danger of falling out with Pete because he took himself off most Saturdays on spying missions to scout potential signings when his place had to be with the team. Pete called the shots during the week and he'd have a laugh with us every Friday as he picked the side before he disappeared, leaving Mick and myself in charge.

By Christmas when Pete was absent and we lost at Newcastle, then 3-2 at home to Shrewsbury, I'd had enough of a crazy situation that demanded Taylor take control on matchdays.

The year ended with Derby still bottom and seven points away from safety, which appeared to be slipping away each passing week.

I told him: "This can't happen, Pete. There's no connection for the lads. They see you one minute, then you're gone. You simply must be here on the training ground and here on matchdays too. You have to see the players you've got now to know if you want to keep them or bomb them out."

To his credit, he immediately took my constructive criticism to heart and we won a few more points to raise morale. A 2-2 draw at Oldham on New Year's Day was followed by a 2-0 home win over an excellent QPR side which went on to clinch promotion as champions.

But it was the draw for the FA Cup which brought a sharp intake of breath among fans in the East Midlands, and I dare say much further afield.

The balls came out of the famous velvet bag for the third round to the announcement: "Derby County will play ... Nottingham Forest." Taylor versus Clough.

Men who had been virtually inseparable were barely on speaking terms, Clough convinced he had been betrayed. I know Brian negotiated Pete's retirement at the City Ground with a sizeable golden handshake – but what irritated him most was that he was getting so little joy from a couple of players he described as "Taylor's dodgier proteges" notably Justin Fashanu, the £1million misfit from Norwich.

The rival managers did their best to downplay the occasion as "just another match" in the lead-up to the tie but who were they trying to kid? Fans at both ends of the A52 were having none of it, and neither were the press.

I was concerned we were too lightweight up front to trouble Forest's defence. Taylor and I exchanged looks which translated into 'just our 'effin luck' when we discovered Davison, who had settled in quickly, was ineligible.

Who could have guessed his appearance for Halifax in the first round in a 1-0 home defeat by North Shields would have such repercussions? Making matters worse, Wolves did not want Richards cup-tied when he was recalled to Molineux, so our attack comprised two youngsters. Andy Hill, a raw local lad from Ilkeston, came in to partner Kevin Wilson.

The team bottom of Division Two kicked off against the side in joint-second place in the First Division and at no stage during the 90 minutes was the difference in status apparent.

A muddy, murky, dank, damp Baseball Ground afternoon when character, spirit, determination and sheer bloodymindedness counted for everything meant John Robertson and Garry Birtles would have to work their socks off if Forest were to make their superior skill the decisive factor.

Gemmill had something to prove to Clough, having been sold by him to Birmingham under a cloud of ill-feeling.

Our driven Scot carried a touch of venom from the first exchanges and Forest were muted in the face of our hostile crowd and in-your-face effort from the magnificent Gemmill, who curled in a free-kick before hobbling off with a hamstring injury. The referee was looking at his watch and preparing to blow for full-time when Hill took a short pass from Mick Brolly and lifted the ball over keeper Steve Sutton to clinch a 2-0 victory.

Our form was hit and miss because the team wasn't balanced or settled. Pete and I craved consistency. Satisfying as it was to beat Forest, then Chelsea in the next round before being edged out of the Cup by Norman Whiteside's late goal for Manchester United, it was an indication something was wrong.

I didn't believe the lads should be relishing big occasions as underdogs, putting the pressure on the likes of Forest, Chelsea and United, then letting their standards drop the following Saturday against the likes of Cambridge, Shrewsbury and Rotherham. We weren't strong enough mentally and to underline that fact, the week after the Forest win we were thumped 3-0 at Carlisle.

Taylor shored up the defence by finding £115,000 to buy Paul Futcher from Oldham, pairing him in central defence with Steve Powell, and out of nowhere, we embarked on a 15-match unbeaten run which took Derby from a precarious position eights points away from safety to the brink of survival.

The tension was ratcheted up when May brought consecutive away defeats at Crystal Palace and Blackburn. We needed a point from our final match against Fulham at the Baseball Ground to be sure of staying up, while Malcolm Macdonald's men would only claim the final promotion place if they bettered Leicester's result at home to Blackburn.

Davison went a long way to cementing his status as a Derby hero when he swivelled near the penalty spot to crash a volley into the roof of the net but the match is perhaps better remembered, bitterly by Fulham, for the way the last 10 minutes were played with thousands of fans barely able to contain themselves behind the touchline.

A leg even snaked out to kick one Fulham player, which was unforgivable, and I had every sympathy with my old England colleague Macdonald as he stood in front of the tunnel shaking his head in disbelief and asking the police why this intimidation had been allowed to happen.

When the referee blew for offside as their keeper punted the ball high into our half there was still over a minute of injury time to play, but that was never going to happen as the mud-caked pitch was engulfed by a frenzied mob.

We were staying up and Fulham were staying down, despite an appeal to have the match replayed, which was rejected by the Football League. That was never likely because results elsewhere meant we could afford to lose a replay and, if they won, Fulham would have more points than Leicester.

I felt shattered in the dressing room afterwards, relief sweeping through me, as Taylor and I congratulated the team on dredging up one final mighty effort.

I can't say I was particularly proud of our supporters, I detest anything connected with hooliganism, but the following afternoon I watched extended highlights on The Big Match and recall Brian Moore saying: "It gives you an idea of the depth of feeling for football in this great old football town if staying in the Second Division can generate as much excitement as this today."

21

Third-class Citizens

HE took a nip of whisky with his coffee at 10 o'clock on a Sunday morning at home in Widmerpool and told Mick Jones to start looking for another job.

I nearly dropped my cup and saucer in Peter Taylor's lounge as he bluntly told our assistant team boss: "I'm sorry, Mick, but you've got to go. We can't afford you."

After taking training the following morning, I tackled the manager and was in no mood to beat around the bush. I said plainly: "If Mick goes, I go too."

Pete fell silent for a moment before trying to soften the blow: "Don't worry, I'll make sure Mick gets looked after."

But he looked crushed, a beaten man, and surprised me by adding: "In fact, Roy, get a settlement for me and I'll go too."

Derby County were in crisis on and off the pitch in the spring of 1984, and Pete wanted a way out. Disillusioned at his failure to mount a promotion drive, he had clearly had enough. He was fighting too many battles on too many fronts, and not winning any of them.

How different it seemed the previous summer when, buoyed by our Great Escape, the season ticket money rolled in and we staked over £200,000 on two controversial signings, winger John Robertson from Nottingham Forest and Bobby Campbell, my former Bradford City centre-forward.

Antagonism between Brian Clough and Taylor went off the scale while Brian was in the Yorkshire Dales on a 100-mile charity walk and phoned home from a pub to discover that Robbo had signed a three-year deal with us.

It was Clough's own fault because he unnerved Robbo with some comments and the player felt the new contract he expected to be offered at the City Ground would mean a drop in wages and reduced security. On the other hand, Pete made him feel loved and wanted again.

Everyone thought my fingerprints were all over the signing of Campbell, when the reverse was true. He cost £75,000 and Derby lost £45,000 when he was hastily returned to Valley Parade after 11 League matches. Following our success with Bobby Davison from Halifax, the expectancy was that Campbell would make a similar impact.

He was, in fact, a disaster.

Taylor, Jones and our valued youth team coach Ken Gutteridge all gave the Ulsterman the thumbs up.

I cautioned against the move but was outvoted. They couldn't understand why I couldn't endorse a man who scored a stack of goals for me, but I didn't think it was wise to take him out of his environment.

Campbell liked to be liked, he relished being a big fish in a small pond and the liberty to go boozing at home in Huddersfield, while I often thought it was best not knowing what he got up to.

He loved his life, although it wasn't the ideal way to live if you were a professional footballer, and he wasn't the best trainer in the world. Very independent and single-minded, Bobby was off the wall and refused to conform.

I rode my luck at Bradford and got the best out of him because Les Chapman acted as the perfect minder.

At Derby, he never understood that we couldn't indulge him or cut him any slack and that he needed to perform in every match and training session. He didn't, so we cut our losses and moved on.

As for Robertson, whose transfer fee was set at £135,000 by a tribunal, some supporters never accepted him because of his close association with Forest.

They questioned why a Scotland international dropped a division if it wasn't "just for the money". The last time they had seen him at Derby, Robbo had underperformed in the FA Cup to such an extent he was taken off.

He needed a cartilage operation in November and was out for two months when we expected him to be missing for four weeks.

Money problems sent the club spiralling into massive debt and the players weren't always paid on time.

Neither were two of our FA Cup opponents, Telford and Norwich, both kept waiting for their share of the gate receipts.

Eventually, the Football Association threatened Derby with expulsion from the Cup if a cheque for the outstanding amount didn't arrive at Carrow Road. We beat that deadline by a matter of hours.

Some of the playing staff weren't the most talented but they did not deserve to be messed about. There were mortgage repayments to be met, food bills and basic living expenses. One month, Derby were on the breadline so Pete, Mick and myself agreed to defer our money so the players were guaranteed their wages. The three of us never did get that month's money in full.

The bank refused to extend the club's overdraft, forcing chairman Mike Watterson and several directors to dip into their pockets to prevent Derby from folding as the debt reached £1.5million.

Even had we been able to afford to buy new players, that option was removed by the Football League after we fell behind with instalments on Robertson.

Then Watterson panicked and issued a writ to recover £33,000 he loaned the club before publicly questioning the manager's credibility. Watterson left and a reluctant John Kirkland took over.

The Inland Revenue, owed £129,000, issued a winding-up notice and then a deal for financial backing from a multinational conglomerate based in Hong Kong collapsed.

If you wanted an omen, it came at Stamford Bridge on the opening Saturday when we went down 5-0 to Chelsea, and our resources were so stretched that I was soon pressed into service again at 35.

With Steve Powell injured, Taylor asked me how I felt about facing Swansea at home, and I was happy to oblige.

One of the lads joked with gallows humour: "We've got a new nickname for you, Roy – Bognor! Because you're the last resort."

I had my hands full with Ian Walsh and Bob Latchford, who scored for the Welsh club, but was pleased to complete the match and delighted that we squeezed out a 2-1 win. I had kept myself basically fit and still looked forward to playing a full part in training, but I was only filling in here and there, making two more starts and five appearances off the bench.

There was no great last hurrah and my final touch as a professional footballer arrived in December at Portsmouth, where I wore the No.12 shirt and we lost 3-0.

An FA Cup semi-final against First Division Watford at Villa Park came tantalisingly into view in March. Our share of the receipts would partially answer prayers for financial salvation and 25,000 raucous Derby supporters would create one hell of an atmosphere.

Watford were good, but no better than Norwich, who had turned up at our place in the fifth round after eliminating Aston Villa and Tottenham, quietly fancying their chances of going all the way, certainly of making class tell with Mick Channon, Keith Bertschin and John Deehan in their ranks.

Like Forest the previous year, they discovered how much Derby relished the role of underdogs as we beat them 2-1.

That vision of embarrassing Watford proved to be a mirage however because we made the classic schoolboy error of getting ahead of ourselves.

The quarter-final draw sent us to Plymouth, languishing near the foot of the Third Division, and we were extremely fortunate to escape with a 0-0 scoreline, yet convinced ourselves we had done the job and that the advantage was all ours in the replay.

Our keeper Steve Cherry suffered an absolute nightmare the following Wednesday – at fault when a corner from Argyle winger Andy Rogers curled over his head and into the net for the only goal of the game.

Cherry held his hands up, openly admitting his costly mistake, but that did not stop him from getting a verbal pummelling from Taylor who was beside himself with anger.

The financial implication of failure, after the carrot of an FA Cup semi-final was dangling so enticingly, was too much for Pete to bear. He turned on whoever else in his eyes had failed to come up to scratch and might as well have lambasted everybody because the whole team didn't perform. They weren't good enough to see it through.

Eventually, Taylor made the mistake of using Archie Gemmill as his verbal punchbag. In front of the entire team, Archie was told that he had shot it, he was a disgrace, his legs had gone totally and that he would never play again for Derby County.

Pete was losing his head, saying outrageous things which made me wince – especially the line, "you'll never play again for Derby County".

I'd heard him use that earlier following one of a number of substandard performances by central defender John McAlle, only to backtrack on his threat a fortnight later when injuries left him down to the bare bones.

Tell a player he has no future and you are unlikely to get a response beyond two fingers.

The club was in danger of stagnating and we were all sucked into the mire. It was an unhealthy environment for players and management alike.

Pete was used to fighting and scrapping, but winning in the end. The odds were beginning to look insurmountable and nothing he tried could dull the pain or paint what was happening in a favourable light.

Without Archie, we caved in at home to Brighton 3-0 and drew 0-0 at Middlesbrough before Pete had a change of heart, begging Gemmill to play the following Saturday at Barnsley, but Archie's pride had been damaged and he turned the tables, telling the manager: "I'll tell you straight now, I'll never play for Derby County again while you are the manager."

Pete watched a thoroughly disheartened side beaten 5-1 at Oakwell with Derby fans demanding to know why Gemmill wasn't playing. Within a week, Pete had been sacked and Stuart Webb, now chairman, asked me to take charge for the remaining nine matches.

Publishing tycoon Robert Maxwell was in the background, keen to relinquish control of Oxford United and take over at the Baseball Ground, which he bought for £305,000 from the NatWest Bank.

At last, it looked as if some serious money would come into the club and I had something to celebrate when I told Gemmill: "I need you against Crystal Palace on Saturday, Archie. It's important you play in our remaining matches if you feel like it." We had a good chat but he needed a fair bit of persuading and coaxing before he agreed.

Archie's experience was vital, and my faith in youth was rewarded when Andy Garner, just turned 18, scored a hat-trick in a 3-0 home win over Steve Coppell's side.

I signed off with a 100 per cent winning record at home as manager in my own right, supervising subsequent victories over

Fulham, Manchester City and Portsmouth without conceding a single goal.

Staying up was a big ask but we gave it a good go in those home games where the fans gave us every encouragement and the players' response was much better.

It was, however, the same old sorry story on the road where we lost at Sheffield Wednesday, Cardiff, Newcastle and Shrewsbury, gaining a solitary point at Leeds, and scoring once in those five away matches which exposed our weaknesses.

We went to play Arthur Cox's Newcastle seeking a miracle against a side on the brink of promotion and featuring Kevin Keegan, Peter Beardsley and Chris Waddle. Everything they did came off, it was a breeze for them and Keegan displayed remarkable fitness and agility, despite being on the verge of retirement as a player.

Ninety minutes later, that talented trio had combined to score all the goals in a 4-0 victory. The packed Geordie crowd, in a promotion party mood, created a fantastic atmosphere in the sunshine and we were, in a sense, lambs to the slaughter.

We knew it was going to be a thoroughly testing afternoon, and it was. There was disappointment on a quiet journey home but I can't say I was unduly surprised – we had not performed well away all season.

The minute we conceded a goal, you could sense everything drain away from players who lacked the requisite character and fighting spirit. They became meek, pallid and resigned to their fate far too often.

After Newcastle, the game was up – we were doomed unless Oldham lost their remaining two matches and we won both of ours.

The last vestiges of hope were extinguished two days later when my old pal Joe Royle got Oldham over the finishing line with victory over Grimsby and Derby had to face up to the harsh reality of a future in the Third Division.

22

King Arthur

FLOYD STREETE didn't know what hit him when he trooped off after a poor first half, head down. There, waiting for him in the dressing room was Arthur Cox, apoplectic with rage.

Our Jamaica-born centre-half didn't so much get it in the neck with both barrels as face a firing squad of expletives as the Derby County manager called him everything from a pig to a dog. "Do your job, why can't you just do your fucking job?" barked Cox.

Floyd was a big, strong, athletic guy with plenty of muscle and didn't take kindly to being bawled out in front of his team-mates, although there were no racial overtones.

If looks could kill, however, they would both have been mortally wounded. Bristling at being belittled, Floyd stood his ground, staring straight at Cox, who was like a bull mastiff with a bone – he simply wouldn't let go. Just as it appeared inevitable they would come to blows, I forced myself between them and the tension passed after a stand-off.

Fortunately, Floyd kept his temper in the face of extreme provocation, defended himself against accusations of dereliction of duty and somehow went back out and redeemed himself in the second half.

Streete was by no means the worst defender I saw in a white shirt at Derby but he was prone to lapses of concentration which caused trouble. It is a major thing for any footballer, or athlete, to be 'in the moment' because opponents are always seeking an edge, and if they spot a player prone to switching off they will take advantage, target him and make his life a misery.

If a perfect storm created the whirlpool which sucked the club down, then a fortunate set of circumstances – including Robert Maxwell's millions – combined to bring the club back to the surface.

Our last Second Division fixture had seen us beaten 3-0 at Shrewsbury, after which Stuart Webb told me: "You're still in charge, Roy. I'd like you to continue to act as manager, hold the fort and see where the team needs strengthening."

Behind the scenes, things happened rapidly. Webb invested heavily, spending £140,000 to take a controlling interest, and the next managerial appointment had to succeed otherwise he stood to lose a fortune.

Webb told me I was in the frame but that he and the directors were considering the merits of another man steeped in the club's history, my good friend and former team-mate Alan Durban, sacked by Sunderland, and Mick Buxton, the Huddersfield manager, who had taken the Terriers from the Fourth Division to the Second. I was relaxed and confident when my turn came to enter the boardroom for an interview, and my mood hadn't altered when I left it.

Webb's deliberations over the three of us stopped immediately when Cox dropped a game-changing bombshell on Tyneside by quitting Newcastle in a contract row. I don't think he was impressed either when he was presented with the budget for new players at St James' Park, particularly as Kevin Keegan needed replacing.

Arthur's pedigree and the vibrant, attacking football he preached made him an irresistible candidate.

It doesn't take much to imagine Webb promoting Cox as a top-of-the-range manager and Maxwell, never a man to settle for second best, delivering the order: "Get him here now, pay him what we wants."

Maxwell demanded the best person for the job and if Webb told him that Cox was that man, then the publisher expected him to be delivered. Maxwell and his money were very persuasive allies.

Fours days after leaving Newcastle, Arthur was installed at the Baseball Ground and we spent two hours over countless cups of tea closeted together in the boardroom. He listened intently as I told him, openly and honestly, everything that was wrong with the club, which players needed replacing, the ones worth keeping and where the team required strengthening.

I honestly thought that meeting would end with Arthur thanking me for my input, shaking my hand and wishing me well whatever the future held in store.

He was a powerful new broom and nobody could have blamed

him for sweeping away everything associated with recent failure.

Around noon, Arthur shocked me by breaking into a grin and saying: "I'd like you to stay, Roy. I'd like you to be my assistant because I think we will make a good partnership. How does a new contract for two years sound?" It sounded very acceptable and Webb wasted little time in organising the paperwork.

As soon as the fixtures came out ahead of the 1984-85 season, I scanned the list to discover when I knew I would be abused, labelled a 'Judas' and have my parentage questioned, and there it was ... Saturday, November 10th, Bradford City (away).

The crowd gave me some fearful stick, and rightly so because of the manner of my leaving Valley Parade. There are times when you have to admit: "I didn't handle that well." That had certainly been one for me.

Walking out of the tunnel and down to the visitors' dugout was not an ordeal I was looking forward to, but something I had to face at some stage in my career and it was never something I would shy away from.

The relationship was still raw and touchy between myself and wounded City fans. Things had yet to heal.

I expected a really rough ride from them and that's precisely what I got.

When it happened, it was extremely unpleasant and I felt very uncomfortable but I had created the problem. It was all of my own making.

In a strange way, anything less than the way those passionate Bradford punters slaughtered me would have been a disappointment. Their vitriol, the spittle and coins, showed how much they felt let down, cheated even, by my decision to walk away from the club after winning promotion. They certainly let me know the depth of their feelings, and rightly so. It was not something I would care to experience too often.

The mood in the Bradford boardroom was totally at odds with the hostility on the terraces and the reception I received, and a beer afterwards, was nothing short of excellent. I had enjoyed a sound relationship with the directors, they wished me well and appreciated what I had achieved.

I took the club up to the Third Division and now, under Trevor Cherry and Terry Yorath, it looked as though Bradford were thriving at the start of a campaign which ended with them going up as champions.

Certainly, they were too good for Derby on the day, winning 3-1. I can only apologise to Bradford supporters and hope they recognise the job I did for their club. Equally, I accept what I did to them was wrong.

Six months later, my heart went out to everyone connected with Bradford as I experienced one of those 'There but for the grace of God, go I' moments when fire engulfed the main stand at Valley Parade, claiming 56 lives.

We had finished the season winning 3-1 at Newport, so it should have been a relaxed journey home from south Wales.

Arthur and I were saying goodbye to staff at Somerton Park and ensuring all the kit was safely stored on board when a couple of players jumped off and repeated sketchy details of the tragedy from radio reports.

I was numb and morose on the way back, trying and failing to get my head around the enormity of what happened at Bradford where the afternoon started so promisingly with promotion celebrations before their match with Lincoln.

When news came through of multiple deaths, I couldn't keep out of my mind the dirty, cramped conditions under the stand. Worse than that, my mind was racing over all the faces I knew at the club, fearing that some of them might have choked to death. It must have been absolutely horrendous for those trapped by locked gates, the victims who took a wrong turn instead of trying to escape onto the pitch. I brought Don Goodman, a young local lad, to the club and he had given a ticket to his former girlfriend. She was among those who died. You never forget things like that.

Back at the Baseball Ground, before then, Maxwell's son Ian had parachuted in as chairman with a £550,000 cash injection to help balance the books, courtesy of the family fortune, and Cox's earliest signings were prudent free transfers. Both he and I recognised that we needed a strong backbone.

Centre-half Rob Hindmarch was well known to Arthur, having played on his patch in the North East for Sunderland. Although his pace was suspect and he got caught on occasions, Hindmarch possessed great presence as a solid, genuine No.5 and became club captain. Goalkeeper Eric Steele and right-back Charlie Palmer travelled up the motorway to join us from Watford.

Kevin Wilson could never be as good as Kevin Hector, but the slender, dark-haired striker brought back memories of 'The King' with a torrent of goals – four against Hartlepool in the Milk Cup, followed by a hat-trick against Bolton three days later. Fourteen games in, Wilson had 13 goals to his name when he broke his arm against Plymouth and when he returned to prove his fitness over Christmas, the decision was taken to accept an offer of £150,000 from Ipswich, who were crying out for a goalscorer to keep them in the First Division.

It was a good opportunity for Wilson to test himself at a higher level and provided Cox with the bulk of the money to replace him with not one, but two quality forwards.

Trevor Christie had scored a stack of goals for Notts County the previous season. Not enough to keep them in the First Division but sufficient to attract the attention of Brian Clough.

That hop across the River Trent hadn't worked out favourably, however, and the emergence of Garry Birtles at Forest meant Clough was happy to accept £100,000 for Christie, who proved to be very decent in the air and formed a good partnership with Bobby Davison.

Gary Micklewhite also dropped down from the First Division, joining us for £80,000 from QPR to patrol the right wing, a bundle of energy who could cross the ball as well as anyone and a willing workhorse with an appetite for winning the ball back. Micklewhite was a tremendous asset who couldn't wait for Saturdays.

Another significant piece in the jigsaw slotted into place in the spring when we paid Bristol Rovers £40,000 for Geraint Williams.

I had to watch him several times to be assured that he was precisely what we needed before being convinced enough to tell Arthur: "He's our man," but the deal still took several months to complete.

Maybe the stocky Welshman didn't catch the eye quite like Christie and Micklewhite, but 'George' as we called him was a good, solid signing who improved, becoming positive on the ball and increasingly mobile.

He was Arthur's equivalent to Dave Mackay's Henry Newton,

equipping Derby with a gritty, physical influence in the middle of the park.

The green shoots of recovery were evident in the spring of 1985 as we ended a campaign of transition in seventh place in Division Three, losing one of our final 10 games – but Arthur was impatient.

His short back and sides haircut reinforced the image of a no-nonsense character who looked as if he would be equally at home on an Army parade ground as the training pitch, where he was single-minded, strong with the players and a fierce disciplinarian.

The players nicknamed him the Sergeant Major, with good reason.

Everybody knew where they stood with Arthur – in trouble if they failed to carry out his instructions. But any bollockings, as in the case of Streete, were never allowed to fester. Arthur made his point, very forcibly at times, and moved on, the ultimate professional.

He didn't suffer fools and within the game he wasn't easy to get on with. In working relationships, he could be quite distant with people, a little bit insular. You had no relationship with Arthur at all if he didn't respect you, and that respect was hard-earned. I was fortunate because he treated me as if I was a member of his own family. He admired me for what I had achieved in football and if there was one character at the club he treated better than anyone, it was me.

In terms of style, John Bond was a very different type of manager and his refusal to be anything other than immaculately turned out amused Cox and myself on one occasion at Swansea.

We were in south Wales for a match which stood very little chance of going ahead because of torrential rain.

Arthur stayed in the dressing room, deadpanning as he said I could have 'the honour' of testing the water on the sodden Vetch Field pitch. Fortunately, I'd left our hotel in an old tracksuit and scruffy training shoes.

Still, Bondy looked at me as if I was something the cat had dragged in as we met in the tunnel before venturing out to investigate the state of play – or rather lack of it – with the referee.

He wore a fur coat over a beautiful pastel-coloured Italian suit topped off with a pair of handmade, light shoes.

By the time we reached the centre circle, I swear Bondy had shrunk an inch or two in the quagmire.

I glanced down to see his shoes were caked in mud which was now creeping up his trouser legs.

The ref told us: "I don't think there's a chance," to which Bond replied: "Well, it's your decision. We don't play, then."

With that, he turned to me and said: "Safe trip home, Roy, and give my regards to Arthur," before trudging off without a care in the world – not even the hefty dry-cleaning bill coming his way.

Cox was scowling in November and looking for the Baseball Ground cat to kick when Steve McClaren, our new £70,000 midfielder from Hull, went down with an injury.

The prognosis was poor. The future England and Derby manager was not going to play again any time soon but I was almost smiling when Arthur rounded on me and said: "Roy, we need someone to dictate in midfield, any ideas?" I replied instantly: "John Gregory at QPR."

Arthur wanted to know more and asked: "Why? What's he going to bring to the table?" and I could feel the manager tense when I told him: "Sign him, just sign him."

He hated riddles and guessing games, so I put him out of his misery and explained that one of the bonuses of watching Micklewhite on several occasions at Loftus Road and beyond was that I had seen another QPR player with the qualities we now needed.

So we splashed out £100,000 on another First Division player and Gregory brought us style as well as substance, that little bit of extra class which took us a cut above most of our rivals. He stroked the ball about beautifully, controlled things, passed with accuracy and imagination, and kept everything ticking over. He complemented the 'dirty' work Williams did so diligently.

I couldn't claim any originality for that line: "Sign him, just sign him."

Peter Taylor, that extraordinary talent-spotter, used it when he came gushing back to meet Brian Clough after watching Roger Davies at Worcester.

And it was exactly the sort of thing Arthur and I would hear from our chief scout Ron Jukes as a prelude to listening to him enthuse over a particular player.

"Sign him, just sign him," said a beaming Jukes following one excursion to Shrewsbury, where he felt central defender Ross MacLaren had outgrown Gay Meadow and was ready for bigger and better things. Shrewsbury were less than impressed at receiving £67,500 at a transfer tribunal for a very capable defender who loved a meaty tackle and served Derby exceedingly well.

I watched the 1985-86 season unfold with growing optimism,

racking my brains for the last time I'd seen a settled Derby team functioning so well, enthusiastic players with smiles on their faces, a potent blend of youth and experience.

Three rounds of the Milk Cup were followed by seven FA Cup ties, culminating in a fifth-round exit at Sheffield Wednesday in a replay, and a stack of postponements led to a tense climax in May.

Reading and Plymouth were up, while we needed to beat Rotherham at home in our penultimate fixture to be sure of pipping Wigan for the final promotion place.

It was 1-1 approaching the last five minutes when we won a penalty, which Christie scored, and I think that everyone in the ground knew then that we were up. It was inconceivable that we would let the prize of promotion slip because all our players knew their jobs – Cox made sure of that.

Twelve months later to the day, he was obliged to jab a finger at several players at half-time against Plymouth, reminding them of their responsibilities before they stirred themselves to win 4-2 and clinch the Second Division championship in front of our ecstatic fans.

Two new full-backs, Mel Sage and Micky 'Bruce' Forsyth bolstered the defence during the triumphant 1986-87 campaign, while David Nish had done us a favour by recommending Phil Gee, a young striker of his at nearby Gresley Rovers.

And as a final flourish, we shelled out £140,000 to Watford for their talented winger Nigel Callaghan in February to provide the attack with an injection of pace and a sharper cutting edge.

Sage was a tidy, compact player who cost £60,000 from Gillingham, while the powerful Forsyth proved to be a £25,000 bargain buy from West Brom reserves. Micky went on to serve the club superbly, making over 400 appearances after arriving as a central defender but swiftly making the No.3 shirt his own.

Gee had combined work as a painter and decorator with terrorising non-league defences. He gave a hint of what was to come in his first season with us, plundering goals galore for the reserves, before stepping up to bag 15 in League action, just four fewer than top scorer Davison.

A first-rate manager, who knew precisely what he wanted and where to find it in the transfer market, supported by the requisite financial muscle proved to be an irresistible combination and Derby were back in the big time following a second successive promotion.

Cox's ability had not gone unrecognised in the West Midlands, where Aston Villa sacked Billy McNeill, after less than eight months in charge, and his assistant Ron Wylie, after finishing bottom of the First Division.

Villa Park held a strong attraction for Arthur, who said: "If you get that job, you're not running a corner shop, you get the keys to a megastore." He told me tales of how he had briefly been Villa caretaker, then coach, in the late Sixties during Tommy Docherty's time – and now it was suggested he was the man to take over as manager in his own right.

I feel certain he would have wanted me to go with him to Villa and I was equally relieved it was never a decision I had to make.

Chairman Doug Ellis went to Watford instead to recruit Graham Taylor for a combination of reasons. Arthur and I were under contract to Derby, where his stock was sky-high and Cox was intrigued by how far he could take the club under Maxwell's patronage.

And having won promotion to the First Division again after performing a similar feat at Newcastle, Arthur was loathe to kiss goodbye to his hard-won lofty status and exchange away matches at Anfield, Goodison Park, Old Trafford, Highbury and White Hart Lane for trips to Bournemouth, Swindon and Shrewsbury.

Arthur was very adept at manipulating stories. He knew the right people in the business and was rigid about the small number of people he admitted to his inner circle.

It had done his reputation no harm to be linked with the Villa job of course, his loyalty rating increased by staying put, and that would have stood him in good stead when he next went in to renegotiate his contract, which he richly deserved, with Maxwell and Webb.

23

Life With The Borgias

JOHAN CRUYFF is negotiating to join Derby County as technical director, trumpets the Daily Mirror. It is April, 1988 – the week after All Fools' Day – and not for the first time Robert Maxwell's antics leave me astonished.

Cruyff is certainly available and on the market because he is between jobs after leaving Ajax.

I imagine guiding one of the world's greatest footballers over the road in Shaftesbury Crescent after training to buy a packet of 20 Gold Leaf for the notoriously heavy smoker before maybe adjourning a few yards to the Baseball Hotel to discuss tactics for a forthcoming trip to Watford over a pint of Bass.

I fantasise about how the Dutchman, Arthur Cox and myself will lead the club to unimagined glory.

It's all madness of course ... yet I doubt whether Maxwell considered it as such, or thought Cruyff was out of his league. He had already plucked two England internationals from Southampton, goalkeeper Peter Shilton on £4,000 a week as a free agent and centre-half Mark Wright for a fee of £760,000.

Cox was bitterly upset, tackling Maxwell directly in private over the Cruyff speculation and risking the chairman's wrath by publicly criticising him for instigating talks without prior consultation. Arthur told me being kept in the dark was a recipe for disaster because it spawned confusion, mixed messages and mistrust.

He was always prepared to fight his corner against Maxwell or anyone else if he felt he was being wronged. Arthur spoke to Maxwell following every home match either in person or by phone and I was present on many of those occasions when the manager responded fiercely to criticism if he felt it was unwarranted.

Speculation about Holland's sharpest football brain arriving in town faded almost as quickly as it arose.

So Derby's 'loss' became Barcelona's 'gain' as Cruyff returned to the Catalan giants as manager, winning a stack of trophies and introducing the close-passing style later adopted to great acclaim by Lionel Messi, Xavi and Andres Iniesta.

To be fair to the old rogue, Maxwell's punt for Cruyff made more sense than his much-derided plan to merge Oxford United and Reading into Thames Valley Royals, but his constant dabbling in the affairs of other clubs, including a bid to buy-out Elton John at Watford, had a negative ripple effect at Derby.

First season back in the top flight, Arthur and I needed as few off-field distractions as possible. We had to concentrate on gaining a foothold in the table, away from the slippery slope of relegation.

My old international team-mate Shilton was pushing 38 yet still, without doubt, he was the best goalkeeper in the country. His dedication and preparation for training and matches was undiminished.

For most of the week, Arthur supervised training and we'd finish off with a small-sided game or use a full-sized pitch – eight versus eight, 11 on 11, maybe even 13 against 13.

But on Thursdays, Peter trained with me exclusively and I worked him mercilessly. We didn't have a specialist goalkeeping coach so I put him through his paces, helping to maintain his reactions with a series of drills.

The other lads finished training and came in, looking at us, shaking their heads and laughing, but Peter stayed out with me for an extra half an hour, sweating like a pig and plastered in mud sometimes, cursing loudly if the ball I fired spewed from his grasp and he needed a second attempt to complete the save to his satisfaction.

Wright was a superb signing, above all of Cox's other buys in terms of quality. He had it all – power, pace, control, he could head a ball and read situations. Mark also had a defect, however. His temper. He was headstrong and when the red mist descended, he became a danger to himself and the team because he risked a booking or worse and could cost us a goal.

Arthur made Wrighty a better player because he calmed him down over time to become more dispassionate on the pitch, he regained his England place and developed into a genuine international.

Maxwell looked upon Derby as an executive toy and after allowing his son Ian to play with the 'train set' for a few years, he decided he fancied a turn as the 'engine driver' once the club was in the First Division.

Getting Cruyff in as a super coach would have pandered to his sense of self-importance and misguided superiority the next time he was hobnobbing with Sir Matt Busby at Manchester United, John Smith at Liverpool or Peter Hill-Wood at Arsenal.

Of course, Arthur and I were extremely grateful for the money to finance the arrival of Shilton and Wright, but Derby were still making too many headlines for the wrong reasons.

The Football League took an increasingly dim view of Maxwell's machinations and proposed a new one-man, one-club rule which had our chairman threatening to pull out of football altogether.

Against this sideshow of threats, injunctions and court action, we suffered an alarming spell in mid-season, losing seven games in a row and plummeting from ninth to 18th place before squeezing to safety and finishing 15th.

Had that run continued, Maxwell might have had a monopoly on the relegation places. Although he never managed to get his hands on Watford, they went down with Oxford.

Bobby Davison found the going considerably tougher at this level and was sold to Leeds for £350,000. Phil Gee and John Gregory finished joint top scorers, with just six goals apiece, which illustrated where improvement was needed.

Maxwell liked nothing better than to play politics and if the subject matter involved his native Czechoslovakia nothing could stop him dabbling.

Cox's face betrayed no emotion when the owner casually informed him: "I've got you two new players. Czech internationals. Can't remember their names. See the secretary, he's got the details." Maxwell did not need to break the news to us because it was plastered all over that morning's edition of the Daily Mirror.

Lubos Kubik and Ivo Knoflicek wanted the freedom to play in the West, to make a decent living for themselves and their families, and Maxwell set the wheels in motion for them to defect. Both players were in their mid-20s, but the Czech football authorities would not sanction them leaving until they had turned 30.

While the rest of their Slavia Prague team-mates were training at a tournament in West Germany, a British agent spirited the pair away by car to Belgium, where they spent a fortnight before holing up in a Spanish fishing village north of Barcelona, spending four months there living in a house belonging to Maxwell's daughter Ghislaine, playing tennis and generally keeping themselves fit for purpose.

When we learned all this, and dodgy documents were mentioned, Arthur and I thought we were trapped in some sort of football version of The Ipcress File and that Michael Caine might walk through the door at any moment, introducing himself as Derby's new foreign scout.

Midfielder Kubik and winger Knoflicek were granted political asylum in Britain, but Slavia Prague officials refused to sanction their transfers to Derby and because they had quit Czech football without permission, FIFA banned them from playing any competitive football for a year.

I really felt for the Czech lads, who were kicked around like political footballs during the months they spent with us training, but with no release at the end of the week, no match to look forward to. Kubik was extremely talented, his qualities stood out in training.

They started off living in the Clovelly Hotel on Broadway in Derby, then got shifted into a flat above an Italian restaurant in Burton Road where we knew they would be well fed and looked after in a more homely atmosphere, before moving into a rented house when one of their families came over to join them.

Cox was not at all enamoured with the situation. Without clearance to play, he felt Kubik and Knoflicek were a waste of space, and he wanted to wash his hands of them. It was a very difficult time for Arthur because he was under instructions to look after them and get them fit.

If only Maxwell had agreed to stump up some money to Slavia Prague, Derby would have benefited from a couple of top-class imports, but he refused to pay the Czech club a penny. It might have been a matter of principle, or he might have felt he'd already paid more than enough in wages and accommodation, and was therefore somehow 'entitled' to take them for nothing.

The mess was finally resolved when the pair did a moonlight flit back to Prague where Slavia did deals to sell Kubik to Fiorentina and Knoflicek to St Pauli in Hamburg. The next time I saw them was on the television, playing prominent roles as Czechoslovakia reached the quarter-finals of the 1990 World Cup in Italy.

Paul Blades, a composed young defender, started to impress at right-back, while we had tweaked and improved our options in midfield and attack.

Oxford's demise was Derby's good fortune as Trevor Hebberd arrived from the Manor Ground for £200,000 to be followed by the high-class Welsh international Dean Saunders for £1million.

I couldn't help feeling sorry for Oxford manager Mark Lawrenson, who didn't have a clue a deal was being conducted behind his back between Maxwell and his son Kevin, the Oxford chairman. Lawro complained he'd been stitched up, only to be unceremoniously sacked for his trouble.

Cox went for the experienced Paul Goddard, from Newcastle for £425,000, as Saunders' strike partner and the two of them were well served by jinking Scottish winger Ted McMinn, who returned to these shores for a fee of £300,000 from Seville, and became a firm favourite with the fans.

It didn't matter who you were, what your reputation, what you had achieved for the club, if Cox could identify a better player in your position – and Maxwell gave him the thumbs up – the deal went ahead.

As a confirmed Liverpool fan, I felt a pang of regret that I couldn't be at Hillsborough one April afternoon in 1989.

The FA Cup semi-final held extra spice for me as Brian Clough was there with Nottingham Forest, bidding to reach his first final. On the other side of the Pennines, Derby were focused on Old Trafford, and an away match against Manchester United.

Arthur and I were happy with the way the lads had shaped up in training during the week. They were ready to take on Alex Ferguson's side, spearheaded by Mark Hughes and Brian McClair, and backboned by Steve Bruce and Paul McGrath.

We gave Fergie's side a good working over, winning with goals from Gary Micklewhite and Goddard.

In normal circumstances, I would have enjoyed a decent drink or two – raising my glass to Clough and Peter Taylor where it had all gone wrong for them after a previous Derby win in the United boardroom.

But now football seemed so trivial, it ceased to matter, as word filtered through of the catastrophe at Sheffield Wednesday's ground which left 96 innocent Liverpool fans dead.

The tragic news came through initially in dribs and drabs that there had been a major crowd incident. People were whispering in corners, eager for information.

Arthur and I had a quick glass of wine with United's assistant manager Brian Kidd while Alex joined us briefly in the backroom used by his coaching staff, after completing all his post-match duties, before we parted company.

The radio was on throughout the journey home and our mood was sombre as the story unfolded and we attempted to absorb the enormity of it all. No one doubted there had been a disaster, but people were reluctant to confirm anything. At first, I thought two or three supporters had been killed accidentally and when the death toll mounted, so did my utter disbelief that in this day and age so many people could have lost their lives, crushed together at a football match.

To my mind, there were tragic echoes of the Bradford fire disaster four years earlier.

I felt a tinge of relief because I knew none of my family were at the semi-final. My brother-in-law Bobby Hargreaves had stopped going to away matches, although he always sought out a ticket for a final. I offered up a silent prayer that no one I knew had been caught up in the horror.

Somehow the focus had to return to football and when it did we managed three more wins, including a fine 2-1 victory at a packed Highbury, thanks to a couple of goals from Saunders, which threatened to deprive Arsenal of the championship, on our way to finishing fifth. But there was no UEFA Cup place on offer because English clubs were still banned from Europe as a result of the Heysel disaster of 1985.

I don't think it was too fanciful to imagine Derby launching a title bid in 1989-90. We still needed a handful of more accomplished players, which was perfectly understandable considering the starting point of the revival but Maxwell suddenly and unaccountably pulled the plug.

He was never in love with football and became thoroughly disenchanted after Hillsborough and the level to which gates dropped. The game had rarely seemed less attractive to casual supporters who stayed away in their thousands.

Maxwell grumbled about "bloody ungrateful Derby fans" when the first home match, in midweek against Wimbledon, was watched by a crowd of 13,874 and there were 13,694 the following month for a 1-0 defeat by Southampton. Derby weren't alone in suffering at the turnstiles, QPR pulling in just 10,565 at home against Luton Town.

A lack of further investment put the brakes on the club's forward momentum and nine defeats in our final 13 matches indicated that a decline was underway.

The disappointment I felt was put into perspective in early October, 1990.

Arthur and I were preparing for an away match at Liverpool when word reached us that Peter Taylor had died, aged 62, at his holiday villa in Costa de los Pinos in Majorca. His wife Lil had been out for the evening and returned to find Pete slumped on a settee.

After first contacting the emergency services, her next call was to summon Willie Carlin, who had a nearby apartment, and he raced round but there was nothing he could do.

I know Willie would have given anything to save him, even though Pete had been responsible for Carlin leaving the club when he sourced Archie Gemmill as a younger, more vibrant midfield general.

I was desperately sad to hear the news and for days my head was full of all the great times Pete, Brian and I had shared in the early days when Derby were kicking up a storm. And my mind shot back to happier times on Cala Millor when Pete was loosely in charge of the team on our sunshine breaks because Cloughie wasn't too keen on flying.

Pete's death didn't come as a total shock, however, because I knew he had been ill for three years. His heart gave out in the end but what got him was pulmonary fibrosis which scars the lungs and progressively takes the victim's breath away.

Back at Derby, Dennis Wise had been coming from Wimbledon in the summer. Cox had set his stall out, told Maxwell that reinforcements were absolutely imperative and been told: "Get on with it, then." Wise's transfer fee, wages, length of contract, everything was in place for him to leave Plough Lane.

Then the owner had a change of heart, everything went quiet and the spiky, little midfield player went up the District Line instead to Chelsea for £1.6million. And instead of playing for us, Dennis made his debut for the Blues against Derby as we lost 2-1 at Stamford Bridge.

Shortly before Christmas, Micklewhite completed what I thought was a remarkable turnaround at home to Chelsea with 15 minutes to go, scoring to give us a 4-3 lead after we had trailed 3-1 at half-time.

Following a tortuous start to the 1990-91 season, six defeats and three draws in the opening nine matches, it seemed for one wonderful moment that Micklewhite was delivering a fifth win in seven games and, with it, mid-table respectability.

What happened next that afternoon – and for the following four months – almost defied belief.

We defended so abjectly that Wise, the smallest man on the pitch, scored a header and left-back Graeme Le Saux tapped one in as Chelsea fought back to win 6-4 towards the start of a club record run of 20 games without a win.

The team surrendered again to lose 7-1 at home to Liverpool and although Southampton were smashed 6-2 when they pitched up in May, Derby were down by then.

It was almost as pathetic as it was avoidable.

We had England players in defence in Shilton and Wright plus a couple of solid, reliable players in attack in Saunders and Goddard, but having successfully established ourselves back in the First Division, the club had been trying to tread water.

And that's an impossible trick to pull off, because if you're not moving forward, ticking over by adding one or two quality players every season, you are in reality going backwards.

Derby needed to strengthen around Shilton, Wright, Saunders and Goddard. Maxwell chose not to do so, and we all paid a high price.

Without further investment, we looked vulnerable and the First Division was a merciless place against teams of superior all-round quality.

Following relegation, Maxwell recouped £5.4million by selling Saunders and Wright to Liverpool – then four months later he was dead, drowned in mysterious circumstances while his luxury yacht was moored off Tenerife. He was facing a financial meltdown.

Lionel Pickering was now the big noise, a committed fan and local journalist who made his fortune from a free newspaper empire, and the boom times were back when he invested £13million to become the majority shareholder.

For an outlay of that magnitude, you could hardly blame him for taking a keen interest in the running of the club.

Cox sussed out the situation and would not entertain Pickering at any price, passing him on to Jimmy Sirrel, our chief scout having retired as Notts County manager.

"Jimmy will educate you and tell you everything you need to know," Arthur explained to Pickering, as if he was doing him a favour. "He has forgotten more about football than I'll ever know."

So Sirrel was lumbered with the job of spending hours talking to Pickering about football in general, our players, youth policy, potential transfer targets – and particularly where his riches were going to be spent and reassuring him that he would be getting value for money.

Pickering's quest for knowledge was insatiable and he was soon dropping by every day seeking out poor Jimmy for discussions that lasted for hours.

Within a fortnight, Sirrel came to us pleading: "You've got to make him stop, Arthur. He's driving me crackers and I can't do my scouting and follow-ups properly." Cox merely gave Jimmy a cruel smile and said: "It's a tough job, Jimmy, but somebody has to do it. Roy and myself are busy men too, you know."

A campaign of massive upheaval on and off the pitch saw Derby go within two points of returning to the top flight automatically at the first time of asking and featuring in the inaugural Premier League.

Despite missing out narrowly to Middlesbrough, promotion through the play-offs looked a distinct possibility when two of our forwards, Marco Gabbiadini and Tommy Johnson, scored against Kenny Dalglish's Blackburn in the first leg at Ewood Park. Leading 2-0 with 75 minutes still to play, what do you do? Stick or twist? The spring sunshine in 1992 scrambled the lads' brains. They became passive, Blackburn seized the initiative and fought back to take a 4-2 lead to the Baseball Ground where we could do no better than win 2-1 on the night. By virtue of away goals, 3-1 would have seen us through and we missed a stream of chances in a one-sided second half.

In the battle of the millionaire owners, Jack Walker went to Wembley where Blackburn beat Leicester 1-0 while Pickering tackled Cox over what needed to be done to guarantee promotion next time.

Eyebrows were raised when centre-half Craig Short arrived from Notts County for £2.5million – the highest fee a club outside the top flight had paid and a British record for a defender. Lionel also bankrolled the purchases of another member of the back four for £600,000, Darren Wassall, who had fallen out with Clough, and the midfield was reinforced by Martin Kuhl, who came from Portsmouth for £650,000 to play alongside Wales international Mark Pembridge, an earlier £1.25million investment from Luton.

Ten home League defeats – matched only by relegated Brentford and Bristol Rovers – proved disastrous as we limped home in eighth place at the end of the 1992-93 season.

We arguably took our eyes off the main business in a season

which featured 64 matches, including nine in the FA Cup and League Cups and another nine in the Anglo-Italian Cup, where we reached the final.

If we weren't going up automatically, Pickering craved a big day out at Wembley and glory through the play-off final.

He did get to go to the twin towers but the Anglo-Italian job proved to be another letdown.

Our opponents Cremonese were backed by a few hundred supporters in a gate of 37,024, which gave an indication of how much a rare trip to Wembley meant to our fans.

Cremonese were a technically gifted team, we knew that because they had come over and beaten us 3-1 earlier in the tournament, but they were also masters of some spiteful dark arts which the Spanish referee refused to acknowledge.

Despite their talent, Cremonese were unnerved by the volume and intensity of our support and went out to win by fair means and foul, which they did, repeating that 3-1 scoreline.

Fourteen months later, I led out Derby at Wembley again, in the play-off final this time, having been assured that I was getting the sack regardless of the result against Leicester.

Arthur Cox had succumbed to a chronic back condition. In football parlance, he had taken the club as far as he could in nine years and agreed a retirement package.

Things weren't falling apart but, equally, Arthur was exasperated by the struggle to put together another promotion-winning side.

With Cox laid up at home in Barton-under-Needwood, I effectively ran the team for several weeks before officially replacing him as manager in October 1993 and celebrating with a 5-3 home win over West Brom.

Our form was very inconsistent, and it was a relief to finish sixth and bag the last place in the play-offs against Mick McCarthy's Millwall.

We were fortunate to beat the Londoners 2-0 at home in the first leg of the semi-finals. They played some very good stuff and I thought we would have our hands full at the New Den. Instead it was the Millwall stewards and the Metropolitan police who were at full stretch dealing with two pitch invasions by the home fans who tried to force the game to be abandoned as we wrapped up a 5-1 win on aggregate.

A nasty night saw our keeper Martin Taylor belted and bumped all over the place by a couple of thugs and there was also an element of racism as our black players, notably a physically shaken Paul Williams, were targeted by hooligans. On our way out of the ground, in the safety of our coach, we saw that the Radio Derby car had been rolled onto its roof – a desperately sad image.

My mood was not enhanced when I was told by an impeccable source that the club were preparing to get rid of me.

Three men wanted me out – but vice-chairman Pickering was not one of them. I found the news very difficult to stomach. We had played some delightful attacking football in between all the nonsense at Millwall and were on such a high that Wembley couldn't come quickly enough.

When I took over the reins from Cox, my first move was to find a right-hand man and I wanted Colin Todd from Bolton, where he was Bruce Rioch's assistant. That plan collapsed when Pickering refused to meet Bolton's request for compensation.

Health problems obliged Sirrel to retire, so I brought in another esteemed former team-mate, Alan Durban, to help me run the show. Durbs was even more shocked than me that my services were no longer required, despite the fact Derby were potentially 90 minutes from bagging a place in the Premier League.

I had been associated with the club for 25 years and I thought I was still doing a good job. For three powerful men, evidently that wasn't enough.

Mind you, I don't know why I should have been surprised.

After all, this was Derby County – the club which could frequently give the Borgias a run for their money when it came to intrigue, politics and infighting.

I didn't have a clue where my future lay after Wembley, where we took the lead against Leicester through livewire Tommy Johnson only to lose to a pair of goals from Steve Walsh.

So much went wrong for us that sunny Bank Holiday Monday afternoon it wasn't true.

Paul Kitson, our very talented striker, failed a fitness test the night before the game, and a fully fit Kitson might have made all the difference.

Williams slipped on the line and ducked beneath Walsh's tame header to give Leicester a soft equaliser; John Harkes missed a sitter when he was clean through and the referee Roger Milford didn't want to end his career on a controversial note.

I happen to like Roger, and consider him a good referee, but he made several quite poor decisions and when the time came to send off Paul Grayson for a clear professional foul on Johnson after an hour, he took the easy option and gave the defender a slap on the wrist in the form of a yellow card. I am a firm believer in officials never retiring with an important game.

Maybe it was simply fate that decided events in Leicester's

favour. They had lost the previous two play-off finals, to Blackburn and Swindon. Perhaps it would just have been too cruel on Little had he completed a hat-trick of failures. He sent out a team against us with the primary intention of not losing, and it worked.

Had we won, the plan was for the team to stop off near the M1 on the way home for a slap-up celebratory meal, but that was hastily cancelled.

Lin had driven our car down to London with Beth, who was on her way back to Bristol University, and the three of us made a pit stop at the Compleat Angler at Marlow off the M4 where we downed a gin and tonic apiece in complete silence. The journey to Bristol to drop off Beth, then the long haul up to Derby, was mentally draining. So much was racing through my mind, yet Lin and I barely spoke. Where would I get another job? How long would it take? Did I make mistakes at Wembley? How could I have affected the match to Derby's advantage?

For weeks that summer I anticipated a phone call requesting me to come in and negotiate the terms of my departure but nothing happened.

It was weird, yet my sense of a reprieve disappeared at a board meeting when Pickering announced: "I want half my money back, I want £6million back."

All eyes around the table turned to me – I knew my remit was now to sell Derby's best players, and my negotiations would be like a suicide note in instalments because flogging our riches would make my job untenable.

Having finished sixth in the table, I needed a few more quality players, not to see our stars packing their bags.

Stuart Webb was friendly with Aston Villa chairman Doug

Ellis, who agreed to sign Johnson and right-back Gary Charles for a combined fee of £2.9million, while Kitson brought in £2.25million from Newcastle where Cox had re-emerged as manager Kevin Keegan's assistant.

After our best players were flogged off, Pickering moaned about the poor campaign we were enduring. I told him not to blame me because I wasn't the one who agreed to the sales, yet he had the effrontery to tell the press that he hadn't wanted to reclaim any of his fortune.

The instability had predictable results and as the 1994-95 season drifted to a close with Derby in mid-table obscurity, the jungle drums started to beat out the message: "McFarland is going".

I knew I was on borrowed time and requested a meeting with Pickering at his home, the elegant Ednaston Manor. Lionel also held court frequently over a few pints at the Yew Tree Inn, which he owned in the village, but on this occasion we were perfectly at ease over a pot of tea.

I said: "Come on, Lionel, we both know the story – my contract is up at the end of the season. I won't be here next year, will I?"

He was reluctant to give me a straight answer to my question, saying: "Roy, I would rather leave it," but I pressed on: "Be fair, there's only two or three games left and I want to plan for the future."

Pickering did indicate that my contract was up but, in fact, it had another 12 months to run. I asked again: "Tell me, Lionel. I won't be here next year, will I?"

He took a deep breath, leaned forward in his armchair and said: "No, you won't be, Roy. I do appreciate what you've done for Derby County, but you're not staying."

No sooner had I thanked him for putting me out of my misery than he launched into an amazing attack on the Gang of Three, the men who had been plotting against me for ages.

"Mind you," he confided, "I'm not sure about some of the people I've got on the board." One he described as "a horrible, slimy little bastard, a conniving, slippery bloke". Another, Pickering said, he could "never trust" while of the third he was simply "unsure". I thanked Lionel again and thought to myself: "I'm glad to be out of this set-up."

Incompatibility on the pitch also played a part in our failure to reclaim a place in the top flight.

The two principal strikers, Gabbiadini and Kitson could not stand the sight of each other, and certainly did not respect each other. Paul felt that Marco was very greedy and that while he was prepared to work the flanks and square the ball, Marco was never prepared to reciprocate.

When your two main forwards won't work together, you have a major problem. Kitson disliked Gabbiadini intensely and they caused a rift in the dressing room with rival cliques forming.

As young players, they should all have been going out together, drinking, eating and celebrating. I tried my best to get the bonding to work but it was an unrewarding task.

As hot-headed and greedy in front of goal as he was, I liked Gabbiadini and I liked the fact he walked around the place with a smile on his face, rather than a scowl.

We possessed youth, pace, a lovely guy in Johnson, a nice balance to the team but it wasn't enough because we lacked a crucial ingredient, a character in the mould of John Gregory to dictate play in midfield and spray passes around.

To his credit, Kitson apologised to me at a golf do just a few years ago. He had kept everything bottled up for years but it all came gushing out over a few drinks as he confessed to having behaved like an idiot at Derby and still felt guilty about the way he had spurned my advice and offers of help.

My professional association with the club ended on April 29, 1995, with the penultimate game of the season.

I wish it could have been a match of some significance – against Liverpool or Manchester United maybe – but our opponents were Southend and, to make matters worse, we lost 2-1.

At the final whistle, I ventured onto that scruffy, dry rectangle which had been the source of so much joy in my career and raised my hands to applaud the fans.

They sensed I was waving goodbye and responded warmly. It was a fitting way to go.

I should have stayed longer at Bradford, and I should never have spent so long as Arthur's assistant.

He was very good at his job, and I learned a hell of a lot from him, but in terms of my career, 10 years as a No.2 to Taylor and Cox was too long and I should have struck out on my own and gone somewhere else.

But despite all the aggravation behind the scenes, this was the club I loved, we were a comfortable fit during the good times – and even the bad times – and my family was here.

Derby made a big play to bring in Steve Bruce from United to replace me but Fergie demanded that he stayed at Old Trafford to see out his playing career.

Jim Smith came up from Portsmouth to take the job instead and played a masterstroke by appointing Steve McClaren as his first-team coach, the catalyst for a successful promotion campaign.

I went to prison.

24

Last In, First Out

SEVERAL Derby players had dealings with a financial advisor, who proved extremely inventive at investing their money abroad before being caught, convicted of embezzlement and sentenced to a spell in the slammer.

He was transferred to Sudbury Open Prison in south Derbyshire, where the inmates threw a dinner party to raise funds for a charity.

I was only too happy to part with some cash in the aid of a good cause and was rewarded with an outstanding meal.

My solicitor was adamant that I had a year's option on my contract when it was terminated, but the club disagreed.

I had not heard anything from either party for some time and was growing concerned when I spotted Derby's legal eagle with me in the nick at the dinner and grabbed him. "Is my solicitor right?" I asked him, and the reply was: "One hundred per cent, Roy."

That was a great relief. I knew I had a safety net and wouldn't have to start scrabbling around for another job.

Derby paid me 50 per cent of my year's money and I thought that settlement was quite fair. I could move on in my life with no financial worries or the possibility of instigating court action. After spending so long at the Baseball Ground, the last thing I wanted was to be walking away with any recriminations and a sour taste in my mouth.

Huddersfield chairman Terry Fisher was on the phone to enquire if I was interested in their managerial vacancy, and I certainly was. Neil Warnock had taken the Terriers into Division One through the play-offs before heading to Plymouth. The Yorkshire club had already moved from their antiquated old home at Leeds Road into the superb new McAlpine Stadium and the future looked bright.

I knew I wasn't the only candidate but after a second interview, from the tone of the directors I met, I was almost convinced the Huddersfield job was mine.

Then came a more tempting offer, courtesy of Bolton chairman Gordon Hargreaves.

Bruce Rioch had worked wonders at Burnden Park over a couple of seasons and was off to Arsenal as a replacement for George Graham. With Colin Todd at his side, Bruce had won promotion to the Premier League and also led the club to a League Cup final, where they were far from disgraced in losing 2-1 to Liverpool.

Toddy was staying and Hargreaves believed that two heads

were better than one as he offered me the post of joint-manager. I had been on the verge of telling him that I was going to Huddersfield, but managing in the top flight again was simply too tempting an opportunity to ignore, especially as it meant working closely with a very good friend. The prospect excited me.

Colin and I had never fallen out or had a major argument and I was sure we could do the business together successfully as equal partners.

While Colin concentrated on the players he knew well who were already at Bolton, I took a slight initiative in the transfer market and spotted a versatile character at Middlesbrough who I knew could provide a bit of steel and do us a job as a deep-lying midfielder or emergency centre-half.

Colin was well aware of the player too, but when the chairman and I instigated negotiations, he was adamant: "I don't want anything to do with that, leave me out of it."

The player was Andy Todd, his son, and Colin had no wish to be accused of favouritism within the ranks.

I cursed the loss of Jason McAteer in early September – even if his transfer raked in £4.5million from Liverpool – but I wouldn't have a word said against the young Irishman, who had a formidable work-rate and could also steal you a goal.

We wanted him to stay, but his head had been turned. He was undoubted Premier League quality and left a conspicuous hole in midfield.

Jason had probably clinched his move to the club he supported while growing up on Merseyside with his performance against Roy Evans' side in the League Cup final at Wembley.

He was already an established international performer who

had sampled World Cup action with Jack Charlton's men in America the previous summer.

At 24, Jason was the perfect age to take the step up in class and I knew how strong the pull was from Anfield because I had often dreamed of running out there in a red shirt to applaud the Kop.

Colin and I spent £1.5million of the McAteer money on Sasa Curcic, from Partizan Belgrade, a gifted Yugoslav who loved his football.

The Bolton faithful were bubbling on his debut in October when Curcic helped us to a very satisfying 1-0 win over Arsenal, but it was soon apparent that for all his creative talent and the excitement he generated going forward, Sasa neglected his defensive duties and had a suspect work ethic.

We badgered him, stressing the importance of doing the dirty, grafting, sweaty spadework as well as the eye-catching stuff, and although he did his best, it didn't make much difference and at times the team carried him.

Scott Sellars arrived from Newcastle and settled in quickly to provide experience and a decent level of industry in central midfield, while Chris Fairclough, another seasoned campaigner who learned his trade under Brian Clough at Forest, gave the club sterling service for several years in central defence.

Two of my undoubted favourite Bolton players, were Scottish strikers Owen Coyle and John McGinlay. Neither of them were the tallest, but they were tireless and their attitude was first class.

Keeping Bolton up at the first time of asking was always going to be a tough ask for anybody, especially following the departures of Rioch and McAteer. It was difficult from the first game of the season, a 3-2 defeat at Wimbledon, and some players found the gulf between the First Division and the Premier League a massive step up in class.

Enthusiasm, attitude and guts can only take you so far. There are some easy games – but none when you're new boys down at the foot of the table.

It was deeply frustrating, the mixture wasn't right on the pitch or in our managers' office.

I had deep misgivings about my partnership with Colin from an early stage. I think we both soon realised our joint-manager venture wasn't working. Responsibility needed to be clearly defined. The buck always has to stop with one man, the manager, and he needs help and support from below.

Several players brought their problems and insecurities to me, and if they didn't like what I had to say, they shuffled off and tried to get an alternative response from Colin. Others that saw me were worried Colin might think they were going behind his back, and vice versa.

At half-time, I'd come in and talk, then Toddy would have his say. It was farcical.

Apart from the Arsenal match, we won one other League match before the new year, way back in August against champions Blackburn before confidence started to erode.

Two victories in the first half of the season looks pathetic, but it doesn't tell the full story. We were on the wrong end of several unjust results and, although the squad was not strong enough, I would not knock the players for their level of performance, spirit and attitude.

If Colin and I did disagree, it was occasionally over tactics for an away match against one of the top sides.

He was always a confirmed 4-4-2 man, but I felt we might have more joy going 4-5-1, which is by no means as cautious as it looks providing your two wide midfield men have the nous to bomb forward when it's appropriate to make a 4-3-3 formation. We also operated with a sweeper, but it was useless fiddling too much on the training ground because players brought up on a strict regime of 4-4-2 became confused.

As defeat followed defeat and autumn turned to winter, with a handful of draws against Everton, Nottingham Forest and Tottenham for comfort, Hargreaves spoke to Colin and myself and left us in no doubt what would happen if results did not improve: "If anyone goes, it's going to be you, Roy. Sorry, but last in, first out."

I wasn't happy, but I understood how football works.

Once you realise it's a 'no', you must accept it. It hurts, but you can't talk yourself back into a job.

The end came on New Year's Day 1996 with Bolton bottom of the table having lost 4-2 at Sheffield Wednesday. I was bitterly disappointed not to have been a success, Colin and I had both put so much effort in.

In terms of arriving at a settlement, Bolton did it right. I had only served six months of a three-year contract but the chairman made me a generous offer and everything was done and dusted in one meeting.

I wished Toddy the very best of luck, and knew he would need more than that to keep the club up, shook hands with the chairman, backroom staff, players and was on my way.

I could not criticise the Bolton players for their efforts, they were nothing but supportive. I was proud to have been in the trenches with them but despite all our frantic digging and fighting, we never escaped those trenches. Relegation became a formality.

A striker of Alan Shearer's genius would have made all the difference – and it wasn't long before I was officially on the Football Association payroll and seeing a great deal of Newcastle's world record £15million centre-forward.

England boss Glenn Hoddle's No.2 John Gorman never forgot how I spoke up on his behalf in the press and said it was shameful that he'd lost a managerial job earlier in his career. We'd bumped into each other over the years, got on well and had a drink or two.

Gorman called to commiserate over losing the Bolton job and to offer me the opportunity to be Hoddle's eyes and ears from the Midlands to the North East as England's northern scout, while Glenn Roeder worked the southern half of the country.

I needed no persuading to accept a tidy little retainer with travelling expenses for 10 months. It was a nice job and now, from the vantage point of the best seats in the nation's top stadiums, I could revel in the talent of players such as Shearer and Paul Scholes, at Manchester United, where before I was in a dugout and cursing those two as they tormented Bolton.

Because I'd been a centre-half, I could appreciate what Shearer brought to the party more than most.

Pele and George Best were exceptional players and, on his day, Shearer was at that level too with his heading ability, shooting power in both feet, tackling, pace to burn and willingness to come back and defend.

You need bravery to hold the ball up when you're leading the line and getting a kicking and elbows in the kidneys, and Shearer had that courage in spades.

I hope Hoddle didn't think my reports from Newcastle matches were one-dimensional because I frequently wrote along these lines: "Alan Shearer's all-round game was again outstanding, with no discernible weak points. He has, if anything, grown in stature as a player since moving from Blackburn."

25

Abbey Returns

TREVOR BENJAMIN was an innocent lad at Cambridge United with more than his fair share of problems, a tough upbringing and an absentee dad.

I spent countless hours training him in the wind and rain, nurturing his development, helping him as much as I could with his personal life, providing a shoulder to cry on and, eventually, having the huge satisfaction of seeing Benjamin develop into a £1million striker by the age of 21, bound for the Premier League.

And that's the moment when it all began to turn sour for me in the Fens.

It started with a row too after Ron Jukes, my old Derby scout, ordered me to apply for the vacant post at the Abbey Stadium.

Ron was quite aggressive, saying: "It will be a good job for you, Roy. Think about it, but you can't afford to wait because they've already done the interviews and Brian Laws is favourite. Get in there now."

I did not take kindly to Ron's bullying tactics and told him so. I certainly wasn't going to rush into anything, reasoning I needed a day or two to decide if I fancied a proposal dropped into my lap without warning.

I knew the England scouting role wouldn't last for ever and that I wanted to clamber back onto the managerial merry-go-round – just at a higher level than Division Three.

Then I had a change of heart and said to myself: "What the hell!" and, at Jukes' insistence, called Ron Atkinson, a former Cambridge manager who had the ear of the chairman, Reg Smart.

Big Ron's endorsement earned me an interview the following day late in 1996 at the Moat House, just outside Cambridge, where I was confronted by Smart and his full board of directors.

They quizzed me long and hard about what I thought of their team, the style of football I proposed to play if fortunate enough to get the job, and what my plans might be regarding promotion and the club's prospects. I returned home around 10.30pm and half an hour later Smart was on the phone offering me the position. Another five minutes and we had agreed the terms of my contract.

A local builder made good, Smart was excellent for the club. Although we were to have lots of disagreements and rows, I had plenty of respect for him because he loved the U's passionately.

I was delighted to be back in business, succeeding Tommy

Taylor who had upped sticks and returned to his east London roots at Leyton Orient.

Tommy was not going to be an easy act to follow as he'd left the side in good shape, sitting comfortably in second place but my debut match in November against Welling in the first round of the FA Cup could hardly have started more encouragingly, Billy Beall scoring after 74 seconds to pave the way to a 3-0 success.

I accepted a few welcoming slaps on the back in the clubhouse, but warned those supporters: "Just don't expect us to score that early every week."

I knew it would take time to adapt to a new environment, stamp my personality on the team, and that I had inherited a few players who rated Taylor and would not turn up their noses at an approach to follow him to Brisbane Road.

One of those was midfield man David Preece, who I considered vital to my plans. He had played for Jim Smith briefly at Derby and the best part of his career at Luton under David Pleat. I needed a reliable assistant who would double as player-coach and successfully sold him the idea over dinner in Northampton with our wives, Lin and Louise, when we talked families, kids, job satisfaction and I emphasised the daily grind of commuting between his home in Luton and Leytonstone.

He was an excellent talent-spotter with first-class contacts and his connections led us to a centre-forward at Walsall whose career was faltering under Chris Nicholl.

Preece took one look at Martin Butler playing in the reserves and told me: "Gaffer, we've got to sign him." I went up to take a look for myself and needed 30 minutes to agree.

I saw Butler score and miss a couple of chances, but at least he was in the right position to have a pop at goal. Also in his favour was the fact he could head, tackle, spin off central defenders and make their life a misery with his movement. He was so enthusiastic, a constant threat, and I told Preece: "This guy would chase a piece of paper."

It didn't take much haggling to persuade Nicholl to sell Butler. We shook hands on a fee of £22,500. If Nicholl was happy with the money, I was simply delighted. Less than three years later, Butler was on his way to Reading, and Cambridge had a guarantee of £750,000 in the bank.

Alex Russell was another diamond, a Scouser after my own heart. He had played over 100 games for Rochdale before we picked him up and provided tremendous guidance in midfield, linking the play with organisational talent. Russell made the game look simple, and that is an art in itself.

I went back to Derby to sign a young central midfielder, Ian Ashbee. He was raw but developed out of all proportion and went on to great things, captaining Hull City in the Premier League.

Ashbee formed a strong partnership with Russell and Paul Wanless, a bundle of energy who brought me goals running from midfield.

We also had a real gem of a left-back in Danny Granville, clearly destined for bigger and better things. When Chelsea appeared waving a cheque for £300,000, the deal was swiftly concluded and I wished Danny all the best, telling him to look and learn from his new boss at Stamford Bridge, Ruud Gullit.

He did, and little more than a year later Danny performed out of his skin as Chelsea beat Stuttgart 1-0 to win the UEFA Cup Winners' Cup in Stockholm.

The exodus of bright young things had started. Cambridge were in no position to refuse decent offers and in my first summer at the club we accepted £250,000 from Watford for midfielder Micah Hyde and £300,000 from Sunderland for central defender Jody Craddock.

You always have mixed feelings when your best talents depart, knowing it's ultimately futile to try and stand in their way. You hope they do themselves justice, yet you're still disappointed because it means your chances of success are diminished.

And managers being what they are, and professional football the hard-nosed business it is, after each big sale the temptation is to knock on the chairman's door and ask him: "What's in it for me? What percentage of that money do I get to buy a replacement?"

My team-building plans were sabotaged by losing Granville, Hyde, Craddock and Matt Joseph, and set me back to such an extent that having finished 10th at the end of my first season, we could do no better than 16th place in 1997-98.

No one wants to hear excuses and I knew I would soon be looking for alternative employment if United underachieved again – but redemption was just around the corner.

Sometimes cup runs obscure the main task in hand, on other occasions they prove invaluable in boosting team morale and exciting supporters.

Cambridge had more chance of flying to the moon than winning the Worthington Cup but our involvement in the competition convinced myself and, perhaps more importantly, the players that we were good enough to win promotion from the bottom tier.

In the space of 18 days we met First Division Watford three

times, starting with a friendly win before knocking them out of the Cup 2-1 on aggregate, and Graham Taylor was magnanimous enough to admit we had been the better side in all three matches, insisting we were a banker bet to go up.

This was a good Watford side, too, which went on to win the play-offs and claim a place in the Premier League.

While the former England manager was encouraging punters to have a few bob on us, not even our most ardent supporters fancied our chances in the second round against Premier League Sheffield Wednesday, who had beaten both Tottenham and Blackburn 3-0 in the League.

I would never ever decry the impact foreign players have had on British football, but sometimes they just don't 'get' matches in our domestic cup competitions.

I noticed Danny Wilson had six continentals on his teamsheet: Italian strikers Paolo Di Canio and Benito Carbone, Norwegian winger Petter Rudi, Dutch midfielder Wim Jonk, Argentinian right-back Juan Cobian and Brazilian centre-half Emerson Thome.

And I wondered just how motivated they would be in front of a sparse home crowd of under 10,000 against Cambridge, a city most of them would be hard-pushed to locate on a map.

I knew Danny would be in the dressing room, doing his best to stoke them up, yet I suspected Di Canio and Carbone might be laughing and joking, and saying: "Yeah, yeah gaffer. Don't worry, we hear you." And that's if they didn't think it was a bit beneath them to be turning out against my lot, put together for the princely sum of £42,000. Their minds might even be on the next home game, against Arsenal. At least, that's what I hoped.

Danny knew the score from his previous job at Barnsley and early playing career, scuffling around at the bottom of football's food chain at Bury and Chesterfield. If your preparation is poor, if you start slowly, take things for granted, no matter how superior your team looks on paper, football has this terrible habit of biting you on the backside.

Wednesday didn't perform like a fraction of an outfit which had cost £22million to assemble, and we held on for 87 minutes for a 1-0 win, courtesy of 'Bruno' – our 19-year-old forward Benjamin, who bore a passing resemblance to Britain's world heavyweight boxing champion.

Benjamin was rewarded for chasing an early sloppy backpass, charging down keeper Kevin Pressman's attempted clearance and getting up swiftly off the pitch to walk the ball into the net.

Danny was unstinting in his criticism of his 'Fancy Dans' who hadn't fancied it enough, but I was more concerned with ensuring the lads knew they still faced a monumental task.

Hillsborough was a most satisfying win, but Wednesday had the second leg to get their house in order and salvage their pride. Our supporters were near fever pitch for the return, swelling the crowd to 8,502, the club's biggest attendance for six years and their mood dipped for only five minutes midway through the second half.

That was the time between Wednesday taking the lead when the ball skidded off Jamie Campbell's head past Arjan Van Heusden for a crazy own goal, and the equaliser.

Then Benjamin was at it again, restoring our overall lead with a thumping header when Alex Russell found him with a free-kick as we edged through 2-1 on aggregate.

The Wednesday ties came during an unbeaten spell which

saw us rise from 11th to fifth in the table before we ventured north again to do battle with another Premier League outfit.

Nottingham Forest were in disarray and bore the hallmarks of a club ripe for a second relegation in three seasons.

Brian Clough had been gone for five years, since when they had gone through Frank Clark and Stuart Pearce as managers before giving the job to Dave Bassett, who was experiencing unparalleled grief with his prolific, but moody centre-forward Pierre Van Hooijdonk.

The Dutchman was on strike in Holland, training with his old club NAC Breda, after being denied a transfer.

Van Hooijdonk's bone of contention was that Forest had promised to make major signings to cope with life back at the top but, not only were those signings not forthcoming, the club's new owners sold his forward partner Kevin Campbell and let captain Colin Cooper move to Middlesbrough.

I didn't have a shred of sympathy for Van Hooijdonk. His actions were unprofessional. He let down his team-mates and the Forest fans. I could have hugged him though, because his absence didn't harm our chances at the City Ground one little bit and we arrived with Forest on the floor following a 5-1 mauling at Liverpool.

The conditions that October evening in the East Midlands were near-perfect for another giant-killing but I had a nagging feeling from the kick-off that something wasn't quite right and I knew what it was.

Injuries meant I had to blood our third-choice goalkeeper, 20-year-old Shaun Marshall, while trainee defender Martin McNeil came in for his full debut because Marc Joseph had damaged his thigh.

The second half was barely a minute old when I got a nauseous feeling in the pit of my stomach as Forest established a 3-0 lead.

Young Marshall had been to blame for one of the goals, but now he started playing like a man possessed, pulling off a string of wonder saves from Marlon Harewood.

I could swallow going out, but not like this. Even with three strikers on the pitch, we weren't giving their keeper Dave Beasant and his back four anything to worry about. I swore quietly under my breath, turned to right-winger Michael Kyd and told him: "Get ready, son. You're going on."

Defender Jamie Campbell came off, but it wasn't really a gamble. We were as good as out anyway. I simply wanted to make Forest sweat a bit because losing to them especially rankled if you had Derby connections.

Kyd was a very handy performer, but we hadn't seen him in action for a couple of months because of a dodgy knee.

Within five minutes, Kyd had set up a goal for Benjamin, then Butler scored and it was 3-3 when John Taylor slotted in a penalty, awarded for handball on the line by Forest's French defender Thierry Bonalair, who was shown the red card.

Now it was the turn of 'Harry' Bassett and his assistant manager Micky Adams to look the worse for wear.

Extra-time could not separate the sides and not until sudden death in the penalty shoot-out did we succumb.

Even then, defeat felt like a moral victory, and I made sure the lads went up to salute our fans, who had provided tremendous vocal support the whole evening despite many of them being soaked to the skin.

It was time to concentrate on the League and, with confidence rarely wavering, we hit top spot in early March with a 3-0 win at Exeter.

While there were rich memories for those U's fans who enjoyed our Worthington Cup exploits at Watford, Hillsborough and Forest, those who made it to Rochdale in a crowd of 1,408 on a Tuesday night in April 1999 will never forget the 2-0 win at Spotland which clinched promotion with three games to spare.

All season our superb level of fitness had enabled us to plunder important late goals, but it looked very much as if we would be frustrated with Dale defiant until the last 10 minutes when I threw on Taylor, our 34-year-old player-coach.

'Shaggy' was so often a game-breaker and now I was crying out for someone to break the deadlock in our favour.

Within moments, he set up the move which saw Benjamin taken down in the penalty area, and Taylor stepped up to score the resulting spot-kick before heading in a corner.

The long trip to Lancashire for a rearranged midweek fixture, allied to the fact that we were virtually up and over the finishing line with matches still to come against Plymouth, Swansea and Brentford, meant the travelling support was around 300. Shortly after Taylor's second goal they halted their conga on the terraces to invade the sandy pitch and swamp the players in Cambridge hats and scarves.

Then it was down to some serious business ... the champagne always tastes best when you have landed a serious prize.

I had heroes all over the park that season, but nobody contributed more efficiently than my three main strikers. Between them, Butler, Taylor and Benjamin were responsible for 44 of our 78 League goals.

Going up as champions would have been ideal, but Brentford

pipped us for that honour by four points after winning the final game at the Abbey 1-0 in a straight shoot-out for the Third Division trophy.

I needed better players, and more of them, if United were to consolidate in the Second Division in 1999-2000 against the likes of Preston, Burnley, Wigan, Millwall and Stoke. That's not being cruel on my promotion winners, it's just the real world.

You go up and players you want to keep are knocking on your door, wanting to know if and when they are going to get a pay rise. My budget wasn't great, neither was the size of the squad, and, ultimately, there were times when we had too many people playing a bit too much football instead of having a rest.

Butler had 14 League goals to his name before Christmas and I expected the phone to ring any minute with an enquiry we would be unable to fend off. Finally, Reading's offer of £750,000 at the beginning of February proved too much of a temptation.

Staying up was an achievement in itself and we managed that by five points, which looked distinctly unlikely in mid-February when a 1-0 defeat at Stoke left us rooted to the foot of the table, eight points from safety. We appeared doomed but the players reacted magnificently.

I may have lacked numbers in the dressing room and on the training pitch, but there was ample character and heart when it mattered. Easter Monday was a strange occasion as we beat David Moyes' Preston 2-0 to clinch safety, bar a freak set of results in the final few games, while results elsewhere meant the visitors celebrated promotion as champions.

Benjamin's stock was rising all the time. He finished with 20 League goals and his partnership with Butler gave us an important cutting edge – but that elusive 'third man', the role previously played convincingly by Taylor, whose career was drawing to a close, was nowhere to be seen.

A third forward reaching double figures might have been the difference between struggling for nine months and a comfortable mid-table finish.

It was only a matter of time before a bigger club made Cambridge an offer they couldn't afford to refuse for Benjamin, but I had no inkling that his transfer would cause such ill-feeling and prove the catalyst for me leaving the club.

Aston Villa had taken a long look at Benjamin, while Sunderland and West Brom were also hovering in the wings.

Meanwhile, Leicester were crying out for a likely lad after selling Emile Heskey to Liverpool for £11million and Peter Taylor, my old England colleague, came on to me initially offering £500,000, which I laughed out of court.

"I'm sorry, Peter, but you're going to have to do much better than that," I told him. "£500,000 puts you way down the list. I'm looking for over £1 million plus add-ons."

Taylor was still deliberating in July when I went on holiday and my final phone call to Filbert Street was to give him my contact numbers in Majorca as we promised to keep in touch and sort things out, manager to manager.

I was very upset to learn that Smart then took it upon himself to ring Taylor and negotiate a down payment of £800,000, rising to £1.25million based on appearances.

All transfer deals were strictly my remit and I was on an agreed bonus when the club made a profit on the sale of a player whose market value I had helped to enhance.

Smart agreed I deserved a bonus – but offered me just one-tenth of what I considered I was due, and that would only have amounted to £2,000. But it was the principle of the thing that mattered most.

I demanded to see the board of directors to put my case, but they were bitter and nasty, insisting that as the chairman had completed Benjamin's transfer, I was lucky to be getting any sort of cut whatsoever.

Feeling betrayed, I told them exactly what I thought of all of them to a man. Not the wisest thing to do.

I pointed out the folly of accepting £800,000 when Taylor had more or less agreed with me to stump up at least £1million up front.

Later I told them that I would not set foot in the boardroom after games, and I didn't.

So there was understandable tension in the air at the start of the new campaign. I was about to board the bus for our trip home from Bournemouth with a satisfactory point in the bag after the first match of the season when a director handed me an official letter from the club.

It warned me that my contract would be terminated forthwith unless my attitude improved. I felt hurt and let down by the contents of the letter as I had always put my heart and soul into the job.

From that day on, it was just a waiting game.

Smart was quickly in again in December to accept Norwich's £350,000 offer for striker Zema Abbey, although I felt we could get more for him.

By this stage, I wasn't remotely interested in any bonus from the sale and knew there would be no cut after what happened with Benjamin. Abbey was a bright boy, a university graduate who got himself an agent, rejected a contract with us and could have left for nothing in the summer – but we still sold him too cheaply.

Smart started coming out with little criticisms and questions which could only have been planted in his mind as former Cambridge manager John Beck, who had enjoyed huge success for a spell with his aggressive brand of long-ball football, appeared on the horizon.

Why was I doing this? Why wasn't I doing that? I can't say I was unsettled any further, but the identity of my successor was already obvious to me.

The end came in February, 2001, when Cambridge sacked me following a run of six defeats in seven games, a spell alleviated only by a 2-0 win at Wycombe. We had dropped to within five points of the relegation zone.

Days of speculation about my future ended with an emergency board meeting, after which the directors issued a statement in which they said: "Roy McFarland will no longer be in charge of first-team affairs with immediate effect."

I say "sacked" but because the U's could scarcely afford compensation they attempted to kick me upstairs in some sort of advisory capacity – but I wasn't having any of that and moved on, while Beck returned to keep the club up.

My last eight months were a trial but the rest of my time at the Abbey was hugely enjoyable and gaining promotion was a fantastic experience. It took maybe two-and-a-half to three years to build the team and get the team right, having lost those great young players at the end of the first season.

That was an achievement that gave me great satisfaction.

26

Tough Torq

"IF you ever get the chance to manage on the south coast, take it – wherever it is". The tip came from Peter Taylor, my old mentor, who was thoroughly content in Brighton in the mid-seventies before Brian Clough persuaded him to return to his Nottingham roots and help Forest win the small matter of the Football League championship and a couple of European Cups.

My mind turned instinctively to Taylor when I fielded a call from Mike Bateson at Torquay offering me the manager's job, and recalled how much Pete had lapped up the sea air and never peddled poor advice. He was right because Lin and I bought an apartment offering a magnificent view of the bay and our quality of life was nothing to be sniffed at.

Bateson was a natural showman and ventriloquist who enlivened social occasions by whipping out Algernon from a suitcase to do a turn. I was first introduced to the menacing-looking dummy, dressed in club blazer and tie, towards the end of a private dinner party at Mike's house. Clearly, Algernon was going to top the bill given the encouragement Bateson had throughout a lovely meal from several directors to "give the boy his chance". Mike resisted with a straight face, insisting: "No, he's fast asleep, I'm not about to worry him," but caved in to the clamour during the coffee, cheese and biscuits. I faced some ugly, frightening characters as a player – but not many who unnerved me as much as Algernon. Conversation flowed around the table but Algernon's eyes constantly swivelled to size me up and I was worried sick I was about to be picked on. Algernon took mercy on me, however, and reserved his choicest put-downs for Mike's wife, daughter and right-hand man Mervyn Benney, who took it all in good heart, as the evening ended with tears of laughter rolling down our cheeks.

When I assessed the Torquay squad I wondered what Peter Taylor would have seen in David Graham, and whether Clough would have persisted with him or driven him to the railway station, bought a one-way ticket to Edinburgh and waited to ensure the Scottish striker boarded the train.

Graham was about to turn 23 and, with serious application and the right mindset, he should have been playing at a far higher level. Rangers had seen enough early potential to give him a start in the game and I struggled to understand why such a talent was at Torquay. He was no dummy but the best player on the books – streets ahead of the others.

Graham possessed a lovely touch, good control and could score goals. But he was lazy and his lack of appetite in matches meant he didn't stamp his authority on proceedings anywhere near enough for my liking.

I told him: "David, if you start playing the way we both know you can, and put in the effort, some big club will come and buy you. Why waste your talent?"

I needed Graham to be a talisman, producing more for a run-of-the-mill side which required a lot of reshaping as David Preece helped me clear out the deadwood and bring in tried and trusted players such as Alex Russell, who followed us from Cambridge, and some eager young thrusters.

Bateson ran the whole show virtually by himself on a shoestring budget but accepted the need to cancel several contracts and pay off a couple of nondescript Frenchmen who were not what I was looking for.

I also needed other places to take the lads apart from our training headquarters at Newton Abbot, a pitch marked out on the dead ground inside the racecourse where the going for footballers was too often soft to heavy in winter and hard at the end of the season.

The club had fallen into a rut and I was very conscious of the need to freshen things up, so we sometimes trained on local parks in Torquay or spent Fridays on the beach doing stretching exercises and the short, sharp stuff.

Golf days were organised – anything to stop the lads growing stale.

The job in Devon was originally mooted a month after I was sacked at Cambridge when Bateson got rid of Wes Saunders.

He already had Colin Lee at Plainmoor as a consultant however and gave him a chance as caretaker manager until the end of the season, which saw the club avoid relegation to the Conference in their last match – a gripping 3-2 win at Barnet which condemned the home side to the drop instead.

Bateson and Lee had a disagreement in July 2001 and it was then I got the call from Mike, who said he wanted an experienced coach who could get a club out of the bottom reaches. He knew I fitted the bill from what I had achieved at Bradford and Cambridge.

Far from harbouring notions of promotion, the season developed into a struggle, although relegation was never an issue because Halifax were so abject and cut adrift by the new year.

I feared the worst, however, after our first three matches, defeats by Bristol Rovers, York and Kidderminster in which we failed to register a single goal.

My old friend the Worthington Cup was responsible for brief respite when we pulled off a fine 2-0 win at Bournemouth that brought us a touch of glamour in the shape of a trip to Tottenham in the second round. My boys thoroughly enjoyed making a nuisance of themselves for an hour at White Hart Lane against the likes of Ledley King, Les Ferdinand and Sergei Rebrov – and so did our fans, chanting: "Are you Barnet in disguise?" when Spurs struggled for a spell.

The American keeper Kasey Keller was making his debut for Glenn Hoddle's team and it can't have been an easy occasion for him, coming just two days after 9/11. Everyone in the ground stood for an immaculately observed minute's silence as a mark of respect after the tragedy in New York, which was felt so keenly by Kasey.

The show had to go on and we gave him a couple of uncomfortable moments. When Chris Perry slammed a clearance into David Graham, the ball ran tantalisingly along the goal-line and then Steve Tully sent in a low centre which David Woozley struck against the bar.

Hoddle introduced Teddy Sheringham at half-time and Spurs increased the pace, winning 2-0 with goals from King and Ferdinand. It was their first step on the path to the final, which they lost 2-1 to Blackburn in Cardiff, while we returned to the coalface, chiselling out precious points.

November proved the bleakest of all months when our sorry 100 per cent record read: played five, lost five.

I had a rueful smile when I spotted an old warhorse using all his experience to plunder the goals for visiting Northampton to send us tumbling out of the FA Cup at the first hurdle. Marco Gabbiadini was still happily putting himself about at 33 while our attack looked chronically short of impact.

I hauled in Graham and Tony Bedeau to give them a good, old-fashioned bollocking about their general lack of effort and passion, and stuck them on the transfer list.

Something must have registered because they were both in the team when the season finished and, in time, Graham got the move his talent warranted when he joined Wigan for £215,000 and helped them into the Premier League.

The collapse of ITV Digital was a huge blow to the finances of Football League clubs and had consequences at Plainmoor where Bateson quickly did his sums and told me: "We've got to save £6,000 a week, Roy. I'm sorry but that means no way we can afford to keep David Preece – he'll have to go."

I asked Bateson not to be so hasty and said: "Why don't we speak to the whole staff and if everybody accepts a small reduction in wages, David can stay," but he was adamant. My right-hand man was out on his ear.

If the chairman believed I would stay at Preece's expense, he was very much mistaken. That would have smacked of disloyalty. The two of us were very much a partnership and I couldn't have looked David in the eye again if I'd stayed.

I resigned in April 2002, three days after a 2-2 draw at Swansea brought the curtain down on a campaign which saw the Gulls finish in 19th place. I used no fewer than 38 players all told but the margin of safety was comfortable. There was certainly no chance of heartbreak on the final day in south Wales.

Torquay was the hardest job I ever had in football and I thought I did a respectable job, although it's not easy to convince people that the final table does have a tendency to lie sometimes.

It was disappointing not to see all the hard work David and I put in bear fruit because Leroy Rosenior inherited a good squad and took them on to promotion a couple of seasons later.

27

Treasure Chest

SOME people were on the pitch ... they thought it was all over when Hurst scored a famous goal.

And while Geoff Hurst's effort to complete an unforgettable hat-trick in the World Cup final in 1966 was toasted throughout the nation, Glynn Hurst's goal will live long in the memory of every Chesterfield supporter at Saltergate on a May day in 2004.

It came in the 87th minute to break the deadlock against Luton and prompted a pitch invasion. After four excruciating minutes of injury time, the referee blew the final whistle – it was all over now – and hordes of fans swarmed on to celebrate the unlikeliest of Great Escapes.

Before kick-off, we had to win to stand a chance of staying in the Second Division and pray a couple of other results went our way. They did: Grimsby and Rushden and Diamonds both losing to take the drop instead as we survived by a solitary point.

I never cease to marvel at football's capacity to lift you from the lowest lows to the highest highs – and I was almost floating that Saturday night, certainly in a better mood than earlier in the season when we conceded five goals inside the opening 20 minutes in a 7-0 hiding at leaders Plymouth. The strange thing is, I never saw that capitulation coming because we'd travelled down to Devon in good spirits on the back of a 1-0 win at Barnsley, our first away victory of the season.

I had been out of work for 13 months when Chesterfield chairman Barrie Hubbard offered me a route back into the game in 2003, signing a two-year contract at a club which had secured its status on the final day of the season with a 1-1 draw at Blackpool.

Knowing the parlous state of the Saltergate finances, I wasn't about to make outlandish claims and raise false hopes by mentioning promotion. Stability and gradual progress was the name of the game.

Saltergate was 20 times worse than the Baseball Ground in terms of facilities and the club was in urgent need of a new stadium.

The project was one of the things that appealed to me about the job but I wasn't there long enough to be in charge when the 10,000-seater b2net Stadium opened for business.

Just like diehard Derby fans never wanted to leave their spiritual home, so Chesterfield supporters had a very fond attachment to Saltergate, but the club had to relocate to move forward and do things on the corporate side.

Chesterfield had been in trouble for financial irregularities under a previous regime, and Hubbard and his associates were keen to restore law and order.

I discovered a very well-run club upheld by traditional, old-fashioned values. The new characters in charge lived locally and first fell in love with the Spireites standing as supporters on the terraces long before joining the board.

I did my damndest to improve the team and, although money was tight, Hubbard always did his best to provide transfer funds. It was reassuring to work for a man who would tell you, honestly: "There's £20,000 in the kitty if you want that money to try for a new player, Roy."

When there was some decent money to work with, I suffered a couple of major blows concerning players who did very well for us. We had taken winger Jamal Campbell-Ryce on loan from Charlton, but he jumped at the chance of bigger wages and playing Championship football at Rotherham.

Then I picked up Sammy Clingan, a talented young midfield player from Wolves, and when his loan with us ended I put in a bid of £80,000 – colossal by Chesterfield's standards – to make the arrangement permanent, only for Gary Megson to wave a cheque for £100,000 in the direction of Molineux. So Clingan, destined to play regularly for Northern Ireland, made his way to Nottingham Forest instead.

The chances of stabilising the club receded before the start of my second campaign in 2004-05 when several key players left for better jobs paying more money.

I wanted an experienced striker and picked up Wayne Allison, from Sheffield United, and thought he might blend well with Tcham N'Toya, a lad from Paris.

Arsenal loaned me Alex Bailey and Mark DeBolla arrived from Chelsea. To my eyes, they were a couple of rough diamonds in need of a polish, and I thought it would be illuminating to see them fighting for their lives every week, playing regularly in front of crowds they weren't used to. Reserve matches didn't mean as much in terms of results.

You often get a measure of a player only when you take him out of his comfort zone, and swapping a London lifestyle for north Derbyshire would certainly do that.

August took me back to Bradford for the first time as a manager in my own right, and I found a friendly face in the manager's office at Valley Parade – Colin Todd.

When Dean Windass scored his second goal to put City 2-0 up, it looked very much as if Toddy would claim the bragging rights, but I made a couple of decisive substitutions and one of them, Caleb Folan, turned the game on its head with two goals after Shane Nicholson had given us a sniff of a chance from the penalty spot.

Despite dropping away in the second half of the season, we survived fairly comfortably with a six-point cushion.

Tottenham kindly loaned me a gifted teenage midfielder early in 2006 for three months with a brief to give him as much game time as possible and toughen him up. Jamie O'Hara impressed with five goals in 19 games and his memory of his debut for us makes me laugh to this day.

Jamie recalls: "I had done well in my first League game against Doncaster. We were drawing 1-1 away. In the last minute we had a free-kick. Everyone went up. I tried to play a short one, dribble around a couple of people and ended up losing it. They went down the other end and hit the post. In the dressing room afterwards the lads were relatively happy and saying a few nice words when the gaffer, Roy McFarland, walked over. He pointed at me and said: 'You do that again and you can fuck off back to Spurs.' That completely changed my mentality. It was a wake-up call. I'll always remember that."

Youth development wasn't what it was, even as recently as my time at Cambridge where I could develop a young player and sell him on. Now clubs simply waited for players to come out of contract and snapped them up, and that made life increasingly tough for the smaller clubs.

In 1997, Chesterfield very nearly beat Bryan Robson's Premier League Middlesbrough, who boasted such exotic talents as Juninho, Emerson, Fabrizio Ravanelli and Gianluca Festa, in an FA Cup semi-final at Old Trafford. But for a debatable refereeing decision, they would have booked their place in history as the first club outside the top two divisions to contest the final.

I was constantly reminded of how close the unfashionable Spireites came to facing Chelsea in the FA Cup final at Wembley as we went on a glorious Carling Cup run in 2006, knocking out Wolves, Manchester City and West Ham at Saltergate before falling just short against Premier League Charlton, losing on penalties following a 3-3 draw.

My hunch that the first-round tie might be decided in similar fashion paid off when we beat Mick McCarthy's Wolves 6-5 on spot-kicks after I'd had the lads doing extra shooting practice from 12 yards in training.

Stuart Pearce needed a trip to our place with City in the next round like a hole in the head. The Premier League strugglers had started the season with away defeats at Chelsea, Reading and Blackburn, and Pearce was haunted by failure at Doncaster at the same stage of the competition 12 months earlier.

He paid us the compliment of picking his strongest side: Nicky Weaver, Sylvain Distin, Micah Richards, Richard Dunne, Stephen Jordan, Claudio Reyna, Trevor Sinclair, Dietmar Hamann, Joey Barton, Georgios Samaras and Bernardo Corradi.

Without labouring the point, it was a formidable line-up especially with Joe Hart, Stephen Ireland, Paul Dickov, Ishmael Miller and DaMarcus Beasley on the substitutes' bench.

I wasn't worried in the slightest because, as rank underdogs, this was a free hit. Lose and nobody would bat an eyelid; win and we'd make the back-page headlines.

Samaras scrambled City ahead shortly before half-time but we stormed back to win 2-1, Folan heading home a free-kick before Derek Niven produced a wonderful volley as City's brittle confidence snapped. Pearce was defiant as much as deflated when I consoled him at the end with the bulk of the 7,960 crowd celebrating as if we'd won the cup.

If I could have hand-picked our opponents in the third round, I would have chosen West Ham. Like City, the Hammers had a track record of embarrassment at the hands of smaller clubs and Alan Pardew's team arrived on the back of seven straight defeats in the Premier League.

Sky sensed an upset too and scheduled the tie for live coverage, which brought us around £200,000 we hadn't budgeted for. That was a massive amount of income for Chesterfield.

The match followed a similar pattern to the City upset, the visitors going ahead before we fought back to win 2-1. Marlon Harewood eased the Hammers' nerves with a classy volley but their jitters returned when Colin Larkin levelled matters and this time Folan scored the winner four minutes from time.

Again, to emphasise the quality of our performance, I think it's valid to look at the team Chesterfield faced that October night: Rob Green, John Pantsil, Danny Gabbidon, Anton Ferdinand, George McCartney, Nigel Reo-Coker, Hayden Mullins, Christian Dailly, Kyel Reid, Harewood and Bobby Zamora. In an effort to turn the tide, Pardew brought on Teddy Sheringham, Matt Etherington and Paul Konchesky while Carlton Cole stayed on the bench.

Pardew is a decent man, a top-class manager and I was relieved our win didn't cost him his job, but the new West Ham chairman Eggert Magnusson sacked him two months later.

I had feared for Pardew directly after the match when Magnusson's predecessor Terry Brown barged into their dressing room and complained they had played like a pub team and that he'd wasted £16,000 on a pre-match overnight stay. Given £16,000, I might have bought a new player or two.

Now we were into the last 16 and the draw pitted us at home to another Premier League outfit.

Iain Dowie's Charlton were not in markedly any better shape than West Ham but they didn't possess so many big-name players and I suspected, as a consequence, they would be ready to put in more of a shift.

Another factor which caused me disquiet was that they had three talented strikers in Jimmy Floyd Hasselbaink, Darren Bent and Marcus Bent. I knew our defenders would have their hands full.

A gripping encounter finished 3-3 after extra-time before Scott Carson tipped the seesaw Charlton's way by saving two penalties in the shoot-out.

It had been a fabulous run, three Premier League teams

hadn't been able to beat us over 90 minutes and we were proud of that. Unfortunately, we suffered an immediate hangover, when Basingstoke Town came up from Hampshire to knock us out of the FA Cup.

Now all that concerned me was winning enough games to stay in League One – and it was bloody hard work getting men who had given their absolute maximum against City, West Ham and Charlton to repeat their efforts week in and week out.

I had been at Saltergate for almost four years when it was time to go in March 2007. I was a little disillusioned after working hard with a small budget and finding the fans on my back even when we were winning. I had taken the club as far as I could and wanted to retire at the end of the season, nominating my assistant Lee Richardson as my successor.

Lee was there when I arrived at Saltergate and was a great help while I settled in. He had been a Chesterfield player and knew the players, as well as the workings of the club, inside out. Besides having his managerial and coaching badges, Lee had a degree in psychology which I thought would help him immensely through the rest of his chosen career.

However, a generally poor run and four successive defeats saw us slump to within a point of the relegation zone and the chairman was keen to see what Richardson had to offer and gave him the opportunity, with nine games left, to keep us up, which he couldn't.

Hubbard was generous in his praise for the job I had done, saying: "Roy helped a club recovering from the shenanigans of a previous regime. During my long involvement with Chesterfield I have made a number of mistakes, but appointing Roy McFarland as manager was not one of them."

28

Goodbye, Gaffer

BRIAN CLOUGH died, aged 69, in September, 2004, leaving behind a fund of memories – happy and sad.

He inspired such loyalty that Nottingham Forest staff and players went to extraordinary lengths to try and keep his battle with alcohol under wraps.

Maybe they did him a disservice. Maybe if Brian had been forced to confront his demons earlier, he could have turned a corner without seeking a drink and come back to us as the bright-eyed manager with a razor-sharp mind I knew at Derby. But Brian was as stubborn as King Canute.

One international star was ordered to pick Brian up from home in the morning and drive him to work in Nottingham, then hang around for hours after training before taking him home. After two or three weeks of being scolded by his wife for acting as a chauffeur, the player confronted Cloughie and told him to find another lackey. That was one power struggle Brian didn't win.

There were always people only too happy to help, or try to help, though.

Enough is enough, a few of us decided on one occasion, and it seemed as if even Brian himself accepted things had to change when he agreed to host a meeting of about 10 concerned friends and colleagues.

John Sadler, who ghosted Brian's column for The Sun, rallied the troops and London Weekend Television presenter Brian Moore came up by train. They were joined by myself, members of the Forest coaching staff and several trusted local journalists. The unwritten agenda started and finished with one item: What to do about Brian's drinking.

Barbara Clough ferried tea, coffee and biscuits into the lounge and it was a relatively pleasant, relaxed atmosphere but trying to pin down Brian was impossible. When Sadler broached the crucial subject, Brian swiftly turned the tables by recounting anecdotes when he'd been boozing with journalists in happier days. There were a few forced smiles.

And when Brian wasn't holding court, he simply wasn't even there – constantly excusing himself and nipping out of the room to seek a top up from his secret supply. A few people didn't realise at first why he kept disappearing mysteriously and they looked very disappointed when the reason was explained to them.

Brian did appreciate why we had all gathered there and listened briefly to our concerns before growing impatient, clapping his hands together and announcing: "Well, we've had enough of that now," and going off on a tangent. He wanted a party, not an inquisition.

He really didn't want to be told what to do. He was always his own man and going to live his life the way he wanted to live it. He decided what was going to happen and he wasn't going to take the advice of close friends or anybody.

After a couple of hours, the meeting petered out. However much frustration we felt, at least we could console ourselves in the knowledge we'd done as much as we felt we could, only to hit a brick wall. Our intention was to formulate a plan of action to get Brian back on the straight and narrow. It was never going to happen.

I was the last to leave but I wasn't going without a parting shot. I turned to Brian on the doorstep and said: "Gaffer, it's about time you packed in the drink." Suddenly, he looked so crestfallen, pitiful and lost, almost like a little boy, that I momentarily regretted my outburst. But Barbara had heard my plea and told him: "Didn't you hear what Roy said – it's got to stop." Deep down, all three of us knew it wouldn't, at least not yet.

My saddest recollection of Brian was the time I spotted him pottering around the cricket pitch at Quarndon. I was walking Snowy, my West Highland terrier, in one direction and we should have met, but Brian, accompanied by his Red Setter looked up and saw me before engaging reverse gear and scuttling away.

All we had been through, all the triumphs and a little despair, it seemed to count for nothing in that instant when he didn't want to know me because he was too embarrassed or ashamed.

We saw each other in the village plenty of times when Brian was pleased to stop and quickly turn the subject matter from football to his family, especially the grandchildren he adored, and enquire about Lin and Beth. We succeeded in flirting around the subject of his drinking. It was the proverbial elephant in the room. Sometimes he was clear and lucid, and it seemed he was making a genuine effort to clean up his act. Other times he was the worse for wear. I would have given anything to hear him say: "Before you ask, about the booze – I've knocked it on the head." But he never did.

Colin Lawrence, a local newsagent who acted as Brian's driver, kept me regularly informed about his health and state of mind. It would have been the easiest thing in the world for me to be knocking on Brian's door every day, but that would have made both of us very uncomfortable. When all was said and done, his house was his home, his castle, his sanctuary, his refuge.

I cannot hold a single grudge, though.

Time is a great healer and the Brian Clough I much prefer to remember was, simply, the greatest football manager in the business when he was focused – and a great man. And let's not forget that he did kick the booze in the end, and following his liver transplant he was clean for the 18 months until his death from stomach cancer.

Brian had a gift for turning boys into men, and made us not only better players but better people.

He was extremely generous with his time, something I witnessed frequently on trips with Derby. We were strolling along the Golden Mile at Blackpool when an old couple approached tentatively as if he was royalty. The players hung back, looking at each other, then up to the sky. We knew our walk was going to be interrupted for a good five minutes while Brian took an interest in the pensioners, discovering their names, where they were from and answering all their questions. "Why does the gaffer always do that?" one of the younger lads asked, and I told him: "Because he is a decent, working-class bloke who has made that couple's day and most probably their holiday as well."

The pair probably dined out for years recounting the story of the day they met Brian Clough.

Cloughie's soft side could be elusive but he put a lot of thought into his actions.

He wanted a tight-knit group of players, the tighter the better – and nothing acts as a firmer bond than happiness, the sound of laughter and a sense of camaraderie. During mid-season breaks, a phone call would go out from Majorca and 16 or so beautiful bouquets of flowers would be despatched by Interflora to wives and girlfriends.

It became a standing joke with the lads that our women were grateful we were so sensitive, romantic and thinking of them when, all along, it was Cloughie pulling the strings to ensure our home lives ran as smoothly as possible.

He explained: "I was a great believer right throughout my career in family life because I'm family life myself. And I knew the best therapy players could have was to be happy with their wives all week. And it was part and parcel of my job to keep them happy. No point sending out anybody to play football with domestic problems.

"I wasn't the ogre that people thought I was. I did my nut on a lot of occasions and did different things. But different things that were all into one pot for the benefit of us all."

Yet Brian had a contradictory nature too, which made him such a fascinating character.

He hated uniformity, liked to disrupt routine and there was a little resentment from married players with kids, such as Alan Hinton, John O'Hare and Alan Durban when he switched training at Derby to afternoons without warning. "I can't get there, I can't go," blustered Hinton, "I've got work to do." Like the other two, Ally's clash of interests involved the school run. Brian told him in no uncertain terms: "Your work is training with Derby County Football Club in the afternoons now. That's if you still want a job."

Footballers can be selfish and single-minded, but Brian wanted us to think more deeply about other people and understand there was more to life than being a professional sportsman. He polished his Derby teams with little touches of care, always asking after our wives and children. He wanted us to be right in mind and body to get the maximum out of us on the pitch.

Wednesday nights were reserved for a beer or two and after training one Thursday, Brian asked me casually: "Any plans for this evening, Roy?" I replied: "Yes gaffer, I'm taking Lin to the pictures." One eyebrow shot up as he said: "Shouldn't you be resting? I only ask because there's a game on Saturday." I did go to the cinema, but I didn't enjoy the film as much as I might have that particular night. Brian had sewn seeds of doubt in my mind, but I looked forward to the option of going out on a Thursday with Lin, either to see a film or maybe to the San Remo, an Italian restaurant. Sometimes it was like being back at school, there was always something else to learn – and Brian Clough was an unquestioned master in the art of education.

29

Going For A Burton

RETIREMENT beckoned. Lin and I frequently visited our holiday apartment in Majorca and I enjoyed playing golf twice a week, taking satisfaction in seeing my handicap go down.

Life at last was a pressure-free zone ... and then bloody Cloughie went and spoiled it!

Nigel Clough's talent to grow a team at Burton Albion over a decade had been recognised by Derby County and, with the family's deep association with the city and club from Brian's halcyon days, it made sound sense to bring in Nigel as manager at Pride Park in January, 2009, after Paul Jewell had been sacked.

Nigel recommended me to the Brewers chairman Ben Robinson, a man I had known and admired for over 30 years, and the notion of steering Albion into the Football League for the first time was irresistible.

"What could possibly go wrong?" I asked myself, studying the Blue Square Premier League table which confirmed that Burton were way out in front with a 13-point lead after winning 10 games in a row.

Well, in fact, plenty could go wrong – and it did on the run-in, although the Promised Land was within sight at the end of March when we beat Grays 4-0 and drew 1-1 with Kettering.

However, four defeats in five matches then had Burton fans, players and management chewing their fingernails as we prepared for the final game, a trip to Torquay, highly motivated themselves as they needed to win to guarantee their place in the play-offs.

One point would be enough to give us the championship and solitary automatic promotion place but, if we lost, Cambridge United could overhaul us with a four-goal swing and they were at home to Altrincham, who were labouring in the bottom half of the table with nothing but pride to play for.

I didn't have time to worry about the irony of Burton's fate possibly being decided by two of my former clubs. I was far too wrapped up in the moment at Plainmoor. Nigel Clough may have been Derby's boss now but Burton were still his baby and he drove down to watch the match with his son, William.

Both he and I would have been mortified if I'd cocked things up at this late stage.

Fortunately, a little tension was removed when Marc Goodfellow scored for us after eight minutes, but Chris Hargreaves equalised for Paul Buckle's team and Elliot Benyon headed them into the lead immediately after half-time.

The pressure was back on now but the news I feared, that Cambridge had broken through at the Abbey Stadium and Altrincham were in danger of caving in, never arrived, and they could only manage a scoreless draw.

Burton lost but everyone in gold and black colours felt like a winner. It wasn't the most stylish of finishes to a season but that was irrelevant. The only thing that mattered was getting over the finishing line and we did that, we crossed it first.

Relief swept over me in waves because the last handful of matches had been nerve-racking and at times the nerves had got the better of us.

In the immediate aftermath of promotion, there was speculation that I might stay on at the Pirelli Stadium in some sort of advisory capacity, perhaps as director of football – but I made it clear to the chairman that I didn't want to upgrade my position as a caretaker to become the permanent manager.

I had made my mind up to retire at Chesterfield and do other things with my life, and I no longer wanted the pressure and commitment that every Saturday brings in the football season when results are paramount, and you 'live or die' a little with every win and defeat.

My experience of managing at the lowest level in the Football League might have identified the right calibre of signing to help Burton bed in safely and avoid any traumas. The last thing they needed was to face a fight to retain their new status.

But I knew that if I stayed at Burton, nothing would be part-time. I'd soon be hurling myself into every aspect of the club and both Robinson and myself swiftly came to the conclusion that my presence would place an unfair handicap on the new manager, who turned out to be Paul Peschisolido.

I'm happy and content to watch Derby County these days in the very capable hands of Steve McClaren, one of the top British coaches in the business with Sam Allardyce and Brendan Rodgers. I never had an inkling Steve would rise to such heights as England manager when he was playing for Arthur Cox and myself at the Baseball Ground, but he has learned his trade thoroughly and benefited from spending time absorbing the way leading continental clubs such as Bayern Munich, Real Madrid and Ajax do things.

I am delighted Nigel Clough has settled in successfully at Sheffield United. He faced an immense job when he started at Pride Park, moving on men he inherited on big wages and replacing them with players who developed under his guidance. Nigel never probably had the promotion everyone in Derby expected to happen and went after four years, leaving a very decent legacy for McClaren to build on.

The last time I tried to turn the clock back was in May, 2006, when I had the privilege of playing the final two-and-a-half minutes of Ted McMinn's testimonial match against Glasgow Rangers at Pride Park which attracted a record attendance of 33,475 at the ground which opened in 1997.

Three days before my combined comeback and swansong at 58, I was out on a training run along The Common in Quarndon when I pulled my calf muscle outside Brian Clough's old house. I cursed my misfortune and glanced down the driveway of The Elms. For a split-second, I half-expected to see a man in a flat hat and green Wellingtons waving his walking stick at me and shouting: "Serves you right, daft bugger. Fancy running at your age!"

I was assisting Arthur Cox again to manage McMinn's Derby

team and noted with satisfaction the warm reception given to Kevin Hector when he came on for a cameo role.

Given my injury and fears the calf might get properly torn, I was resigned to staying on the sidelines but I'm extremely grateful Cox ordered me to play the final minutes. Like Kevin, I was treated like a returning hero as I was transported back in time because a full, rocking Pride Park, with the Rangers fans helping create a fantastic atmosphere, felt like the Baseball Ground where the crowd was so close to the pitch.

As I hobbled into position, Mark Wright told me not to move. I told him not to worry – I couldn't!

But Wright and Igor Stimac almost tormented me with passes to ensure I had quite a few touches of the ball.

Then it was all over.

I was a proud man when Lin and I drove down to Bristol for Beth's graduation ceremony and I never dreamed the roles might be reversed many years later. But that's what happened in 2010 after I received a letter from the University of Derby saying I had been nominated for an honorary degree "in recognition of my remarkable achievement of promoting the good name of football, by example, at national and international level over a period of 40 years."

At first I thought the letter was a hoax and had to double-check that it was not a wind-up, and I felt a little strange at the ceremony dressed in cap and gown, but everyone was wonderfully friendly and put me at ease as I mingled with lecturers, the High Sheriff and the Duke of Devonshire.

So now I can lay claim to being an honorary master of the University of Derby.

If I could teach a youngster coming into the game today anything it would be purely to enjoy the experience.

If it's meant to be, it will happen. Give everything to your dream, whether you're at Liverpool or Burton Albion, and train hard – as if your life depends on it.

The failure rate in professional football is immense with so many boys becoming desperately wound-up.

I found it the toughest aspect of management to look an apprentice in the face and tell him: "You won't be playing at this football club any more."

I can still see the hurt and disappointment in the eyes of several of those I let go. I did my best to soften the blow, adding: "We're not always right, there are always other openings," and there are, of course, but at that moment it seemed as if they felt their lives were ending.

My good friend Joe Royle, a fellow Scouser, always maintained we were never scallies. Maybe I was simply the idiot who couldn't be bothered to take a couple of buses across the city to learn from Tom Saunders, the Liverpool schoolboys coach, who became an integral member of the Anfield boot room.

I didn't have the dedication or enough belief in my ability then.

But I was fortunate that Tranmere Rovers saw my potential.

And I was definitely blessed the night Brian Clough and Peter Taylor swept into my home and did the deal to carry me off on a rich, rewarding and wholly fulfilled career.

Statistics

Playing career

Season by season

1966-67 Tranmere Rovers – 33 League; 3 FA Cup; 2 League Cup; 0 goals
1967-68 Tranmere Rovers – 2 League; 1 League Cup; 0 goals
1967-68 Derby County – 40 League; 1 FA Cup; 2 goals
1968-69 Derby County – 42 League; 1 FA Cup; 8 League Cup; 9 goals
1969-70 Derby County – 38 League; 4 FA Cup; 6 League Cup; 6 goals
1970-71 Derby County – 35 League; 3 FA Cup; 3 League Cup; 2 goals
1971-72 Derby County – 38 League; 5 FA Cup; 2 League Cup; 2 Texaco Cup; 4 goals
1972-73 Derby County – 38 League; 5 FA Cup; 3 League Cup; 7 European Cup; 7 goals
1973-74 Derby County – 38 League; 3 FA Cup; 3 League Cup; 4 goals
1974-75 Derby County – 4 League; 0 goals
1975-76 Derby County – 37 League; 4 FA Cup; 2 League Cup; 4 European Cup; 1 Charity Shield; 3 goals
1976-77 Derby County – 31 League; 5 FA Cup; 5 League Cup; 4 UEFA Cup; 4 goals
1977-78 Derby County – 26 League; 1 goal

1978-79 Derby County – 24 League; 1 FA Cup; 2 League Cup; 3 goals
1979-80 Derby County – 20 League; 2 League Cup; 0 goals
1980-81 Derby County – 23 League; 1 FA Cup; 3 goals
1981-82 Bradford City – 30 League; 1 FA Cup; 1 League Cup; 1 goal
1982-83 Bradford City – 10 League, 1 FA Cup; 3 League Cup; 0 goals
1983-84 Derby County – 3 League (5 sub); 1 League Cup; 0 goals

Derby County honours: Division One champions 1971-72, 1974-75. Division Two champions 1968-69

Managerial career

Promotions: Bradford City – promotion to Division Three in 1981-82
Cambridge United – promotion to Division Two in 1998-99
Burton Albion – promotion to League Two in 2008-09

International career

England Under-23s: 5 caps

November 12, 1968: St Andrew's, Birmingham.
England Under-23s 2 Holland Under-23s 2.
Scorers: Radford, Hurst. Attendance: 24,258.
Team: Peter Shilton (Leicester), Billy Bonds (West Ham), Chris Cattlin (Coventry), Howard Kendall (Everton), Roy McFarland (Derby), John Hurst (Everton, captain), John Radford (Arsenal), Ralph Coates (Burnley), Jimmy Greenhoff (Birmingham), Peter Knowles (Wolves), Alun Evans (Liverpool).
Substitute: Colin Todd (Sunderland) replaced Kendall.

May 22, 1969: Deventer.
Holland Under-23s 2 England Under-23s 1.
Scorer: Kidd. Attendance: 14,500.
Team: Shilton, Wilf Smith (Sheff Wednesday), Emlyn Hughes (Liverpool), Mike Doyle (Manchester City), McFarland, Hurst, Radford, Coates, Joe Royle (Everton), Brian Kidd (Manchester Utd), John Sissons (West Ham).
Substitute: J Greenhoff replaced Radford.

May 25, 1969: Ostend.
Belgium B 0 England Under-23s 1.
Scorer: Royle. Attendance: 11,000.
Team: Peter Springett (Sheff Wednesday), Glynn Pardoe (Manchester City), Hughes, Doyle, McFarland, David Nish (Leicester), Coates, Evans, J Greenhoff, Hurst, Sissons.
Substitutes: Royle replaced Coates; Kidd replaced J Greenhoff.

May 28, 1969: Funchal, Madeira.
Portugal Under-23s 1 England Under-23s 1.
Scorer: Hughes. Attendance: 15,000.
Team: Shilton, Smith, Pardoe, Doyle, McFarland, Nish, Radford, Evans, Royle, Hurst, Sissons.
Substitute: Hughes replaced Radford.

March 4, 1970: Roker Park, Sunderland.
England Under-23s 3 Scotland Under-23s 1
(abandoned after 62 minutes due to snow).
Scorers: Osgood 2, Kidd. Attendance: 12,885.
Team: Shilton, Smith, Derek Parkin (Wolves), Todd, McFarland, Nish, Jimmy Husband (Everton), Alan Hudson (Chelsea), Peter Osgood (Chelsea), Kidd, Dave Thomas (Burnley).
Substitute: Royle for Osgood.

England: 28 caps

February 3rd, 1971: Valletta.
European Championship qualifying.
Malta 0 England 1.
Scorer: Peters. Attendance: 29,751.
Team: Gordon Banks (Stoke), Paul Reaney (Leeds), Emlyn Hughes (Liverpool), Alan Mullery (Tottenham, capt), Roy McFarland (Derby), Norman Hunter (Leeds), Alan Ball (Everton), Martin Chivers (Tottenham), Joe Royle (Everton), Colin Harvey (Everton), Martin Peters (Tottenham).

April 21st, 1971: Wembley.
European Championship qualifying.
England 3 Greece 0.
Scorers: Chivers, Hurst, Lee. Attendance: 55,123.
Team: Banks, Peter Storey (Arsenal), Hughes, Mullery, McFarland, Bobby Moore (West Ham, capt), Francis Lee (Manchester City), Ball, Chivers, Geoff Hurst (West Ham), Peters.
Substitute: Ralph Coates (Burnley) for Ball.

May 12th, 1971: Wembley.
European Championship qualifying.
England 5 Malta 0.
Scorers: Chivers 2, Lee, Clarke (penalty) Lawler. Attendance: 41,534.
Team: Banks, Chris Lawler (Liverpool), Terry Cooper (Leeds), Moore (capt), McFarland, Hughes, Lee, Ralph Coates (Tottenham), Chivers, Allan Clarke (Leeds), Peters.
Substitute: Ball for Peters.

STATISTICS

May 15th, 1971: Windsor Park, Belfast.
Home International Championship.
Northern Ireland 0 England 1.
Scorer: Clarke. Attendance: 33,000.
Team: Banks, Paul Madeley (Leeds), Cooper, Storey, McFarland, Moore (capt), Lee, Ball, Chivers, Clarke, Peters.

May 22nd, 1971: Wembley.
Home International Championship.
England 3 Scotland 1.
Scorers: Peters, Chivers 2. Attendance: 91,469.
Team: Banks, Lawler, Cooper, Storey, McFarland, Moore (capt), Lee, Ball, Chivers, Hurst, Peters.
Substitute: Clarke for Lee.

October 13th, 1971: Basle.
European Championship qualifying.
Switzerland 2 England 3.
Scorers: Hurst, Chivers, Weibel (own goal). Attendance: 47,877.
Team: Banks, Lawler, Cooper, Mullery, McFarland, Moore (capt), Lee, Madeley, Chivers, Hurst, Peters.
Substitute: John Radford (Arsenal) for Hurst.

December 1st, 1971: Athens.
European Championship qualifying.
Greece 0 England 2.
Scorers: Hurst, Chivers. Attendance: 34,014.
Team: Banks, Madeley, Hughes, Colin Bell (Manchester City), McFarland, Moore (capt), Lee, Ball, Chivers, Hurst, Peters.

May 13th, 1972: Olympic Stadium, Berlin.
European Championship quarter-final, second leg.
West Germany 0 England 0
(West Germany won 3-1 on aggregate).
Attendance: 76,200.
Team: Banks, Madeley, Hughes, Storey, McFarland, Moore, Alan Ball (Arsenal), Bell, Chivers, Rodney Marsh (Manchester City), Hunter.
Substitutes: Mike Summerbee (Manchester City) for Marsh; Peters for Hunter.

May 20th, 1972: Ninian Park, Cardiff.
Home International Championship.
Wales 0 England 3.
Scorers: Hughes, Marsh, Bell. Attendance: 34,000.
Team: Banks, Madeley, Hughes, Storey, McFarland, Moore (capt), Summerbee, Bell, Malcolm Macdonald (Newcastle), Marsh, Hunter.

May 27th, 1972: Hampden Park, Glasgow.
Home International Championship.
Scotland 0 England 1.
Scorer: Ball. Attendance: 119,325.
Team: Banks, Madeley, Hughes, Storey, McFarland, Moore (capt), Ball, Bell, Chivers, Marsh, Hunter.
Substitute: Macdonald for Marsh.

November 15th, 1972: Ninian Park, Cardiff.
World Cup qualifying.
Wales 0 England 1.
Scorer: Bell. Attendance: 36,384.
Team: Ray Clemence (Liverpool), Storey, Hughes, Hunter, McFarland, Moore (capt), Kevin Keegan (Liverpool), Chivers, Marsh, Bell, Ball.

January 24th, 1973: Wembley.
World Cup qualifying.
England 1 Wales 1.
Scorer: Hunter. Attendance: 62,273.
Team: Clemence, Storey, Hughes, Hunter, McFarland, Moore (capt), Keegan, Bell, Chivers, Marsh, Ball.

May 12th, 1973: Goodison Park, Everton.
Home International Championship.
Northern Ireland 1 England 2.
Scorers: Chivers 2. Attendance: 29,865.
Team: Peter Shilton (Leicester), Storey, David Nish (Derby), Bell, McFarland, Moore (capt), Ball, Mick Channon (Southampton), Chivers, John Richards (Wolves), Peters.

May 15th, 1973: Wembley.
Home International Championship.
England 3 Wales 0.
Scorers: Chivers, Channon, Peters. Attendance: 38,000.
Team: Shilton, Storey, Hughes, Bell, McFarland, Moore (capt), Ball, Channon, Chivers, Clarke, Peters.

May 19th, 1973: Wembley.
Home International Championship.
England 1 Scotland 0.
Scorer: Peters. Attendance: 95,950.
Team: Shilton, Storey, Hughes, Bell, McFarland, Moore (capt), Ball, Channon, Chivers, Clarke, Peters.

May 27th, 1973: Prague.
International friendly.
Czechoslovakia 1 England 1.
Scorer: Clarke. Attendance: 25,000.
Team: Shilton, Madeley, Storey, Bell, McFarland, Moore (capt), Ball, Channon, Chivers, Clarke, Peters.

STATISTICS

June 6th, 1973: Chorzow.
World Cup qualifying.
Poland 2 England 0.
Attendance: 73,714.
Team: Shilton, Madeley, Hughes, Storey, McFarland, Moore (capt), Ball, Bell, Chivers, Clarke, Peters.

June 10th, 1973: Moscow.
International friendly.
USSR 1 England 2.
Scorers: Chivers, Khurtzilava (own goal). Attendance: 85,000.
Team: Shilton, Madeley, Hughes, Storey, McFarland, Moore (capt), Tony Currie (Sheffield Utd), Channon, Chivers, Clarke, Peters.
Substitutes: Macdonald for Clarke; Hunter for Peters; Summerbee for Channon.

June 14th, 1973: Turin.
International friendly.
Italy 2 England 0.
Attendance: 44,941.
Team: Shilton, Madeley, Hughes, Storey, McFarland, Moore (capt), Currie, Channon, Chivers, Clarke, Peters.

September 26th, 1973: Wembley.
International friendly.
England 7 Austria 0.
Scorers: Channon 2, Clarke 2, Chivers, Currie, Bell. Attendance: 48,000.
Team: Shilton, Madeley, Hughes, Bell, McFarland, Hunter, Currie, Channon, Chivers, Clarke, Peters (capt).

October 17th, 1973: Wembley.
World Cup qualifying.
England 1 Poland 1.
Scorer: Clarke (penalty). Attendance: 100,000.
Team: Shilton, Madeley, Hughes, Bell, McFarland, Hunter, Currie, Channon, Chivers, Clarke, Peters (capt).
Substitute: Kevin Hector (Derby) for Chivers.

November 14th, 1973: Wembley.
International friendly.
England 0 Italy 1.
Attendance: 88,000.
Team: Shilton, Madeley, Hughes, Bell, McFarland, Moore (capt), Currie, Channon, Osgood, Clarke, Peters (capt).
Substitute: Hector for Clarke.

May 11th, 1974: Ninian Park, Cardiff.
Home International Championship.
Wales 0 England 2.
Scorers: Bowles, Keegan. Attendance: 25,734.
Team: Shilton, Nish, Mike Pejic (Stoke), Hughes (capt), McFarland, Colin Todd (Derby), Keegan, Bell, Channon, Keith Weller (Leicester), Stan Bowles (QPR).

May 15th, 1974: Wembley.
Home International Championship.
England 1 Northern Ireland 0.
Scorer: Weller. Attendance: 45,500.
Team: Shilton, Nish, Pejic, Hughes (capt), McFarland, Todd, Keegan, Weller, Channon, Bell, Bowles.
Substitutes: Hunter for McFarland; Frank Worthington (Leicester) for Bowles.

October 30th, 1975: Bratislava.
European Championship qualifying.
Czechoslovakia 2 England 1.
Scorer: Channon. Attendance: 50,651.
Team: Clemence, Madeley, Ian Gillard (QPR), Gerry Francis (QPR, capt), McFarland, Todd, Keegan, Channon, Macdonald, Bell, Clarke.
Substitutes: Dave Watson (Manchester City) for McFarland; Dave Thomas (QPR) for Channon.

May 15th, 1976: Hampden Park, Glasgow.
Home International Championship.
Scotland 2 England 1.
Scorer: Channon. Attendance: 85,165.
Team: Clemence, Todd, Mick Mills (Ipswich), Phil Thompson (Liverpool), McFarland, Ray Kennedy (Liverpool), Keegan, Channon, Stuart Pearson (Manchester Utd), Gerry Francis (capt), Peter Taylor (Crystal Palace).
Substitutes: Trevor Cherry (Leeds) for Pearson; Mike Doyle (Manchester City) for McFarland.

August 8th, 1976: Wembley.
International friendly.
England 1 Republic of Ireland 1.
Scorer: Pearson. Attendance: 52,000.
Team: Clemence, Todd, Madeley, Cherry, McFarland, Brian Greenhoff (Manchester Utd), Keegan, Ray Wilkins (Chelsea), Pearson, Trevor Brooking (West Ham), Charlie George (Derby).
Substitute: Gordon Hill (Manchester Utd) for George.

November 17th, 1976: Olympic Stadium, Rome.
World Cup qualifying.
Italy 2 England 0.
Attendance: 70,718.
Team: Clemence, Dave Clement (QPR), Mills, B Greenhoff, McFarland, Hughes, Keegan (capt), Channon, Bowles, Brooking, Cherry.
Substitute: Kevin Beattie (Ipswich) for Clement.